QUEER NUNS

SEXUAL CULTURES
General Editors: Ann Pellegrini, Tavia Nyong'o, and Joshua Chambers-Letson
Founding Editors: José Esteban Muñoz and Ann Pellegrini

Titles in the series include:

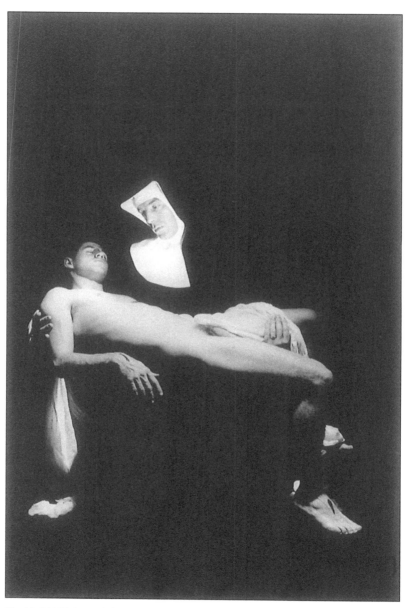

Untitled (*AIDS Pietà*), by David Edwards (Sister Mary Dazie Chain), featuring
Mother Inferior and Barry Lewis.

Queer Nuns

Religion, Activism, and Serious Parody

Melissa M. Wilcox

NEW YORK UNIVERSITY PRESS

New York

NEW YORK UNIVERSITY PRESS
New York
www.nyupress.org

References to Internet websites (URLs) were accurate at the time of writing. Neither the author nor New York University Press is responsible for URLs that may have expired or changed since the manuscript was prepared.

Library of Congress Cataloging-in-Publication Data
Names: Wilcox, Melissa M., 1972– author.
Title: Queer nuns : religion, activism, and serious parody / Melissa M. Wilcox.
Description: New York : NYU Press, 2018. | Series: Sexual cultures |
Includes bibliographical references and index.
Identifiers: LCCN 2017034141 | ISBN 9781479864133 (cloth : alk. paper) |
ISBN 9781479820368 (pbk : alk. paper)
Subjects: LCSH: Homosexuality—Political aspects—Christianity. | Gay activists. |
Gay liberation movement. | Parody.
Classification: LCC BR115.H6 W5425 2018 | DDC 306.76/6—dc23
LC record available at https://lccn.loc.gov/2017034141

New York University Press books are printed on acid-free paper, and their binding materials are chosen for strength and durability. We strive to use environmentally responsible suppliers and materials to the greatest extent possible in publishing our books.

Manufactured in the United States of America

10 9 8 7 6 5 4 3 2 1

Also available as an ebook

This book is dedicated to the promulgation of universal joy and the expiation of stigmatic guilt.

It is written in memory of those study participants who joined the Nuns of the Above during the course of my research:

Sister Karma Za Betch, The Abbey of St. Joan (Seattle, Washington)

Father Oh, Mary!, Abbey of the Big Red Wood (Eureka, California)

All royalties from sales of this book will be donated to the Sisters of Perpetual Indulgence.

CONTENTS

Figures 1–8 appear as a group following page 172.

I cannot remember the first time I saw a Sister of Perpetual Indulgence. On the day in 1979 when three gay men stepped out into the Castro wearing retired Roman Catholic nuns' habits, I was coloring Easter eggs some twenty miles away. No doubt my father, a dedicated Herb Caen fan, read that famed *San Francisco Chronicle* columnist's bemused report on the Sisters' upcoming fundraiser for gay Cuban refugees in October 1980. He and my mother might even have discussed other *Chronicle* articles on the Sisters at the dining table over the years; certainly they recall being aware of the group long before I began my research. Yet I have no memory of such conversations.

My first conscious memory of seeing the Sisters is at the 1995 Los Angeles Pride parade, the year before that city's house came into existence. The Sisters I saw were probably from San Francisco, which may explain why they were so familiar to me. I recall knowing already who they were, and cheering so loudly that they grinned and came over to me on the curb. Most likely I knew of them from earlier Pride parades in San Francisco, but they have been a part of my life for so long that the origins of our first encounter are lost to memory. Having grown up in the Bay Area and come out on a college campus where the LGBT student group was a chapter of Queer Nation, I was perhaps more likely than most scholars to be drawn to write a book about the Sisters.

But having seen even in my undergraduate days the rich potential of connecting queer studies with the study of religion, and having done my doctoral work as part of a research group that encouraged the study of religion in unexpected places, also primed me to see in the Sisters a fascinating opportunity to think about religion, sexuality, gender, embodiment, and activism in complex ways that reflect the equally complex communities in which the Sisters work and from which they draw their members. Such reflections on complexity are a key theme of this book, focused through the analytical concept of serious parody.

Before I move into that analysis, though, many expressions of gratitude are in order. First and foremost, my thanks go to the Sisters of Perpetual Indulgence themselves, both the ninety-one Sisters and Guards who took part in formal interviews with me and the many more who shared thoughts, observations, or simply space with me over the past six years. Tagging along while the Sisters pursue the promulgation of universal joy and the expiation of stigmatic guilt has been the ride of a lifetime, and I am grateful on many levels. The greatest of these is a small act at the 2011 Conclave, by an anonymous Sister, that may have saved my life and that eventually created space for some of the activist work in which I am involved today. For that most of all, without which I most likely would never have completed this book, I am forever grateful.

I am also especially grateful to those Sisters who, in addition to taking the time to meet with me for interviews and to facilitate my fieldwork, shared with me other materials for my research. Thanks to Sister Glo Euro N'Wei for sharing spoken word poetry and gifting me with "Glosaries"; to Sister Vish-Knew, formerly Sister Adhanarisvara and Sister Vicious Power Hungry Bitch, for sharing essays on the Sisters' past and commentaries on their future; to Sister Hysterectoria, a.k.a. Sister Banana Nut Bread, a.k.a. Agnes de Garron, for sharing archival materials from the early days of the order; and to Sister Soami, formerly known as Sister Missionary Position and Sister Missionary P. Delight, for the gift of handmade Sister rosaries and for sharing extensively over the years photocopies, scans, and extra originals from his copious personal archives, as well as for granting me the honor of an overnight stay in his home at the Short Mountain Radical Faerie Sanctuary in Tennessee. Sister Merry Peter gifted me with pearls of wisdom about anguish and joy, and Agnes with insights about how internalized oppression manifests in movement, both of which were part of what enabled me to survive my final years in southeastern Washington. And thanks to Sister Dire-Reahh for Chlamydia and Syphilis, who have a prominent place in my office to this day—but that's a story for another chapter.

Occasionally Sisters are also scholars of gender and/or religion. I've had exciting opportunities to talk with several such Sisters, and have always needed to be dragged away from the conversation when another commitment loomed in my schedule. But I want to recognize one Sister here in particular, one of the first I interviewed and one of those who helped me to understand the order quite thoroughly in a surprisingly brief period of time. Although I count as friends many members of the Order of Benevolent Bliss in Portland, Oregon—and quite a few members of other orders now—Sister Krissy Fiction has played an especially important role in my work and in my personal life, for which I am deeply grateful. Sister Shomi D. Goods came into Sister Krissy's life, and soon thereafter into the order, a few years after my research began, and I have been delighted to come to know her as well over the years. I hope that our friendships will continue long after this book has gathered dust on the shelves.

Even more rare, and invaluable for a scholar researching the Sisters, is the existence of a sociologist of gender and sexuality who is a long-standing member of the order and has also written about it. Jean-Yves Le Talec, a faculty member and researcher at the Université Toulouse 2 and also Sœur Rita du Calvaire, co-founder of the French order, generously spent a Sunday with me in his lovely city sharing Sisters memorabilia and archival materials as well as analytical ideas and concepts. I am grateful to him for his warm welcome of a scholar with shared interest in the Sisters, for his time spent listening to and commenting on my analysis of the order, and for his generously sharing the photo of the first manifestation in Paris that appears herein.

Several founding and early Sisters whom I met after the bulk of the research and writing were completed have gone out of their way to help me get the story right (but never straight). Thanks to Sister Flirtatious Romanovsky of Middlesex, member of the first Toronto house, for the extensive public digital archives that have contributed so much to my understanding of that house, and for feedback and encouragement on earlier drafts of the book. Sister Flirt joined Sister Soami, Sister Vish-Knew, and Sister Hysterectoria in reading a completed full draft of the book and offering helpful suggestions. Sister Soami was particularly diligent in this regard and nearly used up the limited minutes on his phone, to my horror, in offering feedback and additional information as I prepared to make the final edits. Sister Mae Call of the Wilde, co-founder of the Australian order, regaled me with stories of Sydney's activist communities when I met him in Melbourne during the 2016 LGBTIQ history conference at La Trobe University. Also at La Trobe, Sister Mary

Tyler Moore was kind enough to make time in his busy schedule for a chat about the order's early days. Sister Mary-Anna Lingus, also known as Mother Ethyl Dreads-a-Flashback and founder of the London house, responded promptly and enthusiastically to my eleventh-hour request for a Skype interview across the pond just days before the completion of the book's final draft. Sister Enema Mundi, Mother Lateral Thinking, and Sister Onan of the Immaculate Palm replied immediately to Nick Henderson's forwarded appeal from me for details on the founding dates of various Australian houses as I was in the throes of final revisions.

Thanks are due as well to Whitman College, which supported a multi-method, multiyear, transdisciplinary research project bringing together areas of study—particularly queer studies and religious studies—that have tended historically to regard each other with suspicion. That academic hostility makes it extremely difficult to fund a study such as this one, particularly when its scope is international, and Whitman's research support and generous sabbatical program were instrumental to the project's completion. As part of that research support, Whitman funded the work of five undergraduate research assistants during the course of the project. Special thanks go to those five students, Liam Mina, Jack MacNichol, Carly Johnson, Caroline Carr, and Luís Alba-Sánchez, for their tireless assistance with field research, transcription, and analysis and for their patience with the long walks, late nights, secondhand smoke, and highly personal questions that are occupational hazards of fieldwork with the Sisters. Professional transcriptionists also assisted in producing the nearly 1,700 single-spaced pages of interview transcripts on which this book is partially based, and I am deeply grateful for the time and talents of Letta Page, Jeanne Crawford, Michelle Thorla, and Inés Arenas-Embarcadero. At Whitman, talented reference librarian and fellow religionist Ben Murphy responded to my queries about archival collections with enthusiastic and copious assistance, and librarian Jen Pope had an uncanny ability to conjure any book I needed from somewhere in WorldCat. Suzanne Morrissey stood by me when nearly everyone else in our small town and our smaller campus turned their heads or their backs; her support and her belief in me made it possible for me to survive those agonizing final years.

I am delighted to be completing this book as the newly appointed holder of the Holstein Family and Community Chair in Religious

Studies at the University of California, Riverside. Being appointed to this position is a great honor and a great responsibility, both of which I hope I live up to in the coming years. I am thrilled to be back in California, and equally pleased to now be roughly equidistant from three fabulous houses of the Sisters—Los Angeles, San Diego, and Palm Springs. Thanks to all of my colleagues at UCR, in Gender and Sexuality Studies and other departments as well as in my home department of Religious Studies, for their warm welcome.

For archival access I thank the ONE Archives in Los Angeles, whose staff generously accommodated me at the last minute when my travel plans changed, and the San Francisco house of the Sisters of Perpetual Indulgence, particularly Sister Mary Ralph, the Mistress of Archives, who met with me and showed me around their collection. The incomparable Nick Henderson lured me to the Australian Lesbian and Gay Archives a few weeks before completion of the book by sending me tantalizing digital images of archival material; thanks to him, not only do I have a better understanding of the Australian order's history, but I have hundreds of digital archival images scattered on my proverbial cutting-room floor, calling to me to "go forth and write some more." My acquisition of those images is thanks to the extraordinary generosity of Gary Jaynes, who made time in his schedule to be at the archives not once but twice to accommodate a foreign researcher's travel schedule.

I have had the privilege and honor of being invited to speak about this research in a number of venues, and I wish to thank both those institutions and their community members and conference participants who offered thoughtful engagement with my developing work. These include the Université de Neuchâtel and the "Undoing Gender" conference there; the Pacific School of Religion; the Social Science Research Council and its conference entitled "The Politics of Spirituality"; the "Politics of Living Religion/Spirituality and Gender/Sexuality in Everyday Context" conference organized in London by Andrew K. T. Yip and Peter Nynäs; the Ohio State University and its "Queer Places, Practices, and Lives" conference; the Center for Lesbian and Gay Studies at the City University of New York and its "Radically Gay" conference; Barnard College's Center for Research on Women and its "At the Intersection of Queer Studies and Religion" conference; the Women's Studies Department at Hamilton

College; the Women and Gender Studies Department at Hunter College; the Religious Studies Department at Skidmore College; Canterbury Christ Church University's "Queering Paradigms 6" conference, organized by the inimitable Bee Scherer; the Center for LGBTQ and Gender Studies in Religion; the Religious Studies Department at U.C. Riverside; Rice University and its "Being Spiritual but Not Religious" conference; Princeton University and its "Embodied Religion" conference; Saint Mary's College of California; the Faculty of Theology at the University of Oslo; La Trobe University in Melbourne, Australia, and the "Beyond the Culture Wars: LGBTIQ History Now" conference; the "Taking Exception: Queering American Religion" workshop at Indiana University Bloomington; and, fittingly, the University of San Francisco, which holds the honor of being the first academic institution the Sisters ever protested. How things change! To all of these individuals and institutions I am grateful, and I am humbled to find so much interest in and support for my work.

I would like to thank by name several colleagues who have been of especial importance to the development of this work in particular and my professional endeavors in general in recent years. Andrew K. T. Yip has been an invaluable interlocutor over many years now, and I look forward to many more years of comparing notes across the pond on our work with queer religion even as our areas of focus diverge. Bee Scherer is fast becoming a new academic friend as well as colleague. Ann Pellegrini's interest in this project from its early stages was inspiring, and she helped me to begin sorting out how to address the performative aspect of the Sisters. Janet Jakobsen has long been a mentor, and along with Ann Pellegrini remains someone I want to be when I grow up—if I ever do. Rudy Busto has been a fantastic cheerleader, reminding me, "Send me chapters!" even when I was months away from beginning to write. Dennis Kelley offered crucial and eminently timely insights on chapter 4 that enabled me to rethink my approach to the idea of Sisters as sacred clowns. Ann Gleig connected me to the Rice conference, and I'm aware that I owe thanks to others whose names I don't even know for recommending my work in other contexts. Lori Bettison-Varga, whose own work is far from my field but who understands the challenges of being (interpellated as) a woman in academia and who is a sharp strategist when it comes to facing such challenges, has intervened at key points in my career with encouragement and advice. And LGBTQ studies in religion scholars like Mark Jordan, Laurel Schneider, Rebecca Alpert, Jennifer Rycenga, Mary Hunt, Emilie Townes, and Jodi O'Brien, among others, have encouraged and watched out for me since I first began working in the field. Heather White offered informed and sympathetic advice when I faced a tricky challenge toward the end of the writing process. And Anthony Petro, whose current work intersects with mine in fascinating ways, has offered important insights as I have developed the manuscript.

My other fellow queer studies in religion scholars are too numerous to mention—which fact delights me to no end, because such was not the case when I began graduate school. I am grateful to all of them for our growing community; among those who have been there for me at crucial turning points and who have pushed me to think ever more deeply about my work are Claudia Schippert, Horace Griffin, and Robyn Henderson-Espinoza. Thanks to Jason Crawford for being willing to share his dissertation on the Sisters with me; I find our work productively complementary and look forward to the publication of his book. S.J. Crasnow challenged me to engage more explicitly with transgender studies as I thought through the events at Most Holy Redeemer that I discuss in chapter 3; I am always grateful to work with people who are willing to push me, and I thank them for doing me that honor. Drew Bourn was thoughtful enough to send me, unbidden, the transcript of an oral history with Jack Fertig, a.k.a. Sister Boom Boom, from the GLBT Historical Society in San Francisco. Besides knowing San Francisco better than I do and giving amazing history tours, Drew has been fascinating to talk with about my work because of his brilliant mind and his own queer activist roots in the city we both call home.

Jennifer Hammer at New York University Press has been an absolute delight to work with. I was pleased to discover several years ago that we were both interested in having NYU publish this book, and Jennifer's input—always encouraging, always clear, always the right amount at the right time—not only shepherded the book through review but also improved it significantly in the process. Amy Klopfenstein's input and support have also been invaluable as I prepared the final manuscript. Ann Pellegrini has had her eye on this project for the Sexual Cultures series since shortly after I began working with the Sisters, and I am very grateful and a bit overawed to have my work included among such august company. The enthusiastic and insightful comments of two anonymous reviewers for NYU Press—not once but twice!—both encouraged me and assisted me in making further improvements to the manuscript, for which I am in their debt.

Although we teach in widely different institutions at opposite ends of the country, and study regions separated by half the globe in time periods separated sometimes by several centuries, my most valued academic interlocutor remains my brother, Wynn Gadkar-Wilcox. More recently (but quite some time ago now) I gained another academic conversation partner with whom I always have fascinating discussions, sometimes together with Wynn: my sister-in-law Sujata Gadkar-Wilcox. And I already have equally engaging conversations with my niece Ishika as well, although at the moment they tend more toward topics like the opinions of a stuffed animal. We all eagerly await the time when her little sister, Aksita, can also join in the fun.

I learned my curiosity about the world around me and my passionate commitment to justice from my parents, Margaret and Wayne Wilcox. Thanks to teenage visits to the mall with my mom (which deviated in more than one way from most teenagers' trips to the mall in the 1980s), I am an inveterate people watcher and I will always wonder, "What's their story?" How fortunate I have been to find a career in which I have the privilege of asking so many different people that question and receiving thoughtful and generous answers in response. From my dad I get the appreciation of the natural world around me and the interest and fluency in the sciences that led to my undergraduate degree in biology. While I use that training less today, I still spend most mornings recognizing by name the trees and other plants that grace my running path, and I could not write well at all without those grounding moments. Both of my parents were and are my role models as teachers, scholars, and justice advocates; I am the scholar and the person I am today due in no small part to their influence.

My chosen family, Andrea Fazel and Lynnette Hawkins, have had my back for decades and continue to be there for me in both the hardest and the most joyous of times. They were instrumental in my ability to escape a life-threatening situation during the course of this project, and they stood by my side as I celebrated having found the love of my life. I was probably with them the first time I saw the Sisters, and I continue to learn from them about teaching, activism, law, and life. Thank you for everything, my friends.

I learned from Catherine Albanese always to thank the four-legged family members who have taken part in a book's production. Two of those family members are long lost, but they were steadfast companions and one was my canine soulmate. I hope they are happy and healthy wherever they are now, and I still grieve their loss from my life. Still with me, though, is Tukéenen, my fellow survivor, who is always persistent in reminding me to take my eyes off the computer screen and return to the world around me—and isn't afraid to use a gentle claw or two when I'm not paying attention. Kalvin and Max pronounced me trustworthy when I first met them through their human, despite my failure to provide offerings of catnip, and I am immensely grateful for their approval, because that person has become my life partner. We have since lost Kalvin at far too young an age, but he was my steadfast work companion and kept the dog entertained when I was being boring. He is sorely missed. Max comes by at regular intervals when I'm writing, to nudge my elbow and loudly demand that I stop working and feed him cheese. And Raven is my running and former commuting buddy who always reminds me to play—as often as possible, preferably with tennis balls.

One other family member deserves mention for having been a part of this project. He too reminded me to stop working and play, by poking at things on my computer incessantly, banging on the keyboard from my lap, and rewarding me with delighted glee when I stopped staring at the computer screen long enough to run around the living room or peruse the toy bucket with him. He is long lost at this point as well, but if he ever finds this book I want him to know that he is remembered and grieved every second of my life. May the injustices in my own life, and those I've seen around me these past few years, always remind me to strive for greater justice in the lives of others. May there come a day when domestic violence is only a memory in the world.

Finally, my deepest gratitude goes to the love of my life, Nicole Pitsavas, who listens patiently while I spout theory and pushes me to slow down and explain where my ideas are going, who asks questions of the Sisters I haven't even thought to ask and helps me to discover new perspectives, who inspires me with her own passionate commitment to justice, and who keeps me laughing. On a more practical level, I am grateful to her for backing up my weaker Spanish with her native fluency during the interviews with Uruguayan Sisters, for doing a final review of the transcripts of those interviews to ensure that I had heard everything accurately, for double-checking my translations from those transcripts, for taking part in the last-minute archival scan-a-thon that we unexpectedly encountered in Los Angeles and helping me photograph archival documents again in Melbourne, and for the steady supply of See's chocolates that kept the creative juices flowing while I was writing and revising. Nicole stood steadfastly by my side and held me up through a period of devastation when I chose safety and as a result lost nearly everything I held dear. She is truly the miracle in my life and my own universal joy. May it be so for many years to come, whatever else the future may hold in store.

And now—let the nuns begin.

Introduction

"Modern-Day Badass Drag Queen Superhero Nuns"

From the moment I met the Sisters, they were fuckin'
modern-day badass drag queen superhero nuns!
—Sister Saviour Applause, Russian River Sisters of
Perpetual Indulgence

"May I give you chlamydia and syphilis?" politely inquired Sister Dire-
Reahh, of the London House of Common Sluts, as we strolled through
Soho with Sister Cuminja Wrasse in search of a good kebab shop. The two
Sisters had sat down for interviews with me after taking part in a protest
against cuts in National Health Service funding for HIV prevention. We
must have been quite a sight, myself in street clothes accompanied by two
clearly male nuns in formal habits, although relatively few people stared
openly—this being not only England but Soho. Sister Dire, following
the tradition that the U.K. houses of the Sisters of Perpetual Indulgence
inherited from their Australian forebears, wore only dark sunglasses
with an otherwise stern, black-and-white traditional habit reminiscent
of the habits of many Roman Catholic nuns' orders. Sister Cuminja, as a
"dual tradition" Sister with roots within the order from both the United
Kingdom and France, added to that look the white makeup base and colorful facial designs that are the hallmark of the houses in North America,
South America, and mainland Europe.[1] Both sported the muted, low-
profile coronet used by U.K. and Australian houses beneath their veils.

Having already worked intensively with the Sisters for over a year and
a half at the time this conversation took place, I had learned to respond
with aplomb to nearly any situation. I grinned at Sister Dire's request and
replied, "From a Sister, anything!" And I waited expectantly for the punch
line. Smiling, the Sister reached into the capacious purse that is another
hallmark of the order. She pulled out two plush toys: one a pink, snakelike

spiral with two beady eyes at the top, and the other a round green blob with rather innocent eyes, a puckered mouth, and green bits sticking up from the top like mussed-up hair. They are part of a line of plush toys produced by the company Giant Microbes, which creates educational toys in the shape of microscopic organisms—including those that cause sexually transmitted infections. The pink spiral represents the microorganism that causes syphilis; the green, that which causes chlamydia. Sister Dire explained to me that she finds the toys useful in one of the central activities of Sisters around the world: the promotion of sexual health. She then handed me the London house's version of the *Play Fair!* pamphlet, an irreverent and sex-positive guide to sexual health that was first written by the San Francisco Sisters in 1982, when an as-yet unnamed immune disorder was beginning to spread with frightening speed in their community.

Although this encounter took place in London, it could have happened in any of the eleven or so countries, across four continents, where the Sisters of Perpetual Indulgence currently have a "house," or chapter.[2] The Sisters might look a bit different; outside the United Kingdom and Australia, for example, some Sisters have a signature makeup design or "face," and party dresses are more common than black-and-white traditionals. But the playful, sexual humor and the commitment to activism, education, and various other forms of community service are consistent across the order, as are these Sisters' simultaneous camping and claiming of the role of the nun.

Queer Nuns focuses on this unusual approach to activism. As an activist strategy, what I call "serious parody" simultaneously critiques and reclaims cultural traditions in the interest of supporting the lives and political objectives of marginalized groups. Considering themselves quite seriously to be nuns while at the same time parodying the Roman Catholic Church, which has been such a vocal opponent of LGBTQ communities in recent decades, the Sisters of Perpetual Indulgence enact serious parody by combining the familiar tropes of drag queen and female religious renunciant to produce an image and a role that have opened space for both vocal political protest and day-to-day community service and activism, yet have also positioned the order to reinscribe relations of power of which its predominantly white, gay male adherents are less aware. Over the course of this volume I demonstrate both the promise and the pitfalls of serious parody, arguing ultimately for its effectiveness in certain parts of the Sisters' constituencies and for its importance as a strategy of ludic, performative politics that can be enacted by other activist movements facing situations of open and unwavering opposition from culturally powerful institutions. Like any performance, serious parody as a broader activist strategy can either challenge or reinscribe existing relationships of power, and it often does both at once. Thus, in this book I argue not for serious parody as a panacea that can answer every problem encountered by ludic, performative activism, but rather for its possible uses and potential challenges in the efforts of activist groups to work within communities that are opposed and oppressed by culturally significant traditions and organizations—as is the case with queer communities and the Roman Catholic Church.

Encountering the Sisters

Someone encountering the Sisters for the first time might be surprised by many aspects of the experience. Indeed, quite a few Sisters have stories like that of Sister Glo Euro N'Wei of The Abbey of St. Joan in Seattle. An HIV prevention worker even when not in habit, Sister Glo recalled being in face (a synonym for "in habit" in most houses that use white-face makeup) at a gay men's health summit. "I was in the lobby of the hotel waiting for something," she recounted in an interview, "and one of the other participants came up and was like, 'Sister, I just have to ask. What the fuck?'"[3] Sister Glo explained to me that the man was from an Italian Catholic family and simply couldn't comprehend what Glo and other Sisters were doing, or why they might be doing it. Like this man, some observers who are unfamiliar with the Sisters are startled by their appearance itself: people of a wide range of body sizes, shapes, and levels of hirsuteness, wearing dresses and white pancake makeup with bright designs and glitter, or formal habits with large sunglasses and perhaps a bit of lip color or rouge, crowned by coronets of all shapes and sizes and colorful veils cascading down their backs. Many wear heels or impressively tall platform boots, and most carry purses in often quirky designs. In many houses the picture is completed by cigarettes dangling from several Sisters' fingers and by the presence of a few figures clad in black leather, sometimes with whiteface—as they often call their white makeup—and sometimes not.[4] These are the Guards, who ensure that everything runs smoothly and that the Sisters are safe from verbal and physical assault.

Upon encountering Sisters for the first time, a curious onlooker might approach them, asking some version of the question raised by Sister Glo's conversation partner. In a group of Sisters the dynamics of rank might not be obvious to an outsider, but the one answering such questions will nearly always be a fully professed Sister, known as an "FP" or a "black veil" despite the fact that outside the Australian houses and the houses descended from them, most FPs wear colorful veils or more creative headdresses, and rarely wear black. Yet they are entitled to do so, whereas novice Sisters almost universally cover their heads in white.

Figure I.1. Members of the Order of Benevolent Bliss (Portland, Oregon) pause for a photo op during their bar ministry on World AIDS Day, 2009. The member in the cowl is a postulant; those wearing low-profile coronets with white veils are novice Sisters; the one in the black cap wearing partial whiteface is a Guard; and the rest are fully professed Sisters, or FPs. These are the habits used by the Portland house; other houses have different sartorial standards. Note not only the variety of headwear among the FPs, but also the fact that two are wearing white veils. This unusual occurrence is due to the fact that these are the Veil of Shame and the Veil of Remembrance (see chapter 5), worn by these Sisters and written on by community members as part of their World AIDS Day observance. Photo by the author.

Novices are encouraged to speak to the public, but since they are not allowed except in special cases to appear as Sisters, or "manifest," without an FP present, they will typically have a more experienced nun nearby to help them represent the order accurately. Postulants, the rank below novices, generally may not speak to the public. To symbolize this restriction, and the attendant emphasis on listening and learning rather than speaking during this stage of training, in orders whose postulants wear whiteface the postulants frequently "have no lips"; that is, they do not color their lips but rather leave them white (see figs. I.1 and I.2).

The Sisters as a Worldwide Order

While members often speak of the Sisterhood as a single, worldwide order, the use of such language is an acknowledgment of broadly shared goals, values, and history and not an institutional fact. There is no international governing body of the Sisters, and every country or region where houses consider themselves closely aligned to one another manages that alignment differently.[5] One can speak, for instance, of the Sisters of Perpetual Indulgence as a worldwide order, of the French order (which recently included a house near Fribourg, Switzerland) or the German-speaking order (which includes houses in Zurich and Vienna and recent missions in Odessa and Prague despite the language difference in the latter two cities), of the Australian order, or even of the Missionary Order of Perpetual Indulgence, an order of U.S. Sisters who have no immediate access to a geographically based house.

That said, while the San Francisco house has no formal institutional oversight of any other house, its collective opinions carry immense weight since it is the founding house, the Mother House, of the entire worldwide order. The two founders who remain most active in the order also retain significant influence; they are Sister Soami (also known as Mish from his original name, Sister Missionary Position) and Sister Vish-Knew (initially Sister Adhanarisvara and later Sister, then Grand Mother, Vicious Power Hungry Bitch, or Vish). The San Francisco house also holds the trademark on the name "Sisters of Perpetual Indulgence," although it reserves legal action regarding trademark infringement for cases of serious misuse. Thus, while the San Francisco house does not officially set policy for the worldwide order or even for houses in the

Figure I.2. Members of the Erzmutterhaus Sankta Melitta Iuvenis zu Berlin on bar ministry in that city, March 24, 2012. *Left to right*: Mother Katharina Lætitiam Donans, Schwester Francine, Schwester Daphne (*behind Schwester Francine*), and Gardist Heinrich. Postulant Victoria and Postulant Laetitzia are partly hidden behind the four FPs. Photo by the author.

United States, it does have the ability to recognize houses, or to refuse to do so, and to grant or revoke permission to use the order's name. In recent years that responsibility has been taken over by a representative body in North America, the United Nuns' Privy Council.

Most houses of the Sisters are located in cities, although the order has been appearing in less-populated areas in the United States since the early 2000s. The first houses took shape in large, urban areas with sizeable and recognized gay neighborhoods:[6] San Francisco, USA (1979), Toronto, Canada (1981), Sydney, Australia (1981), Melbourne, Australia (1983), Seattle, USA (1987), London, England (1990), Paris, France (1990), and Heidelberg, Germany (1991).[7] Yet in 2001 a new house was founded in the Russian River Valley, a region roughly seventy-five miles north of San Francisco that is known as a gay resort area. The town of Guerneville that is the Russian River Sisters' home of record registered on the 2010 U.S. census as having a population of 4,534—a far cry from San Francisco's more than 800,000.[8] A few years later, the Russian River house sponsored the formation of a house in Eureka, California, a college town of just over 27,000 in logging country near the Oregon border. And while houses continued to form in both mid-sized and large cities around the world, a few came to represent regions rather than specific cities. The Russian River house is technically one such house, as it draws its members from across the North Bay Area and beyond, and the French houses other than those in Paris were intentionally organized based on their regions within the country as the French order began to expand geographically in the mid-1990s.[9] In addition, 2007 saw the formation of the Grand Canyon Sisters of Perpetual Indulgence, which one founder, Sister Odora Flatulotta D'Pew, called "one of the first state houses." Although the house was founded in Phoenix, Arizona, Sister Odora explained, "we wanted to incorporate the fact that we had individuals in Tucson and Northern Arizona."[10] Over the years, each house has taken the form that best suits its members and its community.

As in most organized social movements, occasionally houses experience such severe tensions between their members that they split into two (or, rarely, more) houses. Such schisms generally have one of three results. Most commonly, one of the houses resulting from the schism survives while the other or others fade out. In some cases, as in Seattle in recent years, the two houses exist side by side but only one is recognized by the San Francisco house.[11] And on rare occasions, two houses may be recognized and coexist with varying levels of peace and conflict. To my knowledge, Paris is the only place where this last situation currently holds true. That city is the site of origin of the French order as a whole, but its house split in a schism in 1996, six years after its founding.[12] The new house called itself the Couvent de Paname, after a nickname for the city of Paris, and although tensions continue to arise at times between the two houses, they seem to have staked out different areas of interest and activism that allow them to share the city productively. Notably, this peace seems to have been initially due to the San Francisco house's recognition of the Paname convent,[13] as well as to what Jean-Yves Le Talec circumspectly terms "long negotiations."[14]

While houses occasionally form as the result of schisms, for the most part new houses form either because a fully professed Sister moves to an area in which there is not currently a house or because people who live in that area learn of the Sisters and wish to start a house; sometimes the situation is a combination of these two cases. Outside the United States, the process of starting a house varies from country to country. Some houses, like that in Montevideo, Uruguay, have followed the lead of most of the earliest houses and simply begun manifesting—that is, appearing in habit in their communities—and doing the work of the Sisters.[15] Other houses have begun as "missions" under the guidance of another house. Today most houses go through the mission stage, with other Sisters or other houses (or both) in their national or regional order as their guides to help them with both the administrative and the artistic aspects of becoming Sisters. In a mission house, all Sisters generally begin as novices and then are elevated to fully professed Sisters when the mission is granted full status after a year or more. In North America the San Francisco house grants full status by issuing a document known as an exequatur that gives the new house permission to represent the order.[16] In addition, all U.S. houses must register as 501(c)(3) nonprofit organizations in order to accept and give out the charitable donations that are the backbone of most houses' work in their communities.

In each country there is a different relationship, often at least somewhat formalized, between the Sisters and the state. These relationships span the gamut, however, from working closely together, as the Uruguay house and many of the German-speaking houses do, to refusing all state funding, as many of the French houses do. The former move seems to be more common in regions where there are state-sponsored outreach programs for sexual health and where the state—or at least that aspect of it—is generally trusted by the communities the Sisters serve, in which case the Sisters often partner with or even become an arm of those programs. Greater separation between convent and state is more common in situations where there are concerns about complicity with or co-optation by government forces.

Since 2006, U.S. and Canadian missions have developed under the oversight of the United Nuns' Privy Council, or UNPC. With two representatives from every fully professed North American house, the UNPC was designed to offer more consistent and accessible guidance to Sisters developing houses in new areas. Sister Katie Kizum, who was serving as the UNPC chair at the time I interviewed her, explained it this way:

> The UNPC . . . was founded as . . . a formal way to help mission houses. And as part of that, sort of a natural adjunct, was asked to manage the trademark process. We don't hold the trademark for "Sisters of Perpetual Indulgence"; San Francisco [the San Francisco house] still holds it. But they've asked the UNPC to manage it. . . . We help the missions out and help them move forward. . . . They're forming a business and corporate persona, but they're also learning to be Sisters with a capital *S*, and all the stuff that goes along with that. The Sistory, the spirituality, the community involvement, all of that stuff gets somehow tied together, and yet has to fit into a corporate framework. Which we struggle with on a regular basis.[17]

Indeed, that tension between the ludic engagement of the Sisters in their communities and the twenty-first century routinization of that free-spirited engagement is a central source of the interpersonal strife that can arise at times within houses.

Sister Titania Humperpickle's "SisTree," a genealogical tree of the worldwide order, listed 115 "total world orders, houses, convents, and missions" at the end of 2016, noting that of that number, eighty-four are currently active while thirty-one have closed. Although the list of active houses fluctuates quite frequently, the houses and missions that appeared to be active as of 2016 have their homes in the United States, Canada, Uruguay, Australia, England, Scotland, the Republic of Ireland, France, Germany, Switzerland, Ukraine, and the Czech Republic. The Sisters have an organizational presence in twenty-two states of the United States as of 2016, as well as in the District of Columbia, and no small number of these houses exist in politically conservative states such as Alabama, Georgia, Oklahoma, North Carolina, Tennessee, and Texas. Canada has three active and approved houses as of 2016, including fully professed houses in Vancouver and Montréal and a mission in Toronto, and outside North America the countries with the largest populations of Sisters are Australia, France, Germany, and the United Kingdom. According to the Uruguayan Sisters with whom I spoke, there is also an unrecognized house in Buenos Aires, Argentina, called Las Hermanas de Santa María de Los Buenos Aires.[18]

At the end of 2016 the "SisTree" listed a total of 1,617 Sisters and Guards who have joined the order over time. This appears to include those who have retired or have joined the Nuns of the Above (that is, have passed away), as well as those who have been excommunicated for serious ethical violations such as misappropriating funds for personal use. Although the Sisters do not maintain demographic data on their members, both in my ethnographic work and in the demographic questions I asked of interviewees I observed a predominance of white, cisgender, gay men in the order who identified themselves as either middle-class, working-class, or poor and who came in their own estimation equally from middle-class backgrounds and from working-class or poor backgrounds.

Joining the Order

While every house sets its own policies and procedures, there are strong similarities within and even across national and regional orders regarding the processes involved in becoming a member. A person who wishes to join the Sisters must begin by getting to know them, and becoming known by them. In the North American and German houses, this step is formalized through the declaration of aspirancy: one declares that one aspires to join the order. That person then becomes an aspirant, and must remain active in that role for a minimum period of time and/or a minimum number of events, depending on the house, before advancing to the next stage; a typical minimum in North America is three months' time. Dressing in street clothes and using "secular" names—that is, not yet choosing a Sister or Guard name—aspirants in many German and North American houses appear to onlookers simply as hangers-on or Sister groupies. A few houses require aspirants to wear drag or simply something outrageous, but there is no shared signifier of aspirancy beyond these basic requirements. One cannot with certainty identify an aspirant on sight, but only by being told that the person is one.

More orders worldwide have a stage of postulancy than have an aspirancy; in fact, the French orders combine the two stages into a postulancy of six to twelve months, during which the postulant wears street clothes (plain or outlandish) and accompanies the Sisters.[19] The French houses are not the only ones to require unusual clothing but not habits for postulants; however, in other orders postulants have a shared habit that is often rather simple and drab, such as a black choir robe with a grey cowl. In many houses that use whiteface, one begins to learn the artistic tricks of this sort of makeup as a postulant. However, as mentioned earlier, many such houses require that postulants leave their lips white as an indicator that they are not yet experienced enough to represent the order to the public. Upon elevation to the postulancy, many also take on their first Sister or Guard name, which they are allowed but not required to change as they learn more and advance through the ranks. North American postulancies generally last a minimum of three months; English postulants are in that role for a year and a day unless their postulancy is accelerated; and in the Convent of Dunn Eideann in Edinburgh the postulancy lasts, according to Brother Bimbo del Doppio Senso, "for as long as it takes you to make a full traditional habit."[20] Postulants usually have one or two formally designated mentors, who are variously termed (depending on the house) "sponsors," "big Sisters," or "mothers."

Smaller houses, particularly those in smaller countries, have found these two stages of postulant and aspirant to be prohibitive to their prospective members. Thus, houses such as those in Montevideo and Zurich skip both stages and induct new members directly into the novitiate. All houses, however, share the final two stages of novice and fully professed Sister. Novice Sisters around the world are recognizable by their white veils. Additionally, in many cities a Sister is first allowed to wear the house's coronet as a novice. The Couvent de Paris is one exception to this rule; according to Sœur Néfertata, in that house novices wear a veil with no coronet, while fully professed Sisters, unique in the worldwide order to my knowledge, wear the coronet with no veil.[21] Novices in the orders that use whiteface are allowed to have lips and therefore to represent the order to the public; however, except in the special case of novices who are founding a mission and who therefore have no FPs nearby on a regular basis, novices generally may manifest (and therefore represent the order) only alongside an FP. There are fewer restrictions on a novice than on a postulant or aspirant in the houses that have those prior stages, but there are also greater expectations. Novices must manifest a minimum number of times and/or for a minimum period of time, the latter ranging from six months in many North American orders to five years in the Montevideo house.[22] Like postulants, they work under the guidance and supervision of one or more FPs. In most houses, novices are required to faithfully attend all business meetings, thus proving their commitment to the less glamorous parts of the order's work, and they often are required to complete a novice project. While such projects frequently take the form of organizing an event (often in the North American houses a fundraiser), novice projects can also include anything from reorganizing the house's financial bookkeeping, its archives, or its website to designing a walking meditation based on the oral history of the Sisters.[23]

Upon completing all of the requirements for novices, one either is simply elevated to FP by the house or applies to the house for elevation. At any of these stages one may be denied elevation by one's house, based upon the opinions of the fully professed members. Such denials take place for a wide range of reasons, which vary from house to house and may be perceived as more or less accurate or valid by the person being denied. Nevertheless, the decision stands. Common reasons for refusing elevation include failure to attend meetings or to manifest regularly, interactions with the community or with other Sisters that senior members deem inappropriate, violations of the house's policies and procedures, and even a vague perception among senior members of the order that the candidate is simply "not ready." Upon refusing a candidate's request for elevation, a house may choose to terminate that person's candidacy altogether (which, unlike excommunication, usually does not preclude resuming one's candidacy later, or in another house), or it may require the candidate to remain at the same rank for a longer period of time and then request elevation again.

Upon becoming a fully professed Sister—or in some houses a fully professed Guard—one has full rights and responsibilities in the house. Because of a perception that they play more of a supporting role in the order, Guards are barred in some houses from becoming fully professed; other houses allow them to attain this rank but grant them fewer rights than fully professed Sisters enjoy. While FPs are expected to uphold the mission of their house and the values of the Sisterhood as a whole, they have much greater freedom of expression and activity than do postulants and novices. An FP Sister's elevation is represented nearly universally by the replacement of the novice's white veil with the black veil of the fully professed Sister, but only in houses that retain the traditional black-and-white habit do FPs commonly wear the black veil with which they were elevated. Instead, they wear veils of all different colors and even of different materials. During my fieldwork with the Order of Benevolent Bliss in Portland, Oregon, for example, Sister Dixie Rupt generally wore a feather boa mohawk instead of a coronet and veil, and once, for the Army of Lovers–themed bingo game shortly before Valentine's Day, she showed up with a phalanx of toy soldiers glued down the center of her shaved scalp. Other Sisters prefer garlands of flowers, or they pile colorful feather boas on top of their coronets.

Fully professed Sisters are generally referred to by the title of "Sister" and Guards as "Guard" (novices are "Novice Sister" or "Novice Guard," postulants are simply "Postulant," and aspirants have no special title or name). However, some orders also use the title "Mother," and some have an "Archmother" or "Archabbess." In Australia, use of the term "Mother" originated as simply another clever pun, when founder Sister Volupta was renamed by other members of his house as Mother Inferior.[24] It seems then to have become a term in that country for founding Sisters and for more long-standing members of the order.[25] In the German-speaking and French orders, the usage of the title is much more clearly delineated: a Mother is the founder and/or the current head of a house and an Archmother or Archabbess is the founder and/or the current head of an entire order. Thus, ArchiMère Rita du Calvaire is one of the founders of the entire French order, and she became the Archmother of that order when the original Paris convent began to create new houses in other regions of the country.

Masculine Personas and Guards

While the order as a whole is referred to as "the Sisters," there have been masculine personas since the latter part of the 1980s and Guards in the order since the early 1990s. Masculine personas do the same work as a Sister, but in a persona drawn from the roles open to men in the Roman Catholic Church. In North America one of the earliest such figures was Pope Dementia the Last, who appears to have joined in the early 1990s, and today there are Sisters of all genders and embodiments who have alternate personas that manifest as Brothers, Popes, Cardinals, or Fathers. Complicating this picture are Sisters like Father Oh, Mary!, who explained to me in an interview that despite the title of Father, she was a Sister. "I choose to manifest as a Father for purely physical reasons," she told me.

> I'm HIV-positive for over twenty-five years, and I have pretty severe neuropathy in my feet, and I can't wear high heels. So if I can't wear high heels, I don't want to be a Sister [meaning present a feminine persona]. I want to be a Father, and so that was purely the reason. And also I had done drag for so many years, as a woman, that I wanted to explore the whole genderfuck, kind of Cockettes aspect of drag. It was very appealing to me.[26]

The Australian situation, and historically that in the U.K. houses as well, is somewhat different in this regard. As the Sydney house's website explains, "We . . . use 'Gay Male Nuns' and 'Lesbian Monks' in our terminology, as there are no such animals in the ranks of the Roman Catholic religious!"[27] Mother Inferior explained that historically this approach was meant "to keep the gender statement clear."[28] Yet as structured as this may sound, more than one Australian Sister recounted to me stories of members who unsettled the structure by joining the order in personas that did not match their secular identities—cisgender lesbian women, for instance, who joined as gay male nuns and used the pronoun "he," and cisgender gay men who joined as lesbian monks, using the pronoun "she." Brother Bimbo, from the Convent of Dunn Eideann in Edinburgh, has bridged these traditions of gender in a different way, as the U.K. houses have shifted over time due to influences from the European mainland. When she joined the order, she explained to me, "our house being descended from Australian [houses], . . . women were pretty much expected to be Brothers at that point. But now, since we decided that there was no point to that, because it was possibly emphasizing a duality with which we don't agree, since then all the women in the order have chosen to be Sisters." Brother Bimbo has retained the title of Brother despite being a Sister because of the alliteration in the name.[29] Clearly, genderfuck comes in many forms; even within a relatively small and young organization, the nature of gender subversion changes as the politics of gender shift across regions and time periods.

In addition to male personas who do the same work as Sisters and may in some cases even be Sisters, there is another role that pursues the order's long-standing mission of "the promulgation of universal joy and the expiation of stigmatic guilt" in different ways. As Jean-Yves Le Talec reports, when the French order was founded in Paris in 1990 it included four categories of persona. Three were already known in the San Francisco house that mentored the Parisian founders: Sisters, of course, as well as saints and angels—titles reserved for community members who had significantly contributed to the Sisters' work. The fourth was a French innovation. Termed Garde-Cuisses (Leather Guards) as a pun on the Vatican's Gardes Suisses (Swiss Guards), the Guards were, in Le Talec's words, a response "au souhait de représenter la 'tribu cuir/SM,' et dont le rôle officiel est de 'protéger le corps des nonnes'; leur rôle auprès du public est défini comme équivalent à celui des Sœurs; les Garde-Cuisses sont également maquillés" (to the wish to represent the "leather/SM tribe," and for whom the official role is to "protect the bodies of the nuns"; their role with regard to the public is defined as equivalent to that of the Sisters; the Garde-Cuisses wear similar makeup).[30] According to Le Talec, the San Francisco house was already including the leather community in the 1980s through the role of saints, who generally dressed in leather; the French order simply formalized their involvement by shifting that role to the vowed role of a Guard.[31]

During the course of the 1990s the role of the Guard spread to other orders, partially through the travels of Guards themselves as they moved to other countries and joined new houses. Today Guards are present, though in far fewer numbers than Sisters, in Germany, England, France, Canada, and the United States. Different houses have incorporated the role of the Guard differently, such that Guards wear whiteface in some houses, partial whiteface in some (such as a single band of white across the eyes, or white on only one side of the face), and no whiteface in still others. Guards generally dress in black and often in leather, and in most houses their main role is to support and protect the Sisters of the house. In the Scottish houses, in part because of a need to include people who cannot make a long-term commitment to the order and a wish to honor the hard work of those people, rather than Guards there are henchpeople. These make no formal commitment to the Sisters, but simply show up and help out when they can. They generally dress in street clothes, but at least in 2011 the Edinburgh house had a henchperson who occasionally appeared in habit to make a particular political point.[32]

Taking Vows

At a certain stage of their development, generally upon entering the novitiate, Sisters and Guards take their first vows to the order, to the community, and to themselves. All take vows again upon their elevation to FP. The content and format of the vows vary between and sometimes within houses; whereas in some houses all members take the same vows, and may even reiterate or renew them whenever new Sisters or Guards are elevated, in others each individual member writes personal vows or a supervising Sister writes them. Some vows are truncated, such as those Sister Mary-Kohn described for the Los Angeles Sisters: "I'm a nun; I'll get the rest later."[33] Others are elaborate, lengthy enough that most members cannot commit them to memory, and some even carry a copy of them on a laminated card.[34] In many houses one takes vows twice at each stage of elevation where vows are required: once in private, often shortly after the house decides to elevate that Sister, and once in public. The public vows are often the more elaborate. Two stories from different orders serve to illustrate the wide range of ceremonies for Sisters who are becoming fully professed.

Sister Unity Divine, a founder of the Los Angeles house, had the task of designing the profession ceremony for the founding Sisters, which is still in use for new FPs in the house today. In contrast to their very brief private vows, this house conducts an elaborate and highly symbolic public ritual for each newly elevated member. "We wrap everyone [all new FPs] in a red cloth," Sister Unity explained to me.

> They wear a white outfit, like our traditional white outfit, and a wedding veil. And we lift them in the air, all of us [the existing FPs] together, and when they're halfway up they take their vow. And then we lift them all the way up and we turn them once in a circle. Before lifting them all the way up, we change the wedding veil for their hoobie-doobie [the Los Angeles house's coronet] and black veil, and then we turn them in a circle, lifted above our heads, and then we set them down and open the red cloth, and they present themselves to the world and say their name aloud.[35]

Mother Premonstratensia, one of the founders of the Adelaide house within the Australian order and later a member of the Sydney house, described a very different and uniquely Australian ceremony, although the story begins unremarkably enough:

> When the novice elects are ready, or when the house agrees that they're ready to progress to full profession, the Adelaide house rule specifically says that certain things have to be done. The novice gets to choose the place, the day, and must provide a feast. . . . Once that profession is set up, then the novice and the Mother of the house and the Novice Mistress would normally get together and work out an actual liturgical setting for it. And whilst there are, I would say, standard, generalized vows, which primarily aim at the four tenets of the order as originally designed by San Francisco, clustered around those the novice can place other vows as well. Generally, though, the vows are either fun vows, vows to lighten the burden to some extent, or they're vows of a much more ordinary sort of thing. So, for example, I took a vow of opulence.

Mother Pre explained that like the Sydney house, the Adelaide house had taken the dingo as its symbol because of the ways that animal, similarly to LGBTQ people, had been unfairly maligned and even scapegoated in Australian society. He then returned to his story:

> So . . . my profession was actually done by two Mothers, one from Sydney and one from Adelaide, in front of the dingo enclosure in the

Adelaide Hills, in a private zoo. And there's a wonderful story that at-taches to that, because we were all then in black habit, of course, and there was about eight of us, and this particular reserve contains this very large and somewhat complicated aviary. It's a bit like a maze, it sort of wanders about for a bit. So we entered at one end, all in habit. [It is worth remembering here that Australian Sisters wear a full, traditional habit that resembles that of a Roman Catholic nun; they wear no whiteface, and they usually wear sunglasses.] Unbeknownst to us, coming in from the other direction was a Greek family. And we met in the middle. And they all had video cameras [and] they took lots of photographs of the nuns. So I suspect that somewhere there are relatives in the Peloponnese still scratching their heads, trying to work out what went on! But it was a great, fun event. We also had a little baby with us, and it turned out that the mother and the father of the baby had managed to find a manger. . . . So we put the baby in the manger and we all gathered round, and there were photographs of nuns hovering about the baby in the manger. It was lovely.[36]

Serious, farcical, or most often some combination of the two, a Sister's or Guard's vows are for life. Short of excommunication or apostasy, one never ceases to be a Sister, even in retirement or when out of habit. Nearly universally, the Sisters I interviewed described the experience of taking their vows as deeply moving and even life-changing.

Developing a Name

Upon attaining the level within their house where they must begin to develop a Sister or Guard persona, new members must also come up with a name for that persona. They retain their secular, or non-Sister, names, and members of the order may use both names interchangeably for them, but when out in the community they use only their Sister or Guard name. Some individual members and even entire houses work diligently to keep a Sister's secular name from being revealed.[37] With over 1,600 current and former Sisters and Guards, the task of creating a unique name becomes more difficult every year. In fact, there has been some discussion of loosening that requirement in cases where an estab-lished member is geographically far removed from the new member who wants to use that same name.[38] Generally, though, each Sister's or Guard's name is unique.

Sister names share much in common with the time-honored drag tradition of incorporating witty, sometimes searing, and often sexual puns into otherwise innocuous-sounding names; for this reason, it is helpful to pronounce Sister names aloud in order to understand or guess at their full meaning. Quite a few Sisters also incorporate religious references into this punning. Thus, for instance, the unassuming name of Krissy can become Sister Krissy Fiction, the Nun Who Got Nailed, of the Order of Benevolent Bliss in Portland, Oregon. Here the primary pun is on the word "crucifixion," but what the Sisters call the "tag line" plays on the multiple meanings of the term "nailed"—not only literally nailed, as Jesus was to the cross, but also the meaning of having had sex. Although Sister Krissy did not reference any further meaning when discussing her name with me, one might also hear in the tag line a reference to arrest and perhaps to the long history of police harassment and entrapment of LGBTQ people. And lest one assume that such religious wordplay is simply the result of anti-Christian sentiment, it might be worth mentioning that in her secular life (the term Sisters use for when they are out of habit), Sister Krissy is an ordained minister with the United Church of Christ. While he is not currently serving a congregation because of the economic challenges of ministry, he has in the past served as a youth minister and continues to consider Christianity an influence on his broader religious perspectives.[39]

The two earliest Sisters who remained involved with the order both initially took religiously inflected names. One, formerly a Roman Catholic seminarian until suspicions about his sexual attractions led to his being encouraged to leave, became Sister Missionary Position. The other, of Mennonite heritage but having become a practitioner of Transcendental Meditation, initially took the name "Sister Adhanarisvara" (sometimes spelled Adhanarishvara in archival documents), after an androgynous or intersex form of the Hindu deity Shiva. Sister Adhanarisvara soon became Sister Vicious Power Hungry Bitch, but in the early part of the 2010s she began using the name Sister Vish-Knew, returning again to a Hindu reference in the name of the deity Vishnu.

Other Sisters' names are more direct in their meaning, such as the name of Sister Dire-Reahh, mentioned at the outset of this chapter.

Sister Dire explained to me that, like a number of Sisters, she had her name given to her and then found that it aligned well with the mission of the order:

> I started off, as a postulant, calling myself . . . something like Dire Bolical. It had the Dire in there at the beginning, but it was only until I kind of got to noviceship that Sister Sissi [Sister Sissiphyllis] and Sister Pop [Sister Angelpopstitute] for some reason came up with this Imodium, diarrhea, coming-out-of-your-ass kind of idea. And I think it's because I was a very energetic novice, and early fully professed Sister, where because I was helping to shape the house I was always engaged, always emailing, always telephoning, always organizing. And I have a tremendous amount of energy. And I think they had the idea that I had verbal diarrhea at some point. . . . In the London house . . . there is the idea that we want to kind of reflect our community, and diarrhea is an involuntary part of taking anti-retrovirals. It upsets your stomach and you will have diarrhea. And it's good to explain that to somebody who doesn't understand HIV and AIDS. And say, "There is a purpose to my name as well. It's not just about making you laugh."[40]

Other Sisters' and Guards' names reflect their mission, like Guard Noah Shame of the Order of Benevolent Bliss in Portland, Oregon, or a personal experience or perspective, such as Sister Rhoda N'Lytenment of The Abbey of St. Joan in Seattle. Occasionally a Sister will take a name that references her racial or ethnic identity, like Sister Mary-Kohn of the Los Angeles house, a Chicana Sister whose name is a pun on *maricón*, an epithet in Spanish for a gay man.[41] And some Sisters' names come closer to the names one might hear in a Roman Catholic convent. Sister Mary Ralph of the San Francisco house even took the name of her late biological aunt, a Roman Catholic Sister of Mercy, in recognition that both of them were doing the same work but in different venues.[42] Finally, some Sisters' names offer political commentary, such as the name of Sister Connie Pinko of the San Francisco house, which references the socialist and anarchist tendencies of queer activists and some Sisters in that city.

A note on pronouns is also in order here. Because one's secular and Sister or Guard personas are separate entities, they easily can and often do have different genders. Additionally, the question of pronouns—at least in a language that uses gendered pronouns—is further complicated by situations such as those described above for Father Oh, Mary! and Brother Bimbo, both of whom are Sisters and use feminine pronouns (she/her/hers). In the Australian order and among some of their U.K. descendants, nuns are always "he," because they are gay male nuns (regardless of one's secular gender or sexual identity), and monks are always "she" because they are lesbian monks. Outside Australia, quite a few Sisters have told me that they don't care what pronoun is used for their Sister persona, although I have yet to meet a Guard who does not use masculine pronouns. And some Sisters feel that Sisters are genderless, or perhaps a different gender altogether—that of "Sister." A few of these asked me to use no pronouns at all for their Sister persona. Likewise, I use each person's chosen secular pronoun when speaking of experiences in secular life. Thus, I may write of one Sister as "she," another as "he," and a third using no pronouns at all. I may switch, when writing about a single Sister, between "she" and "he," or between "she" and "they," as I switch contexts between the person's work with the Sisters and their secular life. This is a part of working with the Sisters, and increasingly of working with queer communities in general. Gender is never simple, is rarely predictable, and sometimes is not at all what it may seem.

Motivations and Priorities

People join the Sisters for a wide variety of reasons, having largely to do with one or more aspects of who the Sisters are, the work they do, and the communities within which they work. Since these various factors differ somewhat from house to house, so too do the precise reasons people give for joining. For instance, in Las Vegas, the Sin Sity Sisters focus exclusively on HIV/AIDS services, raising an impressive amount of money each year for their program, which serves people of all genders and sexualities who are HIV-positive and cannot afford medication. Working directly with pharmacies and insurance companies, the Sisters' AIDS Drug Assistance Program, or SADAP, pays for HIV medications for their clients. Logically, then, those who join the Sin Sity Sisters usually have been affected in their own lives by HIV and AIDS, whether because they are themselves HIV-positive, because the disease has affected their friends and loved ones, or both.[43]

Many are drawn to the community service aspect of the Sisters, some through the focus on HIV and AIDS and others through an equally strong commitment to other aspects of the Sisters' work. Three Sisters' stories help to illustrate this.

Sister Angelpopstitute joined the Couvent d'Ouïl in the west of France in 1996 as Sœur Angel, de l'ABBA Tahj-Maale (a play on the French word *l'abattage*, meaning slaughter and referencing homophobic violence in France at the time). Before becoming a Sister, he was already involved in HIV services and support, but having become the director of an important AIDS charity in France, he began to be concerned that the organization was becoming too reliant on state funds and might not retain its own identity and voice. He had already encountered the Sisters the previous year, so when he quit his position with the charity, he approached the Couvent d'Ouïl instead. Sister Angel mentioned multiple times during our conversation the friends and fellow Sisters lost to AIDS. She told me,

> The first thing I did, when I started to think about what's going to be my character, because of all these people that we had lost, so, right? I had brought two golden wings. I didn't even know what I wanted to do. Two golden wings. And then when I was going out as, not a Sister, not even a novice, but a postulant, I was allowed to wear not whatever I wanted, not a Sister outfit, but some kind of thing that I would be recognizable from all other people. So I decided I would actually have these two golden wings, and I had bought at the time two bright red feather boas. I took all the feathers out and I glued all the feathers on the wings, and that's the way it started. And after that, well, that's the kind of angel that I want to be for people. What is very, very important for me is the memory. . . . And that started the journey of Angel as a duty of memory.[44]

Sister Connie Pinko, on the other hand, was a high school student on a trip with their mother to tour potential colleges when they first encountered the Sisters in San Francisco. Sister Connie recounted, "Growing up in a place like Colorado [more specifically, Colorado Springs], where openly gay people aren't there—I was the only openly gay person in my high school growing up—it blew me away that there were these people who were so unabashedly gay." She laughed.

> Like, big homos, and they didn't give a shit what other people thought. And not only that, but they were there doing political work, they were there doing awareness and, you know, amazing, amazing work. Like, donation buckets, everything. And I was in love and didn't really know what to do about it. I thought it was all gay men. And my sophomore year of college at Cal [the University of California at Berkeley], a friend of mine who I had actually known from activist work back in high school told me that he was starting to join the Sisters, and he was a trans guy. And I was like, "Oh, so they let people who aren't just, like, standard gay men in the organization." And he was like, "Yeah, there's women, there's trans women, there's trans men, it's great. You should do it."[45]

After graduation, Sister Connie did.

A number of Sisters spoke of having a calling to the Sisterhood, much as they might in the context of religious nuns' orders, and for a significant minority this calling is an extension or redirection of a calling to more traditional religious leadership. The following conversation began when Sister Kali Vagilistic X.P. Aladocious of the Asylum of the Tortured Heart in San Diego asserted, "I honestly feel that I was born to be a Sister." I asked her to expand on her comment, and then Sister Trystina T. Rhume, who was between houses at the time, and Guard Inya from San Diego each weighed in as well.

> SK: I felt that it was a natural expression of what's inside of me. In a lot of ways a destiny. When I saw a Sister for the first time it was on TV. I wanted to *be* that. By the time life happened and it came around, it was more of an opportunity to express what was going on inside. And so it was taking something deep within me and bringing it forward. And something very natural to me.
> ST: Can I say something to that too?
> MW: Yeah.
> ST: I also had that calling. My father is a Methodist minister, and my grandfather is a Methodist minister, and my great-grandfather was a Methodist minister. And they say some things are just in your blood.

When I was a teenager I was just, I *hated* all religion. But honestly, I do think that it was in my blood. Because when I heard what the Sisters did it was the same thing. I was like, I had always had a calling to *do* something like that, but when you're gay that's just not something that they're going to allow, and I'm not going to hide the gayness in me. And so the Sisters is a perfect fit! You know what I mean? It's a perfect fit! So I get to react to what's in my blood, and do what I think I was called to do in some way, that fits the community that I live in. It's brilliant!

SK: I'm shaman, I'm priest, I'm a nun. One of the things that I've been looking into, it's a term that has been given to me, and then I recognized it but I didn't really understand it, was *heyoka*, which is Lakota for a particular type of shaman work, which is living the contrary. Contrary to that which is happening. It's a form of sacred clown. After a few years of the term being used referring to me, I looked it up and read the definition. And I could remove "*heyoka*" and put "Sister" in there, and it's *exactly the same*. And so people are called to be *heyoka*, it's a deep calling, Creator calls. And so I think it, [*to Sister Trystina*] like you, it *is* in your blood.[46]

ST: It *is*.

SK: It's a calling that, you know, whatever divinity, that pulls out of me.

MW: [*To Guard Inya*] Did you want to take on that one?

GI: Sure. Well, actually, when the San Diego house formed they had three initial Guards, one of whom left very quickly. The two initial Guards that stayed both wished to become Sisters. So they were actually looking for Guards, and I was asked. It took me a few months to ponder it, because if I was going to do this it was going to be something that I was *going* to have a commitment to. It wasn't something that I felt as something that I was destined to, or that was a calling for me, but it has over time very definitely become something that is, it's very much a part of *me*. And it has *become* something of a calling, and a deep commitment for me.[47]

Themes of religion and a sense of calling were not unique to my conversation with Sister Kali, Sister Trystina, and Guard Inya. As a nonreligious order, the Sisters attract members of many religions as well as a high proportion of the "spiritual but not religious" who have captured the attention of sociologists of religion over the past few decades. They also attract a number of atheists and secular humanists. As Sister Edna Daze explained to me in an interview during her novitiate, "If I felt like it was a religious organization, I probably wouldn't have had any interest in it."[48] Like many both in and beyond queer communities, some Sisters have quite dismissive opinions of religion. Others, however, see in the order an important expression of their spirituality, the source itself of their spirituality, or even the focus of their Christian ministry.

There are also those who join because they feel they have taken too much from their communities in the past, and they need to give back. This is particularly the case for the small number of interview participants who spoke openly with me of having struggled with drug use, particularly crystal meth, in the past. Having succeeded in reaching sobriety, they found justice, sustenance, and strength in giving back to the queer community from which they felt they had taken so much at the height of their addiction.

And, last but far from least, quite a few Sisters told me at one time or another that being fun and pretty is a fantastic way to do community work. Sister Anna Wrecks-Ya, a founder of Portland's Order of Benevolent Bliss, spoke of her immediate reaction to the idea of becoming a Sister:

> My very first knee-jerk reaction was, "Wow, I can still be a boy and wear makeup and dresses and have a good time." Knee-jerk. And the moment I spent a minute talking to them, asking who they are, what they do, and what's their purpose, why are they doing this, and they laid the, you know, the condom outreach, and community service and raising money for people who need help, and generally making your fellow man, you know, as a generic term, fellow man's life better, "Whoa, oh, wait, wait, I'm sorry, that was a chest pain I just had. You mean I can dress like this, have as much fun as you do, and do community service and work with my people, in that capacity?" "Oh, yeah." "Whoa." Oh yeah, that sealed the deal.[49]

Sister Nadia Ahnwilda, of Seattle's Abbey of St. Joan, had a similar story. She had lost her best friend Matt to AIDS complications a few years earlier, and she told me, "I've always wanted to do something, to give something back, in Matt's honor. And talking with the Sisters and know-ing what they do, then it just clicked. This is what I'm supposed to do. And so that kind of led me into being a Sister." She then added, "I gotta tell you, though, the glitter pulled me right in. That got me. That put me right over the top. I get to wear glitter! Yaay!"[50]

Family Ties and Community Ethics

It is not unusual for people in LGBTQ communities to form kinship networks based on shared identities rather than, or in addition to, blood relationships.[51] The adoption of Sister Sledge's "We Are Family" as an unofficial anthem and the use of the word "Family" as a coded refer-ence to LGBTQ people are just two indicators of the importance of what some LGBTQ people call "chosen family" in these communities, whose members still experience familial rejection or disapproval all too often when their sexual and/or gender identity becomes known. For many Sisters of Perpetual Indulgence, the order plays a similar role in their lives, and quite a few interviewees called the order a family or likened its dynamics—for good and for ill—to those of a family. Drawing their structure from that of Roman Catholic nuns' orders certainly encour-ages this dynamic, as members speak of "my Sisters," of "my mother in the order," and so on; thus, the Sisters come by their familial model through both the LGBTQ culture around them and their emulation of nuns' orders.[52] Many Sisters and Guards spoke of their houses as their families, but many who spoke of the Sisters as family clearly also had the worldwide order in mind. It is understood within the order, for instance, that a member can travel to any region where there are Sisters and always find an open door and a welcoming host. Some Sisters joked about no longer having to pay for hotels when they travel, and some spoke of their delight in knowing that they had friends around the world whom they did not even know yet, or whom they knew only through social media.

Being part of such a tight-knit community has its rewards, but it also brings challenges whenever members attempt to sort out difficulties such as the ethical dilemmas faced by advocates of a joyous, guilt-free existence who also promote safer sex. In their various regions of the world the Sisters are part of communities that were originally defined, both internally and externally, by sexual attraction and sexual activity.

This definition has played an important role in shaping LGBTQ communities in all of the cities in which the Sisters are active,[53] and is part of the reason why the Sisters' intervention in public health discourse with a wry, sexy, and sex-positive guide to safer sex was so critical in the early days of the AIDS epidemic. It also means that ethical questions around sexual activity and around the use of intoxicants arise for members of the Sisters of Perpetual Indulgence with far more frequency and complexity than in any other order of nuns.

During the course of my fieldwork I saw three key ethical questions arise time and again, not only in different houses but in many different orders around the world. Sometimes they arose as active questions for a house to sort out; sometimes they came up through condemnation as members of one house or order gently poked fun at or flatly decried those of another for perceived violations; and sometimes they came up through the absence of concern, as when a member of a house would say something like, "Well, we're far less uptight than X house. That sort of thing really doesn't bother us." These key questions addressed the appropriateness of and limits to alcohol and recreational drug use when in habit, the appropriateness of and limits to sexual activity when in habit, and whether members of the order have a duty to adhere to or avoid particular practices when having sex out of habit.

The questions regarding appropriate activity in habit come, to be sure, from a very different set of values than they might in other nuns' orders. This is not a question of whether the Sisters approve or disapprove of alcohol and drug use. While there are a number of sober Sisters and Sisters in recovery, neither they nor the order as a whole takes any negative stance on substance use, legal or illegal. Even Sisters who disapprove of such use in their secular lives spoke of reminding themselves, "No guilt!" when they put on their habit and stressed that while their secular persona might disapprove, such is not the proper role of their Sister or Guard persona. Furthermore, most houses are unconcerned by their members having a few drinks while in habit, and many bartenders will offer members of the order free drinks out of respect for the work they do and in gratitude for the clientele they draw.

However, Sisters and Guards around the world are also keenly aware that they publicly represent the entire order, particularly among members of their communities who don't know the Sisters well and to whom they all look alike. Thus, they are quite sensitive to behavior on their own part or on the part of fellow members of the order that may meet with public disapproval. Drinking while in habit may be just fine, but visible intoxication is not. Several Sisters in different houses told me of their distress upon hearing public denouncements of the Sisters for being drunk or high while in habit, and stressed that the commentary attacked the order as a whole even when in most cases the critic had seen only one or two Sisters in such a state. In another context, I witnessed anonymous and frankly cruel derogation of a Sister who had become known for disappearing into the men's room in bars toward the end of a night and returning with her makeup in disarray from performing fellatio. While sexual activity in habit is generally discouraged within the order, in other houses I heard similar and even much more involved sexual activity in habit clucked over with knowing smiles and shaking heads. In this particular house, on the other hand, it was considered—at least by one member, and I gathered more—to be an appalling source of embarrassment to the miscreant's entire house.

More complicated still is the question of whether the ethics of the order should extend into the secular lives of its members. On the one hand, Sisters and Guards are very clear that one takes vows to this order for life, and I heard numerous stories of people striving to meet the values and ideals of the Sisters even when not in habit and not with the order; in fact, many people described their Sister or Guard persona as being a better person than their secular self. On the other hand, many also explained to me that part of what made the time-intensive and emotionally draining volunteer work of the Sisters sustainable was the ability to "take off" the Sister or Guard persona and live as one's secular self the majority of the time. Because the habits and whiteface or sunglasses aid in preventing the community from associating a Sister persona (less so for many Guards) with the secular person, it is possible for many Sisters in particular to take a complete break from the constant availability to the community that is their hallmark when in habit. So do they take a break from the Sisters' values too? When it comes to the promulgation of universal joy and the expiation of stigmatic guilt, everyone I spoke with would answer a clear "No." But what about when it comes to the safer sex that the Sisters advocate? Here the central tenets of the Sisters' mission appear to clash with their concern over public image in the midst of an ethical debate that has preoccupied communities of men who have sex with men at least since the advent of reliable antiretroviral medications: the debate over barebacking.[54]

"Barebacking" is one of the slang terms used to refer to unprotected anal sex between men. Because anal sex between any two people carries a fairly high risk of transmitting infections, especially when the penetrative object is a sex organ rather than a sex toy, public health workers and others who advocate safer sex practices are particularly concerned about the health risks of unprotected anal sex. On the other hand, some gay activists have rightly countered that far more attention is being paid to such sex between men than between men and women, and have argued that the concern (some say panic) over barebacking perpetuates the homophobic association between male-male sex, illness, and death.[55] And while some feel that barebacking is acceptable within a monogamous couple or even a trio, as long as the partners are all HIV-negative or all carrying the same strain of the virus, others argue (as in most safer-sex discourse) that anyone making such a choice is putting his health in the hands of his partner(s) when he trusts them not ever to have sex with someone else without using condoms and without disclosing it. Those male-identified Sisters who have sex with men are in many ways at the center of this debate, being not only a part of the community around which it storms but also part of an order that advocates and educates around safer sex and that has focused much of its work on HIV and AIDS since their discovery.

There are no clear answers to be had, which perhaps is an indication of the complexity of the debate and the honesty of the Sisters' engagement with it. They are clear that when they work with community members who bareback, their task is neither to shame nor to scold but to accept, to educate, and to take a harm reduction approach such as encouraging the person to be regularly tested for HIV or for re-infection with a new strain of the virus if already HIV-positive. And they are clear that as Sisters they do not advocate barebacking, even as they do not condemn those who partake in the practice. But in their own lives, when not in habit, the ethics of the situation are far trickier. I have spoken with Sisters who flatly stated that they would never bareback, Sisters who said that it is a Sister's right to do what he wishes when out of habit but that they hope he will do it quietly so as not to cause a scandal involving the order, and Sisters who privately confided that they do bareback with their partners, in the context of an established and closed relationship. Far from being cloistered nuns, the Sisters are deeply embedded within their communities and experience the same struggles those communities experience, sometimes in heightened ways because of their public prominence and the focus of their work.

Beginning to work with the Sisters of Perpetual Indulgence, either as a member or as a researcher, entails a rather steep learning curve when it comes to terminology and procedures. For someone becoming a Sister or a Guard, this learning is part of the reason for the carefully delineated stages of training, along with the challenges of learning the sartorial and performative aspects of the role. Induction into any new community can be a lengthy endeavor; in the Sisters, with their serious parody of Roman Catholic orders, that process is carefully codified and monitored even as some in all ranks chafe at the constraints imposed by such structure. So how did this serious parody begin, and how did it develop the myriad and often structured forms it takes today? While the Sisters have their roots in the random acts of three bored men in San Francisco, they are also the result of a constellation of factors, from artistic and activist precursors to new religious movements to an epidemic to politics within and beyond gay communities from the 1970s onward. As early member Sister Loganberry Frost put it, much to the amusement of fellow early Sister Mary Media: "Well, it was like this asteroid belt came into the local universe and landed in San Francisco. Didn't really know what was happening. And there were various asteroids, there was the spiritual asteroids, and the political asteroids, and the showgirl asteroids, and the big ego people."[56] The story of those asteroids, and the corners of the universe from which they came, is the focus of the following chapter.

1

"It Was Like This Asteroid Belt"

The Origins and Growth of the Sisters

The tales of Sister Loganberry's "asteroids" begin in the middle of the twentieth century, thousands of miles from the California coast. One of those celestial bodies, Fred, was raised in a working-class German Catholic household that he left in ninth grade to attend a Capuchin Franciscan preparatory seminary near Pittsburgh, Pennsylvania. Several years later, in the midst of the revolutionary Second Vatican Council and partway through his collegiate studies at the seminary, he was asked to leave in order to "make a heterosexual adjustment."[1] He eventually found his way through college, out of Catholicism and the closet, and into a master's program in film and television at the University of Iowa. There he met former Mennonite and anti-war activist Ken Bunch, who had come to work at the university's hospital after embracing his gayness and consequently dropping out of his Mennonite college in Kansas. The two became co-chairs of the University of Iowa chapter of the Gay Liberation Front. Together they organized a series of gay pride conferences, and brought to the university cutting-edge drag films such as John Waters's *Pink Flamingos* (1971) and the Cockettes' *Tricia's Wedding* (1972). Bunch and his friend Tracy Bjorgum became the first same-sex couple to apply for a marriage license in Iowa, and the two also co-founded a drag troupe called the Sugar Plum Fairies; the troupe became known for the pom-pom routines they performed wearing (and then stripping out of) retired nuns' habits that had been donated by a convent in Cedar Rapids "for a theatrical production."[2] In between work, activism, and drag shows, Bunch and another friend occasionally experimented with portrait photography using white pancake makeup inspired, Bunch recalls, by the emcee in the film *Cabaret*.[3]

A third "asteroid" came from yet another part of the country. Agnes de Garron, a former Catholic like Fred, was born under a different name but has been known for many decades as Agnes in honor of dancer and choreographer Agnes de Mille. De Garron settled in Norfolk, Virginia, after being discharged from the U.S. Air Force. Closeted in that city but also tightly connected to a community of other gay men, de Garron was a professional dancer, choreographer, and dance therapist. In 1976 he became the first of these three "asteroids" to land in San Francisco, where he founded a no-experience-required dance company called Reconstellation General Dance. Passionate about helping gay men battle internalized homophobia through dance and movement, de Garron found his activism in his art.

San Francisco itself is another part of the story, another "asteroid." In the early 1970s the city was home to the Cockettes, a radical theater group with many openly gay members that experimented with genderfuck or "skag" drag, flaunting the conventions of gender by mixing markers such as beards and dresses, and that was so well known for its use of white pancake makeup and glitter that some claim it influenced the glam rock movement of the 1970s and 1980s.[4] San Francisco was also seen by many in the mid-twentieth century as a spiritual haven, influenced by the Zen Buddhism of D. T. Suzuki, the growing popularity of Tibetan Buddhism, a variety of Hinduism-based movements such as Transcendental Meditation and the International Society for Krishna Consciousness (ISKCON, better known as the Hare Krishnas), and a wide range of other new religious movements, including Jim Jones's ill-fated Peoples Temple. Among these religious movements, Transcendental Meditation would play an especially important role in the Sisters, as would a movement founded just four and a half months after the order's first manifestation: the Radical Faeries, a neopagan group for gay men co-founded by longtime gay rights activist Harry Hay.[5]

Bunch arrived in San Francisco in 1977, a year after de Garron, and Fred followed in 1978. The two activists from Iowa soon came to know the choreographer through the city's flourishing gay community. The era of the insistently masculine "Castro clone" being in full swing by the time he moved, Bunch had left all of his drag in a trash can in Iowa—except, fortuitously, the borrowed nuns' habits, which he kept "because I thought I might get bored with this whole butch thing, you know, down the road some time."[6] As he frequently notes, his precaution turned out to be both wise and fateful.

"Psychological Car Wrecks": Early Manifestations

April 14, 1979, was Holy Saturday, the day before Easter, in the calendar used by the Western Christian tradition. Down at 272 Dolores Street, in a carriage house apartment behind an old Victorian on the edge of San Francisco's Castro District, Fred and Ken had nothing interesting to do that day. Maybe, they thought, it was time to do something with those old nuns' habits. Bunch recalls, "So I said, 'Fred, the only thing different I have are these nuns' habits, and I'm bored. Let's throw 'em on and go out and just terrorize the town!'"[7] Fred was game, so they called up a third friend and invited him to join in. As they attired themselves, Bunch added the whiteface he'd been experimenting with back in Iowa, along with some rouge and lipstick. He also grabbed a toy machine gun, a sleeker and more compact model than the combat weaponry many children play with today. Fred brought along his Brownie camera, and the three sallied forth into the neighborhood. They walked up through the Castro, then caught a ride with a friend to the gay nude beach at Lands End, where they strolled the cruising paths before posing for their friend to take pictures. They finished the outing at a high-end coffee shop in the well-to-do neighborhood of Pacific Heights. During this initial manifestation, Bunch recalls seeing what he terms "psychological car wrecks" as people gaped at the clearly male nuns, one in makeup and carrying a toy gun, strolling through the city.[8] "We realized we had a stick of dynamite," Bunch recalls, "and that we should do something productive with it. We should use it as a tool for social change, for the change that we want to see."[9]

The next opportunity to wear the habits, and a chance to bring back the Sugar Plum Fairies' pom-pom routine, arose in the form of a gay softball game. The friend who had gone on the first outing was supportive but not really interested in continuing to dress as a nun, and Fred came to the event in street clothes, so Bunch turned to a different friend to accompany him in habit: Agnes de Garron. "I think we were like cheerleaders," de Garron remembers. "We had pom-poms, and we just sat with the audience. . . . It was like this outdoor fun thing. And it was like a tryout for me of, 'Okay, I'll do it, whatever.'"[10] "So we go to the game," Bunch told me. "It's at Kezar Stadium, [an] outdoor stadium [in Golden Gate Park]. And we're running around, and people are cheering, and we're running around the rim of the stadium, and then we run our veils up the flagpole and the game stops because the players can't figure out what everyone's cheering about."[11] Once again, the sight of men in nuns' habits garnered considerable attention and evoked strong reactions—including, Bunch says, the ire of the gay softball league's manager. So, he recalls, "me and Agnes go back to [my apartment] and talk about what just happened. And then we talk to Fred and we talk to Reverend Mother [Bill Graham, who had also been at the game in street clothes], you know, the four of us, and [said,] 'We need to pull our friends together and form an organization.'"[12]

The Castro Street Fair on August 19 offered the four their opportunity, and de Garron recalls making the suggestion that they present themselves as an order.

> At some point I said, "Well, first of all, I've been to New Orleans, and . . . men dress up as nuns and it's a costume, but it's nothing special." I said, "What would be special is if we are an order of nuns. That's something that doesn't exist. And that we're in a convent. And that the only way we can do that is to have a certain amount of people, and this is the amount of people. And that people should all be dressed the exact same way. . . . If you're in an order, you all look the same."[13]

Appearing by name for the first time at the 1979 Castro Street Fair were Sister Adhanarisvara (Bunch), Sister Missionary Position, often shortened to Sister Mish (Fred), Sister Solicitation (de Garron), and Reverend Mother, the Abbess (Graham). "The four of us," recollects Sister Soami (formerly Missionary Position), "all passed out these holy cards inviting people to call Sister Solicitation at this number if you want to join a nuns' group. I think we passed out maybe three, five hundred cards, but no one really responded."[14] When later recruitment efforts proved more successful, the apartment at 231 Ashbury Street that soon came to be dubbed "The Convent" began to receive quite a few phone calls. Sister Solicitation decided that "we need a code so we don't have to take the call. . . . I'm going to give up that name. Nobody is going to be Sister Solicitation, so we can say she's not in." He changed his name to Sister Hysterectoria, although he also came to be known as Sister Banana Nut Bread because of his regular potluck contributions.[15]

Becoming an Order

Sister Hysterectoria remembers an open-ended recruitment process for new members during the fall of 1979, as the initial four Sisters thought through what their order was and what it should do. Reaching out to friends that he and Reverend Mother had met at the first Radical Faerie Gathering in Arizona that September, "I told them that I was trying to get nuns' habits made and I needed people to go for fittings. I said, 'Will you go in and do a fitting for me?' And so they went in and did that."[16] As a choreographer and dance therapist with training in contact improvisation, Sister Hysterectoria was particularly interested in the performance aspect of the new order. He told me that he was inspired by New York City's famous group Les Ballets Trockadero de Monte Carlo, an all-male dance company that performs parodic adaptations of classical ballet as ballerinas on pointe, and by the androgyny of dancer Isadora Duncan's performance style.[17] Putting his gay male dancers in nuns' habits, then, was not much of a leap; neither was recruiting dancers from among friends he had just met at the Faerie Gathering. Those friends, for their part, had come back from Arizona with a commitment to explore their "faerie," feminine side, so they were equally unlikely to balk at the habits.

Because the habits were part of de Garron's dance performances, the creation of the initial set was undertaken by San Francisco's Costume Bank, a city-funded venture to support local performing arts. The habits, designed by de Garron, were simple: black robes with a white rope at the waist and bibs cut from heavy white paper (and repeatedly re-cut whenever they wore out, and soon replaced by fabric). For the wimples and coronets, de Garron explained,

> I went to the San Francisco library, and I looked through period stuff. And . . . I realized that if you were a maiden and unmarried you dressed a certain way. And then women that didn't get married had a choice of becoming a nun, and a lot of them took that. So I took [the design] from the medieval Flemish [maiden's headdress], and turned it over, and made a copy of it . . . and that's what the original design of the headpiece was. I didn't want something like the nuns that I'd known, where you could basically take a sailor hat and put it in the top and wrap it around. It was like, let's have something with much more oomph, if we're gonna do this thing.[18]

Although the Costume Bank made the first set of wimples, as Sisters began making their own habits they discovered that the easiest way to construct the half-spheres that sat over each ear was to cut apart and stuff a bra; to this day the San Francisco coronets are still referred to as "ear brassieres."

Habits made, members recruited (even if initially just as models for fitting the habits), the Sisters still had to decide what the order was going to do. "The first thing that came up," Sister Hysterectoria told me, "was that we were going to do a photo shoot and make postcards." They approached the men who had modeled for the habit fittings to ask whether they would be interested in a photo shoot. "A lot of them, that's how they started getting involved. Some said, 'Well, I'm more than willing to do that, but I don't want to become a nun.'"[19] Others were enthusiastic from the start, and some who were initially uncertain became more interested as the order continued to develop new projects.

With Sister Homo Fellatio and Sister Missionary Position as photographers, an initial set of four images was made into postcards in the

Figure 1.1. Early SPI postcard. Sisters of Perpetual Indulgence, ONE Subject Files Collection, 2012.001, ONE Archives, Los Angeles. Photo © Greg Day. Reproduced by permission.

spring of 1980; a second set of four followed shortly thereafter, and these were eventually supplemented by greeting cards (fig. 1.1). The Sisters exchanged them for a suggested donation, thus offsetting their printing fees and beginning their history of fundraising. All of the images feature men, both bearded and clean-shaven, wearing matching nuns' habits. In the pictures featuring Sister Adhanarisvara she is wearing makeup; all of the others' faces are unadorned, although a few images include one or more nuns in large sunglasses. Most of the images are quite tame other than the genderfuck involved; they show the Sisters kneeling as if in prayer, cheering and shaking pom-poms, gathered in the woods like Catholic dryads, holding umbrellas as if about to launch into "Singin' in the Rain," and lined up like chorus girls on top of Twin Peaks with the San Francisco skyline in the background. One image features a single Sister, skirts hitched up just above the knee, gaily out for a walk with her dog. Only one is risqué; it shows two Sisters flanking a third who is bent over with her habit hitched up and underwear pulled down, baring a behind on which is written, "MERRY XMAS." One of the nuns is eagerly brandishing a small leather switch while the other smiles at the camera. The parodic aspect of the order was coming through loud and clear, and was an important part of its initial work and its initial attraction, both to new members and to their community. The dance performances were taking off, too. But many of them wanted more. The activist Sisters wanted the order to make change in the world; the spiritual Sisters wanted something deeper and more introspective. Some wanted both. And all of these desires began to echo through their work to develop the order, including finally choosing a name.

It may have been November, December, or even January—no one agrees on the actual date and there do not appear to be minutes from the meeting—but at some point in the winter of 1979–1980 there was a meeting of all current Sisters. It took place at the home of Sister Succuba, who had joined the order as Sister Saliva. The meeting took up an important question: what should they call the order? Several members had been raised Roman Catholic, and Sister Mish had attended seminary, so there was a significant knowledge base on which to draw for reference points. Two years after this meeting, a stuffily disapproving article in the *National Catholic Reporter* would observe that "in the same neighborhood" as the Sisters' Convent, "a convent of cloistered Mexican immigrant nuns is located. They are called the Sisters of Perpetual Adoration." The article claims that "neither is aware of the other's existence."[20] Apparently the author forgot to ask the Sisters of Perpetual Indulgence about their awareness, or perhaps he neglected to interview any of the Sisters who attended that early meeting. "We had the Sisters of Perpetual Adoration up the hill from us in the Haight," Sister Soami recalled when I interviewed him. "[They] spent their days worshipping the Blessed Sacrament, and were a cloistered order so you never really saw them."[21] But their name was part of the inspiration for the name of the newer order of not-so-Catholic Sisters.

"We'd all decided that we definitely wanted 'Perpetual,'" noted Sister Hysterectoria, "'cause it's a common [name], the 'Sisters of Perpetual This,' and we liked the word." So each person at the meeting wrote down all the words he could think of that might round off the name. Sister Soami recalls that he came with a prepared list, a column of adjectives followed by a column of nouns.[22] Eventually the entire group was, in the words of Sister Vish (formerly Sister Adhanarisvara), "toying with different words, combinations, whatever." She added, "and it's like, 'I gotta take a pee.' I went into the bathroom, came out and they had the name!" Sister Hysterectoria attributes the idea of adding the word "indulgence" to Sister Succuba, the host for that night's meeting and the calligrapher who designed and created the order's initial banner. Sister Soami again: "So when that combination was Perpetual *Indulgence*, very quickly did we realize, 'Yeah, that's the name.'" A double entendre referencing both self-indulgent pleasure and the Roman Catholic concept of indulgence as release from punishment for sins that have been forgiven, the name echoed and perhaps also helped to shape the order's ministry. Sister Hysterectoria explained, "We *loved* Perpetual Indulgence. 'Cause it *meant* something. It wasn't just a crazy name. You know, it sort of said who we were." Although the Sisters could not then anticipate this need, the name also carried with it a certain flexibility in emphasis; as Sister Vish noted, "later, when AIDS came along, we shifted the meaning a bit. Less on *Indulgence*, more on *Perpetual*. Staying alive to enjoy the fruits of life."[23]

Who they were, though, may have been easier to determine than what they were to be called. Although the order's constitution and rules of order were not formally drafted and signed until July 27, 1980, Sister

Vish recalls that they determined the group's mission statement at the same meeting in which they decided on a name. "The mission statement came out pretty easy," she told me. "To expiate stigmatic guilt and pro-mulgate universal joy, and, you know, we are an order of gay male nuns. Fred was in the Catholic seminary, you know, Missionary Position, and a couple of others were Catholics, and so I think that verbiage came out pretty easily."[24] Sister Soami believes that they developed the mission statement later on, closer in time to the drafting of the constitution.[25] Whether or not the statement took its final form in the winter, however, the spring of 1980 would see the mission of these new nuns take shape in practice.

Making a Name for Themselves: Public Manifestations

The Sisters made their first public appearance as an officially constituted order during an anti-nuclear protest in March 1980 that marked the one-year anniversary of the partial nuclear meltdown at the Three Mile Island power plant in Pennsylvania. "And we thought, 'Oh! That's for us,'" Sister Soami remembers.

> What a great way to announce, "Here we are," under our banner or what-ever. And for the two weeks beforehand we were making pom-poms at the Convent. I composed a Rosary in Time of Nuclear Peril. And Rever-end Mother was going to the planning sessions, at which . . . , in one of them, he was told we should not come. That we were drag queens; that's offensive to women. We weren't germane to the issue. As if anyone on the planet wasn't germane to nuclear power! We knew they were having a lapse of conscience.[26]

The Sisters, as would become their wont, ignored the lack of welcome. Having gotten into habit rather late that day, they missed the rally at City Hall but managed to join in the march. Sister Soami picks up the story again:

> We jumped in between a coffin [that was] entitled "Capitalism," and huge sponges from the Farallon Islands, where San Francisco dumps its [radio-active] waste. And so we jumped in there with our banner, did pom-pom

routines during the long, about mile-long march, maybe, alternating with our Rosary in Time of Nuclear Peril. And by the time we got to the Panhandle [the narrow neck of parkland that leads into Golden Gate Park], the organizers came up to us to join the large circle of organizers, who asked us to recite the rosary one more time. So. We felt we had, in that first entrance, really established the poles of our ministry, which was to be doing something fun and outrageous and humorous, and also informing it with a bed of earnest prayer. And I think that's the winning combination for us: to combine our humor with prayerful acts.[27]

The Sisters marched as a group in the Gay Freedom Day parade for the first time in 1980, and while they may also have appeared at other events in the late spring and early summer of that year, there appear to be no records of those manifestations. But the new order of nuns burst onto the Castro scene and into the local media in August 1980. It was a time of resurgence for evangelical Christianity, and a time of rapid growth in the conservative political, cultural, and religious backlash against the marked social changes wrought by the social and political movements of the 1960s and 1970s. A key branch of the ex-gay movement, one of the organizations that came together to form Exodus International, had taken shape just north of San Francisco at around the same time as the founders of the Sisters were moving to the city.[28] And these evangelical forces, heterosexual and ex-gay, believed that God was calling them to travel to the heart of Sodom and bring the sexual sinners into the light of faith.

The evangelists often set up right in the heart of the Castro, either on the sidewalk in front of the Hibernia Bank building at the intersection of Castro and 18th Street, known facetiously in the neighborhood as Hibernia Beach, or a block up the hill in Harvey Milk Plaza. Singing and praying aloud, they carried the Christian condemnation that underlay so many people's internalized homophobia into the center of the one place where many gay men felt safe and to a plaza named in honor of a recently assassinated Jewish gay rights activist. Beyond being deeply offensive and disrespectful, it was a profoundly aggressive and threatening gesture, and people in the Castro responded accordingly. "I remember being uncomfortable one night," Sister Soami told me, "where all at once it turned into, 'Get out of our neighborhood! Get out of our neighborhood!' [People were] blowing the[ir] whistles. And we would literally just march them down the street and chase them; they couldn't get out fast enough."[29] The Sisters soon came up with a different approach during a particularly intense wave of evangelization. Reporter John Kyper wrote about the event a few weeks later in the *Gay Community News*:

> On Friday, August 22, Castro Street was the scene of a guerrilla theater performance by the Sisters of Perpetual Indulgence, a "convent" of gay male "nuns," who lustily upstaged the nightly prayer meetings that had been taking place in Harvey Milk Plaza. A dozen of the Sisters appeared in the middle of the evening and quickly drew about them an enthusiastic crowd. Seldom does one see so many smiling, laughing people on Castro—though a few seemed grimly annoyed that their cruising as usual was being disrupted by the festivities. At Castro and 18th, a "nun" read a "litany" which included the prayer "Have *mercy* upon the self-righteous who take away our liberty!"
>
> A small group of fundamentalists who had fled the plaza when the nuns arrived subsequently returned with reinforcements, and again began singing and praying on the overpass overlooking the new Metro station. The nuns then marched up the street, bringing over 100 spectators in tow. They mounted the low wall behind the 30 somber Christians and began to dance, to the cheers of the audience. The litany was repeated, to even greater enthusiasm. The circus continued for half an hour, until the fundamentalists marched out, accompanied by whistles and chants of "No more guilt!"[30]

The generous use of quotation marks ("convent," "nun," "litany") in this early media coverage of the order indicates that those whom the Sisters called their gathered faithful were still struggling to sort out the nature of the order that had blossomed in their midst. But part of the genius of the Sisters' use of serious parody in this scene is the way it turned the evangelists' weapons back on themselves. Just as the missionaries' "love the sinner, hate the sin" approach thinly cloaked virulent homophobia within apparently well-meaning prayers for the heterosexual conversion of the gay men around them, so the Sisters' prayers for divine mercy toward the self-righteous cast biting critique within an ostensible concern for the evangelicals' souls.

The same Christian group was slated to rally at the more central San Francisco location of Union Square the following day. Sister Soami recalls the scene vividly:

> That Saturday afternoon in Union Square they had a Christian rock band and they were giving witness. They were giving *their* witness. We typically showed up a little late, the Sisters, by the time we got it all together to get down there. And the gay community that was more responsible, and wanting to get them out of the area, were there sort of chomping at the bit, being angry in the corner, but all at once we showed up. And they smiled, and they were relieved. And we, rather than just sort of getting with them and being onlookers, jumped into the midst of all these dancing Christian youth. And flirted with them. And invited them to keep on dancing, and danced with them. And it just blew everyone's mind. And the gay people quit being angry and blowing their whistles, and maybe ventured forth into joining the party. And to me, I thought that was a real, again, a power point of what our strategy needs to be when confronting people who are violent and hateful to us.[31]

Other members of the order who took part in these actions also recall the nonconfrontational approach taken by the order as unique and valuable. Sister Mary Media observed that the Sisters "kind of provided a community voice in response to these people. It was like a campy, alternative way of expressing resistance without doing it in a hostile or violent way. I mean, the Sisters went down and danced around the Christians who came down to spread their hateful message. And I think the community saw that and felt that we were on their side and we were providing a voice."[32]

Sister Soami's and Sister Media's observations on the Sisters' counter-demonstration highlight the importance of these actions in bringing together the final piece of the Sisters' activism: joy. The postcards had made the Sisters' parody clear; the Three Mile Island protest demonstrated their seriousness, bringing humor together with "prayerful acts." But the ethos of the order seems to have gelled in these guerrilla street theater actions against homophobic Christian witness. Here, for the first time, the promulgation of universal joy and the expiation of stigmatic guilt were on full display, hand-in-hand, brought to life through serious parody. It was a complex and novel combination; no wonder, then, that even a sympathetic reporter struggled to describe what exactly he was seeing.

Growing Activism

After what some call the "first routing of the Christians," both the Sisters' visibility and their activities picked up rapidly.[33] In October 1980 they joined forces with the Metropolitan Community Church of San Francisco, a part of the denomination founded twelve years earlier in Los Angeles by the Reverend Troy Perry to serve LGBT Christians.[34] At MCC's church in the Castro the Sisters organized a bingo game—a traditional churchly activity, but of course with a few risqué twists—followed by a dance. All proceeds went to MCC's program supporting gay Cubans who had come to the United States as refugees in the Mariel boatlift that year. The bingo game, the start of a long history of raunchy bingo fundraising in the order, garnered the Sisters their first coverage in the mainstream media. Their mention at the top of the famed gossip and humor column of San Francisco legend Herb Caen is worth reproducing here in full:

> If anyone is collecting tidbits for a time capsule which, when opened 100 years hence, would suggest what San Francisco was like in October, 1980, it would be hard to top or even explain this announcement of an event beginning at 8 o'clock tonight:
>
> "The Sisters of Perpetual Indulgence invite you to a bingo/disco benefit for the Gay Cuban refugees. The bingo (which will be called in Spanish, English, and sign language) begins at 8 p.m., followed by a disco and salsa dance. The Sisters will be available to absolve you of your sins, and there's a no-host bar. Metropolitan Community Church, 150 Eureka."
>
> Who are the Sisters of Perpetual Indulgence? For the delectation of historians a century hence, Sister Missionary Position explains that "We are an order of gay men dedicated to the promulgation of universal joy and the expiation of stigmatic guilt. We have 17 sisters and two novices who spread joy and put on theatrical presentations. Some of us do have regular jobs to support our habits." And with that sly pun, we slide off in the direction of the nearest no-host bar, singing along with Charles Pierce, "Saaaan Fraaancisco, open your golden gay . . ."[35]

It should be noted that Caen himself was a notorious punster; clearly he couldn't resist following up Sister Mish's pun with one of his own.

The October bingo game was followed two days later by the Sisters' participation in a protest against the University of San Francisco, a Roman Catholic institution that had refused to recognize its gay student organizations.[36] November brought a performance called "Mainstream Exiles" that included Sister Hysterectoria's choreography,[37] and a march against violence in honor of the anniversary of Harvey Milk's and George Moscone's assassinations, at which the Sisters performed a "Litany for Justice for All."[38] By December the gay press was turning more intensive attention toward the Sisters, with articles by Vinnie Hansen, Greg Day, and Mark Thompson appearing in rapid succession in the subsequent months.[39]

The following year brought tireless manifestations at performances, protests, festivals, and everyday occasions; the *San Francisco Examiner* even termed the Sisters "ubiquitous."[40] Among other manifestations in 1981, the Sisters featured in a short film produced through the Stanford University Communications Department, in which they danced to Tom Lehrer's "Vatican Rag";[41] Sister Lida Dogslife organized a charity dog show;[42] the Sisters attracted international press attention and earned approving commentary from San Francisco religion reporter Kevin Starr, who was chastised by many readers and by his own Roman Catholic Church for his pains;[43] members of the order played a softball game against the Gay Men's Chorus to raise funds for the first Gay Olympics (now the Gay Games);[44] and they closed out the year with police harassment. On Christmas Eve, Sisters Adhanarisvara and Missionary Position were cited for "peddling" because they and Sister Pius Peak from Denver had set up a confessional booth on Hibernia Beach and were distributing postcards, t-shirts, and "holy ashes from the Folsom Street fire" for a suggested donation.[45] Their rising profile in the local, national, and international press in 1981 also led to the founding of the order's second and third houses during that year.

Sending Out New Asteroids

If one can speak metaphorically of the early Sisters of Perpetual Indulgence as the product of multiple asteroids landing in the right place at the right time, then one might also say that in 1981 the celestial body formed by these asteroids was spinning fast enough to loose new asteroids of its own; they landed first in Toronto, Canada, and Sydney, Australia.

Apparently inspired by press coverage of the San Francisco Sisters, an initially unaffiliated group of gay male nuns manifested for the first time at the inaugural Lesbian and Gay Pride Day in Toronto on June 28, 1981.[46] Sources from the first Toronto house are relatively rare, but an internal document that introduced new Sisters to the house's procedures lists eight original members: Sister Appassionata della Bawdy House, Sister Opiate of the Masses, Sister Robbed at Birth, Sister Florida Naranja, Sister Intelligentsia, Sister Exposia, Sister Rosa Relentless, and Sister Hair Apparent.[47] Contact between the Toronto and San Francisco houses was spotty; "they actually wrote to us and asked permission to use the name," recalls Sister Hysterectoria, "and we never replied. So they just did it anyway."[48] Sister Flirtatious Romanovsky of Middlesex, who was a member of the original Toronto house as Sister Flagellation of Forbidden Fruit, recounts that "after that first manifestation Sister Mary Media, a member of the San Francisco Mother House and a Toronto native visited and, in the words of founding Sister Soami DeLuxe (ne Sister Missionary Position) 'brought word back to the Mother House you were A OK.'"[49] The Sisters of Perpetual Indulgence were beginning to move beyond their status as a solitary house of nuns and a part of San Francisco's local color; they were on their way to becoming an international order.

In 1980, before the Toronto house manifested, Gary Schliemann came from Sydney to California for a long-term visit. Sister Soami recalls that he was particularly interested in the Radical Faeries; he visited founders of that group in Los Angeles and attended the second Radical Faerie Gathering.[50] Schliemann also traveled to San Francisco; when he asked Harry Hay to recommend a place to stay in that city, Hay gave him a phone number for the Sisters. Shortly after arriving in San Francisco Schliemann ended up, like many friends of the Sisters in those days, donning a habit. He took the name of Sister Gazella Gardenia (fig. 1.2), and manifested with the San Francisco house before returning home to Sydney early in 1981.[51]

In the meantime, another gay man in Sydney had started to wear a nun's habit in public. Raised Roman Catholic, he had undertaken a novitiate in the late 1960s and early 1970s in an Australian Premonstratensian

Figure 1.2. Sister Gazella Gardenia, later Sister Mary Medusa, best known as Sister Mae Call of the Wilde, in an early manifestation with the San Francisco House, ca. 1980. Reproduced by permission of Gary Schliemann and Soami Archive.

monastery in Wisconsin. His sexuality was evident even when he started at the monastery, he recalls in retrospect, at least from the day when

> we were told, "No, you need secular clothes to go out in. You can't go out in habit. You must dress like other people. Now here's thirty dollars, go and buy shirt, trousers, and boots and things." And I came back, unconsciously camp, having chosen this shirt, it was 1971 or 1970, great pointy collar, blue and yellow tiny flowers, and a big three-button cuff with big poufy sleeves and pleats, and they must have thought then, "This one! Here's another gay one. Look at this one, what he's picked." And tight white jeans![52]

In addition to a budding recognition of his sexuality while at the abbey, something else happened to this young novice. It took place on Holy Innocents' Day, when "the abbey had a muck-up day, based on a medieval tradition of the whole system of hierarchy being inverted for the day. So the youngest novice became the abbot. One of my classmates made up a nun's habit. And I remember thinking, 'That looks really lovely!' " He left the abbey expecting to "get rid of the sexuality and come back and live the life I wanted to live as a member of a religious order."[53] But gay liberation had begun, the idea of wearing a nun's habit had been planted, and he went instead to study at the University of New South Wales.

In April 1981, when Gary Schliemann was interviewed for the radio program "Gay Waves," he discussed his time with the Sisters in San Francisco.[54] Sydney's gay community being a small world, someone surmised that there might be a connection between the gay man wearing a nun's habit and the one talking about all the gay men in San Francisco who also wore nuns' habits. The two got together to compare notes. "I looked at the stuff [Sister Gazella] had brought back," recounts the former monastic, "and I thought, Och! This is shocking, you know? They have weird-looking wimples, and they've got beards! What's this about? And some of them had white makeup on."[55] But he was intrigued by the idea of an order of gay male nuns, and Sister Gazella was interested in continuing his ministry in Sydney, so the two began organizing and soon attracted the interest of two more potential members. After an initial manifestation of the original two members in habit as part of a performance of Sydney's famous Gay Liberation Quire, the Sydney house of the Sisters of Perpetual Indulgence officially began with a springtime picnic involving four gay male nuns on October 17, 1981. The former monk became Sister Volupta but was renamed within a few months by other members of the house as Mother Inferior. Sister Gazella became Sister Mary Medusa, soon to be renamed Sister Mae Call of the Wilde. The other two founding members, or Ancients, of the Sydney house who attended the picnic in habit were Sister Sit On My Face, known in the house as Somfie, and Sister Gerontophilia Extravaganza. According to an early timeline written up mostly by Mother Inferior and shared within the house by Sister Cum Dancing, the picnic took place at Sydney's Long Nose Point, where the new order "close[d] the afternoon with some sinining [sic] and serenading ferry passengers."[56] There have been Sisters in Sydney continuously since that day.

The appearance and ministry of the early Toronto and Sydney houses demonstrate a similar serious parody approach to that of the San Francisco Sisters—an approach enhanced in Sydney by the close ties between the Sisters and the campy, activist Gay Liberation Quire.[57] Mother Inferior visited both the San Francisco house and the Toronto house in 1983, and in a conversation with me he reflected on his observations of the budding order. Being a bit more traditional and conservative than most Sisters, he found himself more impressed with the Toronto house than with the drug use, makeup, and increasingly sexualized drag that had become standard in the San Francisco house by that time. "But I did meet [San Francisco Sister] Bobbi Campbell, Sister Florence Nightmare," he explained to me, "and I began to see, this is a very strong community. And it strengthened me. When I went back, I had a greater sense of identity."[58]

All was not lost, then, for Mother Inferior's trip to the Mother House. In Toronto, though, he found greater reassurance that he was part of a worldwide order that was aligned with his own values and priorities. "I was *very* impressed with them," he told me.

> And I found that they were more in tune to us [in Sydney]. Understated. Although there was one, . . . Sister Atrociata von Tasteless! He put things on the top of his veil, like a frying pan, or a Chinese hat, or a pineapple something-or-other. He was very funny. . . . Their names, and the photographs that they had taken of them in certain sites in Toronto, had local humor. And so I came back with this sense, "We really have a good role here. This is wonderful; we belong to this international group who are welcoming and hospitable. This is *marvelous!*"[59]

While the Sydney Sisters grew rapidly, even forming a second Australian house and the fourth house of the entire order in Melbourne in 1983, the Toronto house received less community support than did any of the other three. In 1982 a supportive article in the gay magazine *Body Politic* led to a virulently negative response, not only among the city's heterosexual leadership but also from the gay community's most prominent religious voice, MCC Toronto pastor Brent Hawkes.[60] Whereas MCC San Francisco had already joined forces with the Sisters a year and a half earlier to raise funds for the church's gay Cuban refugee program, and the pastor of MCC Sydney would invite the Sisters to attend a service in July 1983,[61] Reverend Hawkes went on record against the order.

At a time when assimilationist politics were again overtaking lesbian and gay communities, resistance from a leading gay pastor may have played a role in undermining the Toronto house. It lasted another four years, but after persistent negative feedback from some in the community (and it is evident that not all felt this way), the Sisters published a notice in *Body Politic* announcing that they were disbanding as of October 1, 1986. "The Sisters are very proud of their accomplishments," the opening paragraph explained, "and feel that needs still exist within our community. However, it seems as if our message has been overshadowed by our appearance. Our image has blinded many to the work we were doing."[62] "I joke [that] it's a terribly Canadian thing," says Sister Merry Peter with a smile. "You know, 'Ooh, I'm causing ruffles! Oof! Well, close that down!' And then they disappeared."[63] Not two years after that disappearance, as a young graduate student interested in gay male spirituality, he would run across a shoebox of newspaper clippings about the defunct house in Toronto's LGBT archives and become fascinated by the Sisters.

Pandemic: The Impact of AIDS

In the early 1980s, as the Sisters were expanding rapidly in San Francisco, something far more foreboding was spreading there as well that would challenge the promulgation of joy and the expiation of guilt, within and beyond their order, more than any homophobic religious group or politician ever could.[64] At the beginning of the decade, doctors in cities like San Francisco, New York, and Los Angeles began to take note of several rare conditions that were occurring with disturbing frequency in patients who appeared to be otherwise healthy. Two of the most obvious were a rare form of pneumonia—pneumocystis pneumonia—and a rare form of cancer called Kaposi's Sarcoma that soon came to be called the "gay cancer" or simply "KS." Patients with these symptoms also had other opportunistic infections that either were startlingly uncommon— like a microorganism usually found in pigeon droppings—or were seen only in people with severely suppressed immune systems, and the doctors who began to track the suspicious recurrence of such symptoms saw these patients' bodies break down rapidly and the patients die despite the doctors' best efforts. The only link that researchers could find was that many patients who had some or all of these symptoms were gay, others used intravenous drugs, and some were part of both groups.

Early in 1982 the complex of illnesses began to be known as GRID, or Gay Related Immune Deficiency; later that year it was officially named Acquired Immune Deficiency Syndrome, or AIDS. The new disease came to devastate socially and economically vulnerable communities across the world, including communities of gay men, communities of color, sex workers, injectable drug users, and poor communities with little access to health care or safer-sex supplies. In the early 1980s, though, its initial name of GRID linked it inexorably and ineradicably to all LGBT people in the popular imaginary and thereby fanned the flames of homophobia, biphobia, and transphobia that activists had been trying so hard for so long to stamp out.

Sister Soami remembers that Bobbi Campbell already had Kaposi's Sarcoma lesions when he joined the Sisters of Perpetual Indulgence. A public health nurse in his secular life, Campbell took on the name of Sister Florence Nightmare, RN. Though well-known within the Sisters, Sister Florence Nightmare is better known internationally as Campbell, having appeared with his partner Bobby Hilliard on the cover of *Newsweek* on August 8, 1983. "We just knew something was happening, something sexually related," recalls Sister Soami, even back in 1982.[65] Especially in the years following the Stonewall Riots and in the wake of the sexual revolution, gay men in many large cities had created a culture that celebrated sex between men. Because many of the sexually transmitted infections that were common at the time were curable even if unpleasant, and also because they were pushing back against long-standing, concerted, and violent repression, there was little concern and in fact frequent disdain in this milieu for safer sex practices. Add to that the alcohol and drugs that attended any party scene, straight or gay, in the 1970s and early 1980s, and the result was not good news for sexual health—especially with a virulent, deadly, sexually transmitted retrovirus on the loose that had a lengthy incubation period and hadn't even been identified.

A very early Sister re-enters the scene here. The third man who went on the initial manifestation with Sister Adhanarisvara and Sister Missionary Position took the name of Sister Roz Erection but never really became involved in the order. Like Sister Florence Nightmare, though, he was a public health nurse, and the two of them got the idea to write a hip, sexy, funny guide to safer sex that gay men would actually read and take seriously, and that would contribute to the Sisters' mission of promulgating universal joy and expiating stigmatic guilt. The result of their efforts, in collaboration with a doctor (William Owen), a cartoonist from Toronto's *Body Politic* (Gary Ostrom), the design talents of Sister Mary Media, and several other Sisters (Sister Lida Dogslife, Sister Blue Nun, Sister Marie EverReady, and Sister Francis Diana), along with widespread fundraising, was a pamphlet entitled *Play Fair!*, the first safer-sex guide designed for gay men by gay men, presented to the public at San Francisco's Gay Freedom Day on June 27, 1982, as part of a "Mass in a Time of War against V.D." (figure 2 of the color insert, top).[66]

In the early 1980s, as AIDS continued to spread and neither cure nor treatment nor even reliable prevention was yet in sight, the Sisters focused increasingly on safer-sex education and fundraising for HIV/AIDS care; many houses still prioritize sexual health as their main focus today. Since its introduction, *Play Fair!* has been distributed by the Sisters free of charge, often accompanied by safer-sex supplies such as condoms and lube. The early Toronto house produced its own version of *Play Fair!* entitled *Cum Clean*,[67] as did a number of later houses, and in 1999 the San Francisco house revised the *Play Fair!* pamphlet to be inclusive of all genders and bodies.[68] In 2002 Seattle's Abbey of St. Joan took over the publication of *Play Fair!*, producing a Spanish version in 2010, and the London House of Common Sluts began printing its guide in 2009.[69] In keeping with the more inclusive focus of the twenty-first century versions of *Play Fair!*, today some houses also pass out "bliss kits" that offer safer-sex supplies for a variety of bodies and activities.

Through the Keyhole

Like many gay organizations in the early 1980s, the Sisters soon started to lose members to AIDS, including Sister Florence Nightmare in 1984. The ranks of the Nuns of the Above—those who had passed away—swelled long before the order should have had to even create that status. As the Sisters grew rapidly in numbers, came under increasingly intense and persistent media attention, and came to expect more and more of themselves and each other, as their members started to sicken, die, and suffer the depression, grief, trauma, and guilt of those who survived, cracks developed and widened in the social edifice of the Mother House and between its members, the gay community, and the larger Bay Area public.

"In the early '80s," recalled Sister Vish, "when we had thirty, forty members and they were burning out, they were telling me, 'It's time to stop. It's over. We've done it all.' And my response was, 'No, we're just starting.'" As AIDS hit full-force, "it was a war zone on the streets, with ill people here. And my whole vision was, we['ve] just got to get through this brief period. We just have to get through this keyhole. And on the other side of the door, boom, it's going to take off again."[70] At the start of 1982, everyone in the order could see this rosy future. The Sisters were outspoken and often effective political activists for a variety of causes, yet they were also taking care of themselves and each other through dance, meditation, and ritual. Their regard in the community had grown steadily; despite ongoing Catholic ire they had captured the interest and goodwill of many in the larger heterosexual community; they commanded respect on the streets and could parlay that respect to help raise significant funds for important community causes; and many people still expected that KS and pneumocystis pneumonia would turn out to be just another STI like the relatively minor, treatable infections they already knew. "February of '82 was the pinnacle of our acceptance in this community," opined Sister Vish; Sister Soami sees the peak lasting through that year.[71] The Gay Olympics was still fundraising, and the Sisters played another game—basketball this time—against the Gay Men's Chorus to help them out, raising nearly $2,000.[72] "Everyone afterwards [was] like, 'You missed it?'" recalls Sister Vish. "'Oh my God, you cannot miss the next one.' Right? Cute little mascots. Great fun, they know how to throw a party, you know, something unusual."[73]

Sister Adhanarisvara and Sister Missionary Position had also had that run-in with the police at the end of 1981, which led to their being invited to take part in a meeting between representatives of the gay community and San Francisco mayor (later U.S. senator) Dianne Feinstein regarding policing in the Castro. Sister Adhanarisvara arrived directly from work and was not in habit, but Sister Missionary Position came fully manifested; the former was allowed into the meeting while the latter was asked to remain in the hallway. After the official meeting, both

Sisters met informally with the mayor. Other leaders of the gay community explained to her who the Sisters were and lauded the work they were doing. Feinstein, for her part, responded negatively, telling the two founding Sisters, "When I see you, I see *red*." Although Jewish, Feinstein had been schooled by Roman Catholic nuns, and like the Catholics who castigated *Examiner* religion reporter Kevin Starr for finding the Sisters inoffensive, she saw mockery where many others saw camp.[74] The Sisters, in response, decided to hold a Red Party.[75]

By this time in the history of the order, two members had joined who were to become central to the story of its next several years: Sister Sadie Sadie the Rabbi Lady and Sister Chanel 2001. The latter was a celebrity in the gay community even when out of face: he was Gilbert Baker, designer of the now-ubiquitous rainbow flag. He had a flair for visual impact, moving quickly, for instance, out of the traditional Sister habit and into more glamorous apparel. He also had a talent for producing extravagant events. He and Sister Adhanarisvara, both powerful personalities and ardent activists, began to clash.

Sister Chanel was the coordinator of the Red Party, which had been scheduled for May 1 as a reference both to labor movements (referencing "red" communism) and to the neopagan holiday of Beltane, a celebration of fertility in all its forms. The order had rented out "a beautiful Victorian ballroom built in 1909": the Russian Center on Sutter Street.[76] Proceeds were to benefit the upcoming Gay Olympic Games and Golden Gate Performing Arts. Presumably, the tsarist loyalists and their descendants who contributed to and ran the Russian Center found the press release's brief references to "post-revolutionary vigor" in "a pre-revolutionary setting" relatively harmless. But problems arose when the decorations went up. Prominently displayed on the front of the building were a number of flags. "So, Red Party, [Sister Chanel] finds . . . eight national flags with the most red in them," Sister Vish told me wryly. "The ones with the most red. Well, the most red would be communist China, and would be [the] Soviet Union. [Chanel] hangs the flags out in front of the Russian Center."[77] Other sources say there were three flags, but all agree that the Soviet flag was one of them. In addition, Sister Chanel convinced the owners of a homemade rocket to lend it to the Sisters for the night; it was set up in front of the building on a flatbed truck. And that evening, unbeknownst to the Sisters, the Russian Center Ladies' Committee had its annual board meeting. When the committee members arrived they were understandably horrified, and by all accounts Sister Chanel's handling of the incident was rather far from diplomatic.[78] A little over two weeks later, the headline in the *Examiner* read, "Russian Center's Ladies See Too Much Red and Bad Habits," beneath an image of two Sisters shouting angrily.[79] The decline, in the eyes of some at least, had begun.

Not that it was all bad. For Sister Vish, regardless of the ongoing tensions she had with Chanel, there was an advantage to the Red Party gaffe and subsequent controversy. "The community split" over the issue, she recalls, with the less radical among them exclaiming, "'Oh! They're offending us, they're embarrassing us.' [We thought,] 'We're ruining it for everyone? What are we ruining?' So that's our new bumper sticker: 'Ruining it for everyone.' . . . And from that point on . . . people realized we had politics. That there was a political message here. There was more to it than just being funny little mascots."[80] The Sisters continued to be prominent in the community, running fundraisers like the Second Annual Dog Show and Parade (in a sign of the times, that year it benefited the Kaposi's Sarcoma Cancer Clinic) and releasing the *Play Fair!* pamphlet. But the press coverage trailed off, and the membership began to do the same.

One area in which the Sisters did receive positive media attention in the latter part of 1982 was the race for city supervisor positions. According to Jack Fertig, his involvement in the race as Sister Boom Boom, the "Nun of the Above" candidate, started as a campy form of humor. Sister Boom Boom, who was also known as Sister Rose of the Bloody Stains of the Sacred Robes of Je-EE-sus (with at least the final word intoned in plainchant), served as one of the emcees for the 1981 softball game between the Sisters and the Gay Men's Chorus. "And right there in the middle of everything," he recalled in a 1998 oral history interview,

> I just, you know, just sort of a comic, I said, you know, I was thinking of running for supervisor. Yeah, it's like I asked everybody, which supervisor can make the Muni run on time and more effectively and everybody says Nun. You know, what supervisor can cut taxes and deliver more services, and they said Nun. What supervisor can solve the housing crisis? Nun. Well, that's a mandate, maybe I should run. What do you think? And everybody would cheer.[81]

Sister Boom Boom received the requisite number of petition signatures, and her name was placed on the ballot.

A photogenic nun already, and prone to showing off shapely legs in fishnet stockings and showgirl-style shoes, Sister Boom Boom was even more eye-catching because she, like many nuns in the order at this point, had adopted Sister Adhanarisvara's practice of wearing whiteface with eye makeup, sometimes false eyelashes, rouge, and lipstick. As Sister Hysterectoria explained to me, in the low-resolution black-and-white print of a newspaper, "this *reads* really well."[82] Bemused reporters wrote stories about the gay male nun running for supervisor,[83] and campaign posters featured a smiling Sister Boom Boom flying over City Hall on a broom that emitted lavender smoke spelling out the words, "Surrender Diane"—complete with a misspelling of Dianne Feinstein's first name (figure 3 of the color insert).[84] When the dust settled, the Sister had received 23,124 votes, "within a few percentage points of election."[85] The following year, a conservative supervisor instituted a provision that candidates must run under their legal names; it came to be known as the "Boom Boom law."

But while Sister Boom Boom rose to fame—buoyed, Fertig said later, by alcohol and drug addiction—the seams of the San Francisco Sisters were fraying. All of these rising tensions began to manifest more clearly in 1983. Sister Chanel, for instance, resigned from the order that spring, in the process unintentionally giving Sister Adhanarisvara the name by which she would come to be known for decades. Sister Vish remembers that at a general membership meeting, or GM, in the Convent, "Chanel stood up and made this long speech about resigning from the order. And then after everyone left, I go in and I find a letter on my bed. 'You vicious, la-la-la-la-la, you power hungry fucking bitch!' So the next GM I show up and say, 'I have a new name. It's Sister Vicious Power Hungry Bitch.' Everybody's like, 'Yeah, right on! That is you! That is you! That's it, that's it!' "[86]

Other Sisters, particularly those who were involved with or strongly influenced by the Radical Faeries, had growing concerns about the order's procedures. Faeries are essentially anarchist, and they value consensus decision making even when the process is time-consuming. The Sisters' Constitution and Rules of Order, ratified in July 1980, provided for the semiannual election of three "Mistresses of Order to assure the perpetuity and gentle guidance of our young order of indulgent nuns."[87] Sister Soami remembers that these Mistresses "were gently trying to guide us to consensus decision making, as opposed to the tyranny of democracy." Other members of the order had little patience with this process and preferred adherence to Robert's Rules of Order; those who valued consensus felt that their voices were not being heard and their views were being ignored. "And indeed it just precipitated at one point three of the Mistresses just threw up their hands."[88] The Sisters had their first schism. According to Sister Soami, the schismatic group, made up of Sister Homo Fellatio, Sister Viola Tricolor, Sister Kaye Sera, and Sister Francis Diana, called themselves the Little Sisters of Immaculate Sin, and concentrated more on the spiritual side of the Sisterhood. They manifested for about a year and then drifted apart.

Sister Hysterectoria and Reverend Mother found their interest in the group flagging for related reasons. "We didn't leave the order," Sister Hysterectoria explained to me; "we stopped going to the meetings. Because they were just fighting. It was like two people [Vish and Chanel] fighting over how they were gonna run stuff. Didn't interest [us] at all, and it was nothing to do with anything that we had been doing, the Sisters. People were just fighting for power. So we just stopped going."[89] The two manifested on their own occasionally, and still did events with other Sisters at times, but they moved out of the Convent and drifted away from the order. Sister Hysterectoria recalls this entire time period being "so painful for me . . . that I realized I needed to move out of San Francisco to NYC in the mid 80's for my own well-being."[90] Early in 1984, Sister Missionary Position left San Francisco with his partner, Crazy Owl, to take the latter's alternative health education program on the road. Within a year Sister Mish had settled at the Short Mountain Radical Faerie Sanctuary in Tennessee. Thus, by the middle of 1984 three of the four Sisters considered to be founders were gone from the order. Only Sister Vish remained, still fighting with Sadie and Chanel and joined by, in her estimation, three other members. They were entering what she called "the keyhole."

Looking back, Sister Vish can see strengths even in these strained times. Having returned to a membership nearly the size of the original order, "We could do what the fuck we wanted!"[91] They mandated whiteface and began admitting women, following but likely unaware of the lead of the Melbourne house, which had admitted the first "female gay male nun" in 1983 (Sister Very Maculate; see figure 1 of the color insert).[92] Sister Mysteria of the Holy Order of the Broken Hymen was the first woman to join the San Francisco House, and likely the second one in the entire order; a local dominatrix, she could easily hold her own against any residual sexism stemming from years of tensions between gay male and lesbian communities. Sister Blanche de Roote, also a woman, joined shortly thereafter. The Sisters did not manifest nearly as much during this period, and their manifestations were generally far more low-key—not the big productions of years past. When significant events did take place, such as the 1987 exorcism of Pope John Paul II, they flew Sister Mish out from Tennessee to join in, and occasionally when they needed to add to their numbers they skipped a few steps of the formal membership process. Stories abound from that time period of Sisters who were "black veiled on a bar stool" before a protest or other event.

The final straw for Sister Boom Boom came in 1986, just a short time into her sobriety, when against her better judgment but as a favor to Sister Vish she agreed to emcee yet another basketball fundraiser. Part of her ability to keep Boom Boom's vibrant personality going had come from drugs and alcohol; now sober, she recalled in 1998,

> I couldn't do it, it just was not there. I did my best to hold it together and do what I had to do, and then Sadie comes up. . . . She and Sister Chanel 2001 set me up to hit me in the face with a big old cream pie. I was not happy to begin with. This puts me over the edge. . . . I just jumped on Chanel. We had a wig pulling, eye scratching knock down fight right there. We were pulled away. And I was taken backstage to clean up. I just went home.[93]

The basketball game was Sister Boom Boom's final manifestation, although having converted to Islam toward the end of his life, Fertig appeared in Sister space once wearing a chador, at a private party during the order's thirtieth anniversary celebration.[94]

The public skirmishes between Vish, Boom Boom, Sadie, and Chanel, which did nothing for the order's reputation in San Francisco, culminated with the latter two Sisters putting together their own protest of the pope's visit in 1987 and constituting themselves as the "official Papal welcoming committee." Sister Soami, in town for the protest, remembers watching the news that evening.

> And the press is there talking to Chanel. [The reporter] says, "Explain this to me. You're supporting these nuns," which were the Roman Catholic nuns [opposing] the Central American wars, "but you're against these nuns," and he's pointing to the Sisters of Perpetual Indulgence who sort of look like [Chanel]. And he says, "It sounds like there's a war between the nuns!" And Chanel says, "You're right. It's a war. It's a war of the drag queens!" It's riveting TV. I mean, and it's true! And I laugh. And I say, "Oh, I wish we weren't doing this."[95]

The "war of the drag queens" was finally resolved through court-ordered arbitration. In 1987 the Sisters of Perpetual Indulgence, with Sister Vish at the helm, became a legal corporation and trademarked their name, thereby achieving two results. On the one hand, they finally had effective tools to prevent the sullying of their reputation by people who refused to support their mission or who even actively opposed it; on the other hand, they had become a legal entity, which some members considered a betrayal of their anarchist roots.

At their nadir, at the center of the keyhole, the San Francisco house was publicly castigated by its own former members—not for what it had been, as is often the focus of religious apostates, but for what it had become. In an April 1987 article dramatically titled "Walking on the Waters of Babylon: A Meditation on the Death of the Sisters of Perpetual Indulgence," Harry Kelley, also known as Sister Kaye Sera, bemoaned "the real damage, the meanness of spirit, that seems to have settled upon them. 'Sisters of Perpetual Indulgence, *Inc.*, indeed!' We have become the very thing we sought to fight against." Admittedly, the piece is a heartbreaking and grief-stricken dirge that is difficult if not impossible to read dry-eyed; it is more about the deaths of so many individual Sisters than the dying of the order itself. Yet part of what Kelley mourns is what the Sisters were, something that for him in 1987 they no longer can be. "It grieves me today," he writes, "to see what has happened to my Sisters. The damnation of the downtrodden: vituperating each other in the media, suing each other in the courts, even throwing pies in each other's faces in efforts to publically humiliate and shame. As we dance on the edge of the pit of despair, we ought to be able to depend on the kindness of friends."[96] Two years later, in 1989, Sister Boom Boom—now known again only as Jack Fertig—wrote a far more caustic piece for the *Bay Times* following the Sisters' tenth anniversary party. He set the tone with his opening lines: "It was the Sisters doing what the Sisters do best. Fortunately, a tenth anniversary is a perfect occasion for nostalgic self-congratulation. Admittedly I can hardly claim objectivity, but I did go for more than just an opportunity to dish a bunch of tired old sluts."[97] Apparently he found no other opportunities, because dishing is precisely the focus of the entire article.

Despite these commentaries, by 1989 things were looking up. The first AIDS medication, AZT, had been approved in 1987. The drug made people sicker than AIDS made them at times, but it offered a hope that many had not felt in years. New Sisters had begun to join the order; an article written in honor of the upcoming tenth anniversary lists five new members of the San Francisco house in addition to Sisters Mysteria and Blanche.[98] In the aftermath of the Toronto order's closure, Sister Mish veiled that graduate student from the University of Toronto and sent the newly professed Sister Merry Peter back to revive the ministry in that city. Mother Theresa Nervina founded a house in Seattle in 1987, the second house in the United States. And in December 1989 Sister Hysterectoria joined forces and sewing machines with other Radical Faeries in New York City to produce a set of sixteen or so habits, which first hit the streets of Manhattan for the famous Stop the Church protest at St. Patrick's Cathedral, thus initiating the formation of the NYC (dis)Order. The Sisters might well have commented wryly, with Mark Twain, that reports of their death had been greatly exaggerated. They had made it through the keyhole.

An International Order

The 1990s were a time of steady growth and expansion for the order, primarily outside the United States. Although the international houses and orders waxed and waned, split and merged, they persistently spread what the French orders came to call "la bonne parole"—loosely translated, the Good Word—of joy, no guilt, and safer sex across an increasingly vast geographic terrain.[99] Despite tireless work in her community, Sister Merry Peter did not manage to recruit other Sisters during her time in Toronto; it would be the early 2010s before a mission formed and failed in that city, and the future of its successor is still uncertain. Instead, the next house to be founded after the NYC (dis)Order took shape in London. Its founder had moved all the way from Sydney on a mission to establish a new house of Sisters.

Glenn Palmer first encountered the Sisters in Sydney in the mid-1980s. "Like most people who see the Sisters for the first time, you're in awe, I guess," he recalled.[100] But despite being drawn to the order, he felt that he needed a specific reason to join; he found that reason when another member of the order, a fellow student at the University of Sydney, ran for the student council as a Sister. Brought into the order at a 1988 fundraising dance in support of the fight against Section 28, the U.K. law that banned the teaching of gay-related content in schools, Palmer had his formal vestition as Novice Sister Mary-Anna Lingus in the middle of the university quad shortly thereafter. Joining his classmate on "the SPI ticket," he ran for the presidency of the student council. Although he failed to gain that office, he was awarded a seat on the council, becoming the first Sister known to have been successfully elected to a governing position outside the order itself.

After graduation, Palmer took a position as an AIDS counselor, and soon he felt the travel bug biting. Speaking only English and not particularly inclined to move to the United States given the politics of the late 1980s, he set his sights on the United Kingdom. He also felt the need to remain connected to the Sisters, and in the late 1980s there were no houses outside North America and Australia. But in London a veteran gay activist had learned of the existence of the Sisters and was manifesting independently; a brand-new gay-themed television program on the United Kingdom's Channel 4, called *Out on Tuesday*, picked up on the phenomenon, and a friend of Palmer's who had recently traveled to the United Kingdom brought home a videorecording of the show. "Someone needed to bring this person a habit pattern!" recalls Palmer, and he began making plans to move. Mother Inferior insisted that he must be an FP in order to start a new house, so on June 26, 1990, Novice Sister Mary-Anna Lingus became Sister (later Mother, as the founder of a house) Ethyl Dreads-a-Flashback.

The new FP headed first to the annual meeting of the International Lesbian and Gay Association (ILGA, now the International Lesbian, Gay, Bisexual, Trans, and Intersex Association), held that year in Stockholm at the beginning of July. There he conducted a workshop on the Sisters, speaking, as he recalls it, primarily to South American delegates, who seemed rather horrified by the order but whom he couldn't entirely understand due to language barriers. Arriving in London, he stayed initially with an ILGA official and first manifested at a barbecue she hosted. He manifested as well for an interview with London's *Pink News*, but remembers the first "proper manifestation," and his first as Mother Ethyl Dreads-a-Flashback, taking place at "a kiss-in that OutRage! had organized in Piccadilly Circus." The new house soon had novices, and it also drew in others who had been manifesting in the United Kingdom prior to Mother Ethyl's arrival. One of these was Sister Mary Henry of All Angels, who had been part of an earlier, short-lived London house organized by another Australian nun, who had since returned home.

Mother Ethyl's arrival in the United Kingdom was both timely and prescient, for unbeknownst to him, plans were also in the works for a new house in mainland Europe. In September 1990 Sister Vish, Sister X-plosion (also known simply as Sister X), and Sister Psychadelia toured the continent, manifesting with the nascent London house during their stay in that city. When they came to Paris they visited with a young French reporter who had encountered the Sisters a few months earlier in San Francisco. He and two interested friends manifested with the San Francisco Sisters for the first time on September 11, 1990 in Paris (figure 4 of the color insert); this manifestation marked the founding of the Couvent de Paris by Sœur Plat du Jour Tous Nos Prix Sont Nets, Sœur Thérèse Ravière de Cul et Lard, and Sœur Rita du Calvaire de Marie-Madeleine-Car-Elle-Aussi-A-Beaucoup-Souffert (the reporter). They were joined later that evening by a fourth founder, Sœur Marie-Mongolita des Fientes.[101] Jean-Yves Le Talec, also known as Sœur Rita du Calvaire, now a sociologist of gender, notes that the Couvent de Paris took the opportunity offered by the presence of U.S. Sisters at their investiture to convene the first international Conclave of the Sisters of Perpetual Indulgence on June 1, 1991, the day before their investiture Mass.[102] The second Conclave was hosted by the London house the following year, and was attended both by French Sisters and by members of the third major European order to be founded in the early 1990s—that in Germany.[103]

Within a few months of the investiture Mass in Paris, and with no knowledge of that event at the time, a Sister of Perpetual Indulgence manifested in Heidelberg, Germany. Unlike the Paris Sisters, the Sister who would become the German Archabbess encountered the San Francisco house not in person but rather through the writings of an author who had followed the order from its inception. "I found a book, *Gay Spirit: Myth and Meaning*, [edited] by Mark Thompson," she explained when we spoke. "And I read the book, and I was intrigued by the ideas about sexes. And Mark wrote about the Sisterhood in decline in the eighties. It's a very interesting article. . . . And the creativity popped out, and I was completely inspired."[104] The Archabbess laughed. "So I grabbed some old bed sheets. Black ones, it was the eighties, everyone was black, black, black, black. Clothes were black, everything was black."[105] Managing to find some white fabric as well, she made herself a habit and wore it to the Heidelberg AIDS foundation on September 21, 1991. She drew some strange looks, but eventually was able to obtain donation cans to collect money for the foundation. A few others soon became interested in the Sisters, and together they formally constituted the Heidelberg house on Beltane (April 30), 1992, forming missions in other parts of Germany in short order thereafter. In 1997, when the Archabbess relocated to Berlin, the Heidelberg and Berlin houses merged to make Berlin the Mother House of the German-speaking order.[106]

The history of the house in Colombia, which also seems to have begun in the early 1990s, is particularly difficult to trace. Hermana Dolores Raimunda of the Orden de San Felipe y Santiago de Montevideo (Uruguay) recalls being in contact with the Colombian Sisters when his own order started in 2000. He believes that the Colombia house was founded in 1992; the Montevideo Sisters lost contact with that house around 2004.[107] Although the San Francisco house is aware of the Colombia house's existence, I have been unable to find any other information on it. However, it is entirely possible that the founders of the Colombia house were among the South American delegates attending Sister Ethyl's workshop in Stockholm in 1990; perhaps the audience was not, or not to a person, as horrified as the Sister recalls.

Following the 1991 Conclave in Paris and the 1992 Conclave in London, the third international Conclave and the first to draw attendance from at least three continents (North America, Australia, and Europe) was held in Paris in 1997. There had been a schism in the Paris convent the previous year, creating a second convent in the city, the Couvent de Paname. Talks between the schismatic Sisters and the larger French order led to the Paname convent officially joining the order in 1997, and by June of that year it was hosting a well-organized Conclave. Preparations had been under way since 1996, as indicated by a preliminary program released on December 20 "of the year 27 After Stonewall."[108] While the French order had expanded during the 1990s into eight separate convents around the country, AIDS hit it in the middle of the decade in ways similar to the setbacks San Francisco had experienced ten years earlier. By 1998 the count of French houses was back to seven, as the Couvent de Paris was declared temporarily dormant.[109]

The Australian order expanded further in the 1990s, holding its First National Convocation in Adelaide in 1994; according to Mother Premonstratensia, an Adelaide Ancient, that house had been in existence since 1991 or 1992.[110] Other houses are known to have formed in Canberra, Darwin, Freemantle, Newcastle, Perth, and Warburton.[111] The order even made its way across the water to New Zealand, as there was media coverage of a house in Auckland during the mid-1990s.[112]

While the Sisters were busy taking over Europe and Australia, and making inroads into New Zealand and South America, they were reestablishing themselves more slowly in the United States. The San Francisco house was growing again, reinvigorated in part by the rise of the radical street activist group Queer Nation; a reversal in the public condemnation of drag as RuPaul became an MTV celebrity; and the rise of transgender activism. Sister Gladass of the Joyous Resurectum, who joined the San Francisco house in 1990, moved to Los Angeles a few years later and began to gather contacts from drag, theater, and Radical Faerie circles, resulting in the formation of the Los Angeles house on December 10, 1995. This was the second house to open in California, and the first U.S. house to be founded after the Sisters' legal incorporation, so somewhat to their dismay the founding Sisters in Los Angeles found themselves assisting the San Francisco house in ironing out some of the wrinkles in their legal process.[113] That clarity came none too soon, because the Seattle house became the next to go into schism, producing The Abbey of St. Joan in 1996 and eventually the revived, unrecognized Sisters of the Mother House of Washington (SOMHOW) in 2009.

The Sisters' twentieth anniversary party was a far cry from the struggling celebration, and celebration of struggle, held in 1989. Banished to an out-of-the-way bar for its tenth anniversary celebration, for its twentieth the San Francisco house received permission to close a portion of Castro Street for a block party on Easter Sunday. Concomitant with the twentieth anniversary celebration, they hosted an international Conclave that was attended by Sisters from the extant U.S. houses, far-flung former members of those houses, and Sisters from across the globe. The queer nuns were ready for their century to begin.

Critical Mass: Twenty-First Century Queer Nuns

The story of the Sisters in the first decade and a half of the twenty-first century seems to be that of a maturing social movement. The multi-house orders outside North America—Australian, British, French, and German—established themselves firmly during the 1990s, and although their membership and house locations have shifted since then as Sisters move, retire, and join and as local politics and community needs change, in general they continue to be active and engaged. In South America the Colombia house has dropped out of sight, most likely due to ongoing political upheaval in that country, but the Montevideo house, though small, has remained strong and active since 2000, and the unrecognized house in Buenos Aires likewise seems to be thriving. San Francisco Sisters have told me of interest from several other countries in South America, but as of this writing none of that interest has taken the formal shape of a mission.

The Canadian houses have likewise been slow to develop. The first house to open in Canada after the closure of the Toronto house in 1986 was the Abbey of the Long Cedar Canoe in Vancouver, which received its mission status in 2010 and its exequatur in 2012. The relocation of prominent French member Sœur Mystrah to Montréal in the early 2010s led to the formation of a mission there under the aegis of the French order; that house was elevated to fully professed status on August 9, 2016.[114] Other Canadian missions have taken shape as well, but so far none has been able to get off the ground sufficiently to move beyond mission status.

The story in the United States presents a striking contrast to these other scenarios; it is one of rapid and widespread growth during the first decade and a half of the twenty-first century. Only three new U.S. houses formed in the two decades between the origin of the San Francisco house and the end of the 1990s, but the 2001 founding of a house in the rural gay resort area of the Russian River, just north of San Francisco, seems to have sparked an ever-growing chain reaction. By 2005 several groups in different cities were requesting mission status at nearly the same time, leading the existing U.S. houses to develop the United Nuns' Privy Council in order to formalize the formation process and relieve the San Francisco house of the responsibility of oversight. Many major cities in the United States are now home to a mission or a fully professed house; the San Francisco house itself lists nearly ninety fully professed members, although not all of them are active.

Sisters in the United States are often eager to weigh in on the causes of this growth; some attribute it to the rise of the Internet and others to social media. Still others, noting the bump in growth during 2005, attribute the Sisters' success to liberal despair following the 2004 election of President George W. Bush to a second term in office. And a few point to the widespread news coverage in 2007 of Sister Σplace. and Sister Delta Goodhand taking communion in habit at Most Holy Redeemer Roman Catholic Church in the Castro. While each of these factors has likely played a role, at least in recruiting individual Sisters to the order, the date-specific explanations fail to account for houses that were founded at other times, and the Internet and social media explanations fail to account for the differential levels of growth between the U.S. houses and orders in other regions of the world where the Internet and social media have been equally influential. Most likely, as with fluctuations in other orders, the expansion of the U.S. houses in the 2000s and 2010s is due to a combination of factors, including those listed above but also having to do with national politics around LGBT issues, HIV/AIDS, and religion;

the increasing encouragement given to new houses in the United States to set their own procedures and priorities based on the needs of their communities; and perhaps also the existence of the UNPC. In the 2010s, what can be said for certain is that, having traveled through Sister Vish's keyhole and out the other side, the Sisters of Perpetual Indulgence with their promulgation of universal joy and expiation of stigmatic guilt through serious parody appear to be here to stay.

2

"We ARE Nuns, Silly!"

Serious Parody as Activism

The "Our Bother" is an early prayer attributed to Sister Francis Diana of the San Francisco House. It was introduced alongside the Sisters' original *Play Fair!* pamphlet at the 1982 San Francisco Gay Freedom Day festival as part of the Mass in Time of War against VD.[1] The rhythms, if not the words, may sound familiar to readers with some exposure to Christian ritual:

> Our Bother, which plagues our pleasures,
> Horrid be thy shame.
> Your time has come,
> You're on the run,
> As we cure you now and forever.
> Let us spread affection without infection,
> And let us play fair with others
> As we would have others cum clean with us. (Frequently.)
> We lead ourselves into indulgence,
> And deliver ourselves from ill health.
> For ours is the choice,
>   the consideration for our contacts,
>   and the health care for all.
> As it was in the beginning,
> could be now,
> and soon shall be,
>   Nookie without drips or itches,
>   scabs or scabies,
>   herpes, hep, or guilt!
>   AMEN[2]

At first glance, the Our Bother may remind one of the *Hers* ("the word *Hymns* is just so sexist!")[3] of the Church Ladies for Choice, such as the rendition of "Kumbaya" quoted by Benjamin Shepard:

> There are bigots, girls, *Kumbaya*
> At this rally, sisters, *Kumbaya*
> We will mobilize, *Kumbaya*
> Get your dresses, *Kumbaya*
> Tease your wigs, women, *Kumbaya*
> Paint your nails, ladies, *Kumbaya*
> We'll demand our rights, *Kumbaya*
> Time to redress, *Kumbaya*[4]

Others familiar with performative modes of protest that mobilize religious themes in parodic ways may hear instead, or in addition, echoes of Reverend Billy and the Church of Stop Shopping—especially the Stop Shopping Choir's foot-tapping rhythms.[5] Parodic usage of the dominant religion in support of progressive causes is nothing new, even though the Sisters predate both the Church Ladies and Reverend Billy. There is one critically important difference, however, between the parody enacted by the Sisters and that of the other two activist groups: the Church Ladies do not claim with any sort of seriousness to actually be church ladies, nor does Reverend Billy claim to be a real evangelical preacher. The Sisters, on the other hand, are quite serious that they are nuns.

Take, for example, the response from The Abbey of St. Joan in Seattle to a common accusation leveled against the order: "We are often asked, 'Why are you mocking nuns?' Well, we ARE nuns, silly!"[6] Yet it is also difficult to deny that there is an element of parody in the figure of the corseted, fishnet-stockinged, cigarette-dangling, glitter-bestowing nun. This combination of gleeful parody, however marked or intentional on the part of any individual Sister, with the absolutely serious claim to be nuns in their own right is an example of what I term serious parody.

The Sisters can easily be, and indeed have been, identified with a larger tradition of joyful, playful, and performative activism that has played a prominent role in radical and progressive politics, and particularly in queer politics, in the latter part of the twentieth century and into the twenty-first. With influences ranging from the Cockettes to *Cabaret* to the Gay Liberation Front to the remnants of San Francisco's hippie culture, the order came into existence in a time and a place that were rich with what Sara Warner calls political "acts of gaiety" and Benjamin Shepard terms "ludic" protest.[7] Warner, focused on lesbian activism, understandably ignores these mostly-gay nuns. Shepard mentions them only very briefly in passing, seeming to assume that they are a small-scale version of the larger movements that draw most of his attention.[8] This lack of attention, importantly, prevents either scholar from seeing the key ways the Sisters differ from otherwise analogous groups like the Lesbian Avengers, Queer Nation, or the Church Ladies for Choice.

Another potential lens through which to read the work of the order is José Esteban Muñoz's concept of disidentification. Drawn from the work of Michel Pêcheux, the concept is complex, and Muñoz offers several different explanations of it as he sets up his argument in the book by the same name. In the Pêcheuxian sense, Muñoz notes,

> disidentification is the third mode [the first two are identification and counteridentification] of dealing with dominant ideology, one that neither opts to assimilate within such a structure nor strictly opposes it; rather, disidentification is a strategy that works on and against dominant ideology. . . . This "working on and against" . . . tries to transform a cultural logic from within.[9]

Elsewhere, Muñoz calls disidentification a "survival strategy" and explains that it "scrambles and reconstructs the encoded message of a cultural text in a fashion that both exposes the encoded message's universalizing and exclusionary machinations and recircuits its workings to account for, include, and empower minority identities and identifications."[10] Particularly because Muñoz stresses that his use of disidentification can apply to any disempowered group, even if he finds it most clearly represented among queers of color, it is worth pondering whether his analysis can also apply to the Sisters.

In many ways, Muñoz's concept fits. The Sisters are engaging with the cultural image of the nun and are resignifying it to allow for the concept of queer, noncelibate nuns. And yet, the cases Muñoz considers differ in important ways from the work of the Sisters. Some of them involve disidentifying with figures that are dangerous to people like the performer, such as Vaginal Creme Davis's white supremacist character, Clarence.[11] Others involve embodying damaging stereotypes in disidentificatory ways so as to challenge them, such as Carmelita Tropicana's embodiment of the stereotype of Cuban *chusmería*.[12] While both performances enact forms of parody, much as the Sisters parody nuns, neither quite enacts the *respectful emulation* of their target that the Sisters enact of nuns. While the Sisters' serious parody draws on political "acts of gaiety" and "ludic" protest, and while it bears similarities to disidentification, it adds the unusual twist of not only parodying or camping but also reclaiming in all seriousness cultural figures that have proven oppressive to queer individuals and communities.

Seriously Parodic, Parod(ox)ically Serious

Serious parody, as I conceive of it, is a form of cultural protest in which a disempowered group parodies an oppressive cultural institution while simultaneously claiming for itself what it believes to be an equally good or superior enactment of one or more culturally respected aspects of that same institution. In the case of the Sisters, this means enacting parodies of Roman Catholic rituals and figures such as nuns and priests while also claiming in all seriousness to be nuns. Despite the presence of male personas in the order, I have never heard a member claim to actually be a priest, monk, cardinal, or pope; rather, such personas are usually masculine manifestations of an underlying identity as a nun. And while Guards partake in the parodic work of the Sisters, particularly through their names, other than the original French pun on the Vatican's Swiss Guards there is no claim among the Guards to be carrying out the duties of otherwise-religious figures; thus, my claim that the order is engaged in serious parody applies most clearly to the Sisters themselves.

There seems to be little doubt that what the Sisters do is parody, at least in part. Linda Hutcheon describes parody as "a form of imitation, but imitation characterized by ironic inversion, not always at the expense of the parodied text," adding that "parody is, in another formulation, repetition with critical distance, which marks difference rather than similarity."[13] Drawing on both Hutcheon's and Judith Butler's work on parody, Dennis Denisoff notes that one particular aim for which parody has proven to be especially well suited is the undermining of normative idealizations by oppressed groups and individuals trying to negotiate their own positions within society.... Through its reliance on double meanings, parody effectively questions the possibility of any such thing as an 'original,' with the term coming across for many gender and queer scholars as a misnomer for the privileged codes of the dominant ideology.[14]

One argument that some Sisters make against the claim that they are "mocking" nuns is precisely what Denisoff indicates here: that there is no original to mock. Sister Krissy Fiction made this point in an interview with me. "You know," she observed, "the Roman Catholics, they haven't cornered the market on nuns. There's Episcopalian nuns, there's Buddhist nuns, and there's us. So there's all different kinds of nuns. I think that's the confusion, is that when you say the word 'nun' in our society people automatically think of Roman Catholic nuns. Which we're not, obviously."[15] Importantly, Sister Krissy's argument may challenge the claim that the Sisters are mocking nuns, but it also affirms that they are parodying nuns—at least in Denisoff's definition of parody.[16]

As Jean-Yves Le Talec writes, "C'est sans doute l'une des clés de la compréhension profonde des Sœurs de la Perpétuelle Indulgence: non pas malgré, mais en même temps qu'elles sont des personnages de parodie, du grotesque, elles sont *aussi* de vraies nonnes." (This is without doubt one of the keys to a deep comprehension of the Sisters of Perpetual Indulgence: not despite, but at the same time as they are figures of parody, of the grotesque, they are *also* real nuns).[17] Later, he describes the Sisters' ritual evocations of Roman Catholicism through communion and confession as being "entre parodie et mimétisme de la religion catholique" (between parody and mimesis of the Catholic religion).[18]

Parodic Nuns

The parodic performativity of the Sisters has maintained a presence in the order throughout its existence, but it was most extravagantly evident during the first decade or so. September 1987, for instance, brought Pope John Paul II to San Francisco. This was a time of rapidly growing tensions between queer communities, AIDS activists, and the Church; just the previous year the Church's Congregation for the Doctrine of the Faith, whose prefect would later become Pope Benedict XVI, had issued yet another homophobic statement, this one insinuating that gay rights activists were to blame for both homophobic violence and the spread of AIDS. Shortly before the pope's visit, further anger had arisen among AIDS activists across the United States at the appointment of New York's Archbishop John J. O'Connor to the Presidential Commission on HIV. The archbishop was a key author of the vocal stance that the U.S. Catholic Church was taking against condom use, framing AIDS, Anthony Petro writes, "as a national moral crisis."[19] With the leader of the entire Roman Catholic Church coming to their city, the Sisters were primed to respond.

"By this time our public relations abilities were really refined," recalls Sister Vish. "We had a couple of our saints, who were public relations people, put together all of these professional, glossy press packets." Several weeks before the pope's visit, the Sisters held a press conference at Saint Mary's Cathedral (the Cathedral of Saint Mary of the Assumption), one of the locations where the pontiff was scheduled to speak on September 17. Sister Vish recalls that "something like fifty" members of the press attended. The Sisters discussed their concerns with Roman Catholic teachings, and then offered a spectacular political gesture. Again in the words of Sister Vish:

> I said, "And now, I will march to the cathedral to post our demands on the cathedral door, just like Martin Luther." This is all on the evening news. And so it shows me with this long black gown and black veil marching to the doors to post my demands that the archdiocese rescind their invitation to the Pope to visit San Francisco. And I put it up with a Lee press-on nail.[20]

"Nailing" their "theses" to the doors of the church in a parodic and undeniably campy way, the Sisters leveled deadly serious criticisms at the Vatican in the ludic guise of parody.

On the day of the pope's visit, San Francisco traffic was snarled due to road closures for the papal procession. The Sisters took over Union Square and staged a Mass Against Papal Bigotry, during which they exorcised the pope of the demons of homophobia and canonized slain San Francisco gay political leader Harvey Milk (figure 5 of the color insert). Photos from the Mass show a large white cross in the background that reads in stark black capitals "2000 YEARS OF OPPRESSION." Seated in front of the cross is the partner of a member of the order, dressed to represent the pope and flanked by large signs with images of Pope John Paul II circled and crossed out in red. During the part of the Mass in which Milk was canonized, the signs were reversed to show the words "SAINT HARVEY MILK," and a large banner bearing Milk's picture was unfurled in front of the cross. Downstage, along with their signature calligraphed black-and-white banner, are Sisters of Perpetual Indulgence in their traditional black-and-white habits. The order was small by that time, but the visual impact of the Mass made its weakened numbers irrelevant, and the overall impression is quite striking. To top off the event, large trays of condoms in gold foil were distributed as communion wafers.[21]

Not to be outdone, a few years later the Australian order drew on another aspect of Christian tradition to lambaste the deeply homophobic, conservative Protestant politician Fred Nile. In the 1989 Sydney Mardi Gras parade, they marched with a giant papier-mâché model of Nile's head ensconced like a roast on an even larger silver platter and surrounded by a decorative and bounteous, albeit fake, fruit garnish (fig. 2.1). Evoking the figure of Salome, though much more modestly dressed than she is typically portrayed to be, and placing Nile in the role of John the Baptist, the Sisters engaged in a sharp critique of both the politician and his religion by reinterpreting this well-known Christian story through the lens of those harmed by homophobic renderings of Christianity.[22]

While such large-scale and dramatic protests are rarer in the order today, the San Francisco Sisters staged a die-in at their thirtieth anniversary celebration in which red ribbons bearing homophobic Church pronouncements were pulled from the mouth of an effigy of Pope Benedict and read aloud, while in response Sisters chanted, "Words kill!" and fell to the ground.[23] A few months later, in Oregon, in the face of persistent conservative Christian protests at Portland's Pride parade, the Order of Benevolent Bliss carried out a similar action that was recorded by a bystander and posted on YouTube.[24] And on a smaller scale, acts of

Figure 2.1. The head of conservative Christian politician Fred Nile on a platter, surrounded by Sisters, in the 1989 Sydney Mardi Gras parade. Photographer unknown. Australian Lesbian and Gay Archives (ALGA). Reproduced by permission.

parody happen every time the Sisters manifest. When asked by members of their community for a blessing, for instance, many members of the order reply, "Go forth and sin some more!" They may even place a smudge of glitter on the forehead of the supplicant. Yet, even amidst this parody, the Sisters reference the historic roles played by nuns in political protest. Their blessings evoke hilarity, yet also address their mission of the expiation of stigmatic guilt. There are no sins in the Sisters' view of the world save for homophobia, transphobia, sexism, and the like; the point of blessing community members by inviting them to "sin" is to challenge the very notion that their pleasures are sinful. And so we return again to the Sisters' serious side.

Serious Nuns

As quickly as one can name examples of the early order's use of parody to protest religious homophobia and other social and political ills, one can also point to far more sober, even if still lighthearted, adaptations of

Roman Catholicism to serve the needs of the Sisters' communities. The Condom Savior Mass, for instance, was developed by the San Francisco house but first enacted during the investiture of the Paris convent in 1991 using the same gold-foiled condoms as the 1987 Mass against Papal Bigotry. I rely here on Le Talec's retelling of the Condom Savior Mass, "au cours de laquelle le préservatif prend la place de l'hostie consacrée" (in the course of which the condom takes the place of the consecrated host).[25] The consecration proceeded with the following liturgy:

> Before man is life and death, whichever he chooses shall be given him.
> Immense is the power of the wisdom of the Condom Savior; he is mighty in power.
> The latex host is my flesh, for the life of the world.
> Just as the Father who has life sent me, I have life because of the Condom Savior and the man who feeds on me will have life because of me.
> This is the bread that came down from heaven, and, unlike your brothers who ate and died nonetheless, the man who feeds on this bread shall live forever.[26]

Le Talec continues: "La consécration est suivie d'une distribution de préservatifs au public, qui s'accompagne d'un serment *I took the Vow.*" (The consecration is followed by the distribution of condoms to the public, accompanied by an oath, *I took the Vow*).[27] In later iterations of the Mass in the United States, participants received what amounts to a prayer card (fig. 2.2). A piece of card stock folded in half to the size of a business card, it read on the front, in large and ornate letters, "I TOOK THE VOW"; on the back it listed contact information for the San Francisco House and for Sister Mish's residence at Short Mountain Sanctuary in Tennessee. Inside was the text of the Condom Savior Vow, which matches nearly exactly that quoted by Le Talec and that reproduced in a San Francisco Sisters newsletter in 1993:

> We have gathered today to consecrate and receive the Holy Communion Condom. As I take it onto myself, so shall I keep its ritual sacred. The condom is part of my life—part of my responsibility now. If I desire to live, and let my sex partners live, I must sanctify my vow to hold the

I TOOK THE VOW

The Sisters of Perpetual Indulgence

CONDOM SAVIOR VOW

We have gathered today to consecrate and receive the Holy Communion Condom. As I take it onto myself, so shall I keep its ritual sacred. The condom is part of my life -- part of my responsibility now. If I desire to live, and let my sex partners live, I must sanctify my vow to hold the condom savior sacred. My seed is under siege by a horrific virus. Let me not become horrific as well with careless disregard for my life and the lives of those with whom I share the divine gift of love.

I VOW TO LOOK INTO MY HEART AND FURTHER INTO MY SOUL, WHERE I KNOW THAT MY HUMANITY AND SALVATION DEPEND ON HOW SACRED I HOLD THE CONDOM VOW.

LATEX=LUST • LATEX=LIFE • LATEX=LOVE

© 1991 Text by Sister X

The Sisters of Perpetual Indulgence

SAN FRANCISCO ORDER
584 Castro, Suite 392
San Francisco CA 94114-2588
(415) 864-6722

LIBERTY MISSION
Short Mt. Sanctuary
Rt. 1, Box 84-A
Liberty, TN 37095

Figure 2.2. A prayer card from the Condom Savior Mass in San Francisco, ca. 1991. Reproduced by permission of the Sisters of Perpetual Indulgence—San Francisco House.

condom savior sacred. My seed is under siege by a horrific virus. Let me not become horrific as well with careless disregard for my life and the lives of those with whom I share the divine gift of love. [Le Talec's version and the 1993 version add here: My life is to promulgate universal joy and expiate myself from stigmatic guilt. In my Creator's likeness, I am alive and I must protect the handiwork.]

I VOW TO LOOK INTO MY HEART AND FURTHER INTO MY SOUL, WHERE I KNOW THAT MY HUMANITY AND SALVATION DEPEND ON HOW SACRED I HOLD THE CONDOM VOW.

LATEX = LUST * LATEX = LIFE * LATEX = LOVE

Both Le Talec and the "I Took the Vow" card attribute this text to Sister X, originally a member of the San Francisco house who helped to start and then joined the Paris convent before succumbing to complications from AIDS in 1993; some houses today still print the words "Condom Savior" on the safer-sex kits they distribute during their manifestations (see figure 2 of the color insert, bottom).[28]

At first glance the Condom Savior Mass might appear to be the height of parody, even of sacrilege. What could be more offensive to the Roman Catholic Church than a group of ardently noncelibate, queer nuns consecrating the circle of a rolled-up condom in place of the perfect circle of the communion wafer? Even more, in referencing "the man who feeds on me," the consecration liturgy hints at homoeroticism in the very heart of Roman Catholicism: the doctrine of transubstantiation, which holds that Catholics consume the body and blood of Christ not symbolically but literally during communion.

The homoeroticism of the Christ figure is not a new theme; one need only look to the writings of any number of queer Catholic or ex-Catholic commentators to find an ample supply of such references.[29] Replacing the host with a condom, though, is quite an innovation. In the 2010s, with ongoing and justified concern among queer activists over the biopolitical enforcement of AIDS prevention, some might cringe at terms like "responsibility" and the linkage of condom usage to one's very humanity. Yet the impact of the Mass becomes clearer when one considers the climate in gay communities in the early 1990s. Just five years before the Condom Savior Mass was first celebrated, as Deborah B. Gould recounts in her history of ACT UP, queer folks [in the United States] were facing a devastating crisis with numerous medical, social, and political dimensions. The number of AIDS cases had surpassed thirty thousand, the majority of whom were gay and bisexual men, and more than half of them had died. . . . The thousands of deaths were all related: each death was another member lost to an imagined gay community . . . and the accumulating bodies were decimating real lesbian and gay communities. Many gay men were losing their entire networks of lovers, friends, and acquaintances to AIDS.[30]

Moreover, as it became clear that AIDS was sexually transmitted, many gay and bisexual men felt a lifetime of cultural and religious guilt descend on them once again: they had sinned, and here was their punishment. No wonder the Sisters' *Play Fair!* pamphlet, right from its 1982 origins, listed guilt as a disease transmitted through the "Judeo-Christian tradition of morality; Catholic schools; 3 to 4 hours of TV a day when young"—in other words, through religious and popular culture.[31] By 1991, when the Condom Savior Mass was introduced, many more had died and been diagnosed. There was medication, finally, but AZT made one just as sick as, if not at times sicker than, AIDS itself, and there was no preventative other than celibacy or safer sex practices. The Sisters, dedicated to the promulgation of universal joy and the expiation of stigmatic guilt, preferred to recommend the latter.

In light of this historical context and of ongoing scholarly interest in the mobilization of affect in social and political activism,[32] it is not difficult to imagine a member of the Sisters' "gathered faithful" out for a night on the town, alone yet surrounded by the ghosts of his now-dead lovers, friends, and playmates, maybe having left at home a friend or lover too ill to go out, maybe worrying about his T-cell count, maybe simply scared, angry, and grief-stricken. In such a context, to take a heartfelt vow to wear condoms during sex might seem like a confirmation of one's own and one's partners' value; to intone with others in the bar that "in my Creator's likeness, I am alive and I must protect the handiwork" might be a powerful affirmation. Jesus may offer Christians eternal life, but for a gay or bisexual man of any religion, or none at all, at the height of the AIDS pandemic the Condom Savior's offer was likely far more credible.

Today the Sisters still engage in resignifications of Roman Catholic rituals through serious parody. Many houses, for instance, offer "confession" on a formal or informal level. Some simply speak of being available to "hear confessions"; others may have a "confessional" in a bar or at a festival. Some community members approach these opportunities lightheartedly and come just to take part in the parody, but many more take them quite seriously and bring to the Sisters stories and secrets they do not share with anyone else. I heard a number of stories about such "Sister moments," whether they took place formally under the rubric of confession or informally as a part of the order's broader ministry. For many Sisters these encounters are quintessential examples of the order's mission, an important part of their reason for becoming and remaining a member.

Sister Mona Little-Moore of the Order of Benevolent Bliss told me of her first Sister moment, which took place when the Portland, Oregon house was still a mission and all of its members novices:

Our very first World AIDS Day [as a house], we did a candlelight vigil down at Pioneer Square and then we did this walk up to Silverado [a gay bar]. That was supposed to be a celebration of light. That was Sister Miso's novice project, I think. So she had this big piece of canvas, and that was our Wailing Wall. People were supposed to write messages [on it] to loved ones that have moved on. And I noticed this guy sitting in the bar by himself, so I went over and talked to him, [told] him we had the wall there and stuff. He actually said he wanted to go up there, but he just was kind of hesitant. So I took him up there and he wrote his message. I had walked away, and I saw him back at the bar and he was still just sitting there, so I went back up, and he just had tears in his eyes. I was talking to him a little bit, and it turns out that his partner had been [HIV] positive for twenty-five years and had committed suicide two weeks before. He said he didn't know how to express his feelings, and he said the Wailing Wall was just perfect. But he started crying, and I just held him for a good fifteen minutes. You know, he just cried and cried and cried and cried. And [I] looked at what he wrote, and it was just so angry to start with, but then towards the end it was like, "I miss you and I love you," and I mean, it was really, really nice.

Later in our conversation, Sister Mona returned to the story:

> Six months later, I was at Silverado as Ken [Mona's secular self] with
> Tasha [Sister Tasha Salad, also out of face]. This guy recognized us and
> came up to us, and he says, "Do you remember me?" . . . [Tasha] knew
> immediately who it was, but [the man] started saying [to me], "You're the
> one that had talked to me and held me while I cried." I went, "Absolutely."
> He said that a month after that, his roommate's brother had committed
> suicide. And he said he would not have known how to help his room-
> mate if it weren't for what I did for him. So he spent the rest of the day
> hanging out with us at the table, laughing and joking with us. And every
> time he sees us, whether I'm in or out of habit, he always runs up and
> gives me a big old hug and hangs out with us. To see this person that was
> just absolutely destroyed, and crying uncontrollably, [become] this per-
> son that was laughing and having fun with us was just, that's my favorite
> memory. It was my first Sister moment, and it's the one that sticks with
> me the most.[33]

Someone unfamiliar with the Sisters might well ask what on earth would
prompt a grieving partner to fall sobbing into the arms of a nearly seven-
foot-tall, burly, deep-voiced, bearded creature in a black robe, white
veil, and whiteface makeup. While a number of Sisters offered insightful
reflections on exactly how their roles work, at base they all had the same
answer: they are nuns for the queer community.

Twenty-First Century Queer Nuns

Admittedly, these are nuns who hear confession and say Mass. But those
two activities are hardly the most prominent ways the Sisters' practices
vary from those of the Roman Catholic Church. In fact, no one whom I
have told about the Sisters of Perpetual Indulgence has even mentioned
their borrowing of Catholic rituals when reflecting on the elements of
parody in the order. Perhaps that is because the majority of Sisters are
male-identified, and after all, as Mark Jordan pointed out many years
ago, even the most revered members of the male Roman Catholic hierarchy don brocade skirts on Sunday mornings in order to "promenade,
sing, act, and host a meal."[34] More to the point, though, at the base of

both the controversy around the Sisters and their own ministry is the Sisters' ownership, in the active sense of "owning," of the role of the nun.

Drag Nuns

Some Sisters accept the label of "drag nun"; others, strongly invested in distinguishing themselves from drag queens, do not. However, this disagreement and the use of the appellation itself serve as clues to how the Sisters function symbolically, particularly as queer nuns. An important part of the explanation for the Sisters' success lies in their simultaneous mobilization of two tropes that are recognizable and generally positively valenced within LGBTQ communities in the countries and regions where the Sisters are active: that of the drag queen and that of the Roman Catholic nun. The Sisters are neither of these figures, but in blending them to create something new, the order also creates a figure that is immediately legible within their communities, at least once one understands what one is seeing; the drag reference is evident to most community members, but the nun reference less so when a house favors party dresses over formal habits. In referencing both drag queen and nun simultaneously, the Sisters invoke a persona that is nurturing, selfless, sexy, sassy, and eminently queer.

Through their visual reference to drag, be it the high-glamour drag preferred by many stage performers and widely popularized by the TV series *RuPaul's Drag Race*, the gender-bending performance of skag drag, or the exaggerated femme drag used by some female-bodied performers, the Sisters evoke characteristics often associated with drag queens in the communities they serve.[35] Most commonly these include sexiness and playfulness; one might say that the "parody" part of the Sisters' serious parody arises through their visual evocation of the drag queen image. Mobilizing this visual trope also makes the Sisters immediately legible as insiders to the gay community; thus, the evocation of drag is a visual cue for the "queer" aspect (in the identity sense) of the Sisters' claim to be "queer nuns." Although in some cases, such as that of the early Toronto house, this visual reference can also close off the Sisters' welcome in their own communities,[36] the playful and parodic aspects that the Sisters have inherited from the drag tradition are also visible in some of the earliest images of the order. For instance, one of the greeting cards created by the early San Francisco house portrays Sister Vish in a World War II concrete bunker, smiling seductively at the viewer and aiming a toy machine gun off to the side. The text inside the card reads, "It hasn't been easy preserving my virginity."[37]

The two earliest Sisters who remained with the order, Sister Soami and Sister Vish, both clearly acknowledge the drag aspect of the Sisters' work. Sister Vish told me, "What [we're] wearing is the tool to do the work, and it's a Catholic habit. It's [a] nun, drag nun. You know, it's just the truth. I'd say."[38] And Sister Soami related traditional Roman Catholic habits directly to drag, acknowledging in the process the ethical question that arises in reclaiming habits discarded as oppressive and limiting by Roman Catholic nuns:

> It seems to me very appropriate that people with a drag queen bent would say [of Roman Catholic nuns' habits], "Oh, this is fabulous drag that needs to keep being perpetuated." And how do you justify perpetuating that when these women [Roman Catholic nuns] have said, "Oh, it hampered us, and we have to discard it to work in the world"?[39]

Sydney's Sister Rowena Keeper of the Holy Doiley sees so much drag in the San Francisco–based tradition that he critiqued its usefulness as a reference to the work of nuns. Recall that the Australian houses, like some of their descendants in the United Kingdom, wear solely traditional Roman Catholic nuns' habits with sunglasses and no whiteface. Sister Rowena remarked,

> In terms of the reason why we present and manifest ourselves the way we do . . . it actually is a much, much stronger representation, and far, in our opinions, greater parody of the foibles and failings of faith, particularly from the organized church point of view, that it be recognized for what it is by wearing something that's recognizable. So, in our estimation, while we have the greatest of reverence and respect for our peers and colleagues over there in San Fran with their whiteface, we feel it actually dilutes the message a little bit because it becomes almost a parody of a parody. It becomes more a case of high camp street theater with something that's almost recognizable as a nun because it's so close to the traditional, more recognizable genres of drag than it is a genre of parody of faith and religion.[40]

The balance between these two Sisterly tropes, then, not only can shift but may need to shift in response to the goals and cultural contexts of specific houses and individual members.

If the trope of the drag queen lends the Sisters the parodic side of their serious parody, the trope of the nun brings in the serious side. This is not, to be clear, because all nuns are serious, any more than it is because all drag queens are parodic. Rather, the Sisters are working with popular images, the roles implied and the affect evoked by these tropes or representations that communicate to the people they serve who the Sisters are and what they do. The trope of the nun presents the Sisters as reliable and trustworthy, serious and earnest, engaged in selfless service to those around them. The sharply gendered nature of these imputed qualities is particularly striking; moreover, they serve the added function of distinguishing the image of the Sister from the trope of the drag queen.[41] Several Sisters made such distinctions, including some who, like Sister Anna Wrecks-Ya, themselves perform in drag:

> I, having a drag persona myself, am not bashing my fellow drag queens in any way, shape, form, or fashion. However, drag queens are all about themselves. The attention that they get is all about them. Their shoes, their makeup, their dress, their role, their Grand Empress XLVII of the Rose Duchess whatever, it's all about them. They masquerade sometimes, if they're raising money or they're increasing social awareness or whatever, but drag queens are all about their own love and attention. Nuns are the antithesis of that. We get a lot of attention. . . . But . . . [people are] paying attention to the Sisters, they're paying attention to a collective organization of people that are actively doing good work for the people around them.[42]

In insisting with The Abbey of St. Joan that "We ARE nuns, silly!" the Sisters simultaneously combat some of the negative stereotypes evoked by their mobilization of the drag queen trope and communicate in a single word or image their commitment to community service, healing, education, social justice, activism, and spirituality.

One of the founders of the order in Montevideo, Uruguay, Hermana Prudencia Ernestina Simona Crucifija Cienfuegos, stressed this serious aspect of the Sisters' work: "Eso, para mí, es lo más importante: saber que el trabajo de campo que se hace es reconocido, porque no creen que es sólo una vestidura para un momento. ¡No! Están haciendo algo serio. No están tomando para la chacota o para embromar." (This, for me, is the most important thing: to know that the work that is done in the field is recognized, because [the Sisters] don't believe that this is only an outfit [worn] for a moment. No! They're doing something serious. They're not putting it on as mockery or to make a joke).[43]

The insistence on the Sisters' seriousness, sometimes even in the face of obvious parody, is particularly evident in a story that Sister Soami told me about the early years of the order. On the day of the University of San Francisco protest in October 1980 there was also a jazz concert on campus, and some members of the order decided to attend after the protest was over. Sister Soami recalls,

> I went onto campus, campus security tried to take a hold of me and stop me, and I said, "Take your hands off Sister!" And another woman came up to me, a nun, and said, "Why are you wearing my habit? You!" I said, "Sister, *you* are wearing your habit. I am wearing *my* habit," and left her to deal with that. And sat down and listened to Cal Tjador play. And seeing the president [of the university] in the background being really fuming and upset that I'm there. Sitting beside Father Flynn of the philosophy department, who says to me, "Sister, we saw you from the colloquy room and the comment was, 'Well, at least they're *wearing* the habit!'" And I laughed and, one of the gay people had brought me a Coke. And I offered Father Flynn a sip. And in true Jesuit fashion, he kept the whole Coke. Sister was clearly not offering him a drink of her Coke, she was tending to his needs! But it was a fun afternoon.[44]

Sister Soami's flippant response to the Roman Catholic nun who was offended by his habit, and his chuckle at the priest's snide reference to women religious turning to secular clothes after the Second Vatican Council just a decade and a half earlier, are counterbalanced here in interesting ways by his wry comment on a priest apparently making sexist assumptions about the proper role of nuns—even gay male ones. At the same time, the entire part of the story that focuses on Father Flynn shows a Roman Catholic priest affirming in some way Sister Soami's status as a nun; although priestly affirmation of the Sisters seems to be fairly rare, the approval of Roman Catholic nuns is highly valued by many members of the order.

From Genderfuck to Religionfuck

In addition to the clear aspect of genderfuck in the Sisters (including in the above story, since pictures from the USF protest show Sister Soami—then Missionary Position—with his customary bushy beard, traditional habit, and unadorned face), Sister Soami's story demonstrates that a similar confounding of *religion* is also taking place in the order. For the sake of argument and comparison, I playfully call this confounding "religionfuck."

The performative approach to gender known as "genderfuck" is so named because it "fucks with" gender: it disrupts taken-for-granted ideas about the predictability of the relationship between gendered traits and appearance, physiological sex, and sexual desire. For many practitioners of genderfuck, mixing sex and gender signals by wearing a beard with a dress or presenting as hypermasculine but with a soprano vocal range is a performative intervention that unsettles and even undermines cultural assumptions about the links between body, gender, and desire. Furthermore, the apparent incongruity inherent in genderfuck is the basis of both the amusement and the outrage that such performances can elicit from viewers.

If genderfuck challenges and even undermines cultural assumptions about the ways genders, bodies, and desires cohere, then religionfuck might be said to challenge and undermine cultural assumptions about the ways religious identities, roles, practices, beliefs, and appearances cohere. Religionfuck makes use of performance to raise pointed questions about ostensibly "proper" religious embodiment and the authority of religious establishments to dictate the boundaries of religious roles. Is being a nun, Roman Catholic or otherwise, defined by the things that nuns do? If so, why can't a person with a beard and a penis do those same things and also be a nun? Why can't a person with breasts wear a corset and stilettos—or a cardinal's vestments and a large dildo—and do those same things and also be a nun? Every manifestation of a Sister, regardless of the embodiment, gender identity, sexual identity, or religious background of the person manifesting, raises provocative and

profound questions about the connections or disconnects between desire, gender, embodiment, and religion. Likewise, the Sisters raise questions about who can even be considered "properly" religious. For years
I have faced in my own research the common assumption on the part of
both queer urban intellectuals and heterosexuals of all stripes, including some in my own fields, that queer people who are religious must be
both terribly oppressed and part of a negligibly small group. Neither is
true as a general rule, and regardless of the individual religious or spiritual predilections or aversions of the Sisters' membership, their very
appropriation of religious habits and, even more to the point, religious
roles throws a wrench into the works of such assumptions.

To claim the roles of "queer nuns" is also to affirm the sacredness of
queer bodies in the face of repeated accusations from relatives, friends,
religious leaders, politicians, door-to-door evangelists, and religious
teachings (among others) that queer existence embodies sacrilege. Even
for an atheist, the power of such resacralization may be difficult to over-
estimate. I would suggest that some, maybe even many, members of the
communities the Sisters serve experience resacralization when they see
members of their own communities carrying out sacred and respected
roles in the face of religious rejection, condemnation, and shaming.
More than genderfuck, more even than religionfuck, the Sisters both
delight and inspire many in the communities they serve because their
resacralization of queer bodies through traditional religious imagery
playfully but persistently defies the religious and cultural power brokers
who have shamed and oppressed those communities.

Not a dismissal of religion, but similar rather to the powerful reclaiming of Jesus as black in African American communities and as a black
woman by such artists as Renée Cox, the reclaiming of the Virgin of
Guadalupe as a family member and a feminist and queer Chicana icon
by artists like Yolanda López and Alma López, and the reclaiming of
Lilith as a feminist figure by commentators as disparate as scholar Judith
Plaskow and the creators of the Lilith Fair, the Sisters' self-presentation
as nuns claims a place in the sacred for their own bodies and identities
and those of their communities. The queer Pietà on the frontispiece of
this book is just one example out of many of the Sisters' involvement in
this type of artistic reclamation. In recent years, as is so richly displayed
on the cover of this book, digital artist Max Koo has been reimagining

classic works of Christian art such as Leonardo DaVinci's *Last Supper* and Giovanni Battista Tiepolo's *Expulsion of the Money Changers from the Temple* in Sisterly versions that cast two of the founding Sisters in the role of Jesus. No wonder, then, that like the work of many of the above-named artists, the Sisters have been met not only with delight but also with horror and outrage. This interpretation may also help to explain why the Sisters have been most successful in countries and regions where Roman Catholicism is a familiar but not ardently protected aspect of the culture, and why they struggle in more devoutly Catholic cultures. Even Uruguay, culturally a very Catholic country, has been described by the Sisters there as less conservative in its adherence to the religion than other predominantly Catholic countries in the Americas.

Closely related to the Sisters' enactment of queer sacralization is the fascination and delight evoked by the perception of some outsiders, and indeed some Sisters, that the order is engaging in queer sacrilege. Queer sacrilege and queer sacralization may in fact go hand in hand, since the sacralization of queer bodies is perceived as sacrilegious by many socially conservative religious organizations and individuals. Ties between sacrilege and the sacred are hardly unknown in the broader study of religion, even when connected directly to sexuality; however, many queer people who lay claim to religion enact what appears to be a new form of these ties when they sacralize sexual bodies that have been officially declared sacrilegious. Taken to its logical end, this linkage between sacrilege and sacralization leads to what we might call the erotics of sacrilege, which appears in such phenomena as people being sexually aroused by Sisters of Perpetual Indulgence in habit (humorously dubbed "clownfuckers" by the order) and the persistent presence of Roman Catholic themes and roles in BDSM dungeons, particularly within queer communities.[45]

Claiming the Nun

The Sisters' claim to the role of the nun is at the heart of their serious parody, of their interweaving of genderfuck with religionfuck. Without this claim, neither their exorcism of the pope nor their Condom Savior Mass would be fully legible. The Sisters whom I interviewed advanced four different arguments, often in combination, to support their claim to this larger world of nuns: (1) the Sisters do the same work as nuns do, they sometimes do it better, and they are more fun; (2) they have more moral integrity than the Roman Catholic Church, especially toward queer communities and toward Roman Catholic nuns; (3) their work is spiritual or even prophetic, like that of vowed women religious; and (4) the Roman Catholic Church has no monopoly on nuns anyway.

Doing the Work

Aware that the Sisters consider themselves to be nuns, and also that they are often accused of mocking nuns, I asked Sisters at every opportunity how they respond to this charge. By far the most common answer was that they do the work that nuns do, but often better and with more fun. Not one to miss an opportunity for serious parody, Sister Dominé Trix replied with an explanation that is well known in her Seattle house: "Well, honey, we do the same things that the nuns do, you know. They take vows to support the community; we take vows to support the community. They take vows to feed the sick and the homeless and the dying; we take vows to feed the sick and the homeless and the dying. They take vows of chastity; we raise money for the community."[46]

In addition to the claim to be more fun that is embedded within the sly rejection of chastity that breaks this string of parallels, Sister Dominé's well-rehearsed response also summarizes the serious claim that many Sisters make: they are nuns because they do the work. This claim makes clever use of the Roman Catholic side of an old theological debate with Protestantism over the key to salvation: is it having perfect faith in God, or carrying out good works? The Roman Catholic Church has tended to come down on the side of works over faith; taken to an extreme, which the Church of course would not endorse, this position could be said to allow for people who do not adhere to the teachings of the Church but who carry out the work of nuns to be Catholics in good standing, or even to *be* nuns.

Moral High Ground

Moreover, members of the order often linked their claim that they do the same work as other nuns to a claim that they hold the moral high ground over the Roman Catholic Church with regard not only to queer communities but also to Roman Catholic nuns themselves. Sister Pure Heart, for example, who was raised as a Baptist, offered both the "works" and the "moral high ground" arguments in a single statement:

> Well, nuns do charity work, I do charity work. Help [the] poor, home-less, take confessions, listen to people, and try to give a little bit of advice that doesn't hurt anybody. But, yeah. We do the same things as nuns, just not as formal. You know, more for the queer community rather than just the Catholics, I guess, because Catholics can be a little uptight and not forgiving and not accepting or understanding about the gay com-munity, so it's kind of a cool little mission to help my fellow gay men and women.[47]

Another Sister in the same house, Sister Maria Caffeina Mochalatte, who was raised in a family with both Catholic and evangelical Protestant heritage and who today considers herself (in her own words) a "hereti-cal Catholic," made a similar point but tailored the moral high ground argument from a claim against Catholics in general to a claim against the Roman Catholic hierarchy: "In many ways," she told me, the work of the Sisters

> is not meant as disrespect. It's actually meant as almost an emulation. More of a, "Hey, nuns do these wonderful things." And, you know, I think half our [here she means Roman Catholic] nuns are on freakin' welfare, because it's not like the Church—the Church doesn't support them like they support priests. Their orders have to support them. And most orders of women are not wealthy. They're just not, and they never have been.[48]

Quite a few members of the order who made such claims to the moral high ground accused the Church hierarchy of abandoning the prin-ciples of its own religion. Notably, this implies that even many Sisters and Guards who staunchly oppose the Roman Catholic Church and Christianity as a whole adhere nonetheless to an understanding of a "true" or "original" form of that religion that is morally upstanding and even admirable. The website of the Sydney Sisters, for example, explains that "some people think that we hate Christians . . . not so." Instead, the text continues, "we merely oppose . . . any set of values that denies natural justice and inspires prejudice—an idea that is supported by true and honest Christianity already, as well as all major religions and philosophies."[49] Leveling moral claims against the Church is central to the Sisters' enactment of serious parody. In claiming for the order those aspects of Christianity that remain deeply valued within cultures shaped by that religion, the Sisters add to their parody a serious claim to be advocates and even at times purveyors of the most authentic, best forms of the religion by which they and their communities have often been repressed.

Spiritual and Prophetic Roles

Although some Sisters are agnostic or atheist and see no connection between their ministry and any sort of religion or spirituality, there are certainly also Sisters who fall far to the opposite end of this spectrum. Some are themselves Catholics, or Catholics who converted to the Anglican tradition in areas where the Anglican Church is socially progressive in order to escape religious homophobia. Novice Sister Petunia Encarnata, for example, is part of the Abbey of the Long Cedar Canoe in Vancouver, British Columbia. Having been raised Catholic, she told me,

> I joined the Franciscans in South America, where I was born, and I went to seminary. But it was too lonely for me. But I spent six months with them, and it was glorious. A glorious experience. So I've always had this attraction to the religious order. Part of it. Of course in the Catholic Church, I could if I could keep my mouth shut. But where's my integrity? . . . So the Sisters appeared in my life. I said it was just, like, perfect. This is my call to be a nun. A nun, what is a nun? A nun is a person that is consecrated to the service of something that is transcendent. For the love of your fellow human beings. But you're consecrated. So that's why I feel that I am [a nun]. Yes. There's no doubt in my mind. I'm consecrated to the heart of God.[50]

Focusing on neither the moral high ground nor the work of a nun, Novice Sister Petunia made a more radical claim that harks back to my argument above about resacralization: "consecrated to the heart of God," Novice Sister Petunia has let the deity decide whether she is a nun, and has simply found in the Sisters an open and accepting form in which to live out the calling she has always had.

Although Novice Sister Petunia was not the only Sister to tell me of fulfilling a call to the ministry through the Sisters (recall, for example, the conversation about this sense of calling between Sister Trystina, Sister Kali, and Guard Inya in the introduction), other Sisters claimed a broader spiritual and even prophetic role for the order. One of the clearest examples of this claim comes from Sister Baba Ganesh, who termed the oral history walking meditation that she designed for the San Francisco house a *hajj*, thus likening it to the pilgrimage in which Muslims retrace the steps of key figures in their sacred history. At the end of a lengthy reflection on the underlying connections between this meditation and other forms of ministry in her house, Sister Baba concluded,

> That is the nature, I think, of the Sister heart, which is the ability to pull disparate, seemingly unrelated things together toward a queer, spiritual, and socially beneficial purpose. So it was the power of those things that all were kind of beyond language. And I think that that is why I'm a Sister. It's just one of the reasons, but that it provides me that opportunity. . . . There's so much connected to the divine. It's in that place of unknowing, it's in that place of tricking oneself out of knowledge and into intuition, that connection can happen, miracles can be performed, the unimaginable is manifest. So I think it's in those liminal spaces that I see a Sister embodied, down to the outsiderness of it. And the outsiderness of it has to do with the fact that I think in general the classic Sister persona is one of a prophet. And prophets don't fuckin' choose, man. You know what I mean? They're made *crazy* by their lack of choice. . . . And there are Sisters who are prophets *and* saints who are conscious of their calling and do those kinds of things.

Sister Baba considers herself to be among those Sisters who are conscious of their calling; when I asked her whether she considers herself "religious, spiritual, both, neither, something else," she replied simply, "I'm a prophet. I didn't get to choose."[51]

No Monopoly on Nuns

The fourth argument that I heard consistently from Sisters as part of their response to the charge that they are mocking nuns moves away from defending their right to be doing what other nuns do, and instead changes the terms of the question entirely. Rather than counter that they are not mocking Roman Catholic nuns, some Sisters simply point out that the Roman Catholic Church has no monopoly on the role of vowed female religious. They then add that their order is just one of the newer groups of nuns around the world, and that they are not mocking nuns any more than any other group of nuns is mocking nuns; they simply look a little different from most other orders of nuns. As Guard Noah Shame of the Order of Benevolent Bliss pointed out, "The Sisters are what they are because they were modeled after the role traditional nuns played. And the Catholic Church doesn't have a patent on that."[52] Another member of the same house, Sister Maya Poonani, explained, "I'm not making fun of anybody. I celebrate nuns for the work they do. We're doing it the same way they do, just we look different. And we're not making fun. If anything, what's the saying about the sincerest form of flattery?" I replied, "Imitation." Sister Maya affirmed, "Imitation."[53]

Emulating the Nuns, Castigating the Hierarchy

In line with claiming the moral high ground even with regard to the Roman Catholic Church's treatment of nuns, the Sisters take a bifurcated approach to vowed religious within the Roman Catholic Church. On one side of this coin is the Sisters' castigation of the male-dominated hierarchy within the Church and their celebration of criticism from that hierarchy as a sign that the Sisters are doing something right; on the other side is the importance they attribute to gestures of approval from Roman Catholic nuns. The most prominent indicator of the former aspect that I encountered during the course of my research was an oft-repeated story that is, as far as I can tell, completely apocryphal. Yet rather than negate its power, if anything the apocryphal nature of the tale indicates even more clearly how important it is to the narrative that members of the order tell to their communities and each other about who they are and what their relationship is to the Roman Catholic Church. As a direct consequence of their 1987 protest against Pope John Paul II's visit to San Francisco, the Sisters claim, the pontiff officially declared the Sisters of Perpetual Indulgence to be heretics and placed them on what most Sisters term "the papal list of heretics."

While there is certainly every possibility that the Vatican is engaged in activities of which humble scholars like myself are completely unaware, to the best of my knowledge this "official papal list of heretics"—a kind of "Most Wanted List" for the Vatican—does not exist. On the other hand, in a country obsessed with both criminality and lists, it is perhaps unsurprising that the U.S. Sisters would come up with such a claim and imagine themselves as heroic, heretical outlaws with a place of honor on this list. More important than the existence of a real papal list of heretics is the role this apparently apocryphal story plays for the Sisters. Many brought it up when I asked an open-ended question about "the relationship, broadly speaking, between the Sisters and the Catholic Church." "We're on the official list of heretics," Sister Nadia Ahnwilda told me brightly. "We made the big time."[54] Others offered it as an observation during my fieldwork, something they thought a religious studies scholar working with the Sisters should definitely know. A few, like me, raised a gentle eyebrow at the claim, as in this conversation between myself and Sister Dominé Trix:

SD: So when I was going through the learning process I was told, "Well, the Sisters are on the Pope's list of heretics," so on and so forth. I later did some research on that, and I don't think we're actually on it.
MW: I don't think you are either, but I haven't been able to find an official list of heretics.
SD: Right, right. And that's why I don't think we're on it.

We both laughed at her wry statement.[55]

Many Sisters, though, are delighted by their ostensible place on the list of heretics, which some have even embellished to place the Sisters in the "Top Ten." Sister Alma Children told me, "As a group, as a whole it's been said that we're on the Top Ten Heretics list. I don't know that that's ever been one hundred percent confirmed or not. I'd like to have that on my card, personally. 'Official Heretic of the Catholic Church!' I'm very proud of that fact if it's true."[56] And Sister Glo Euro N'Wei was positively gleeful about the story: "I find profound joy in the fact that we're listed as official heretics, having been raised Catholic. I'm like, 'Yes! I've made it!' "[57]

For all that the Sisters castigate the male Roman Catholic hierarchy and value its disapproval, their attitude toward Roman Catholic nuns is generally one of respect and even reverence. Just as popular as the story about being official heretics—at least as a story to tell a religious studies professor—were stories told to me often third- or fourth-hand about Roman Catholic nuns approving of the Sisters and acknowledging the value of their ministry and its similarity to the nuns' own work. While the heretics story invoked righteous anger and fierce pride, stories of Roman Catholic nuns' recognition evoked warmth and gratitude, even moving some Sisters to tears.

One of these stories comes from Sister Odora Flatulotta D'Pew, a founder of the Grand Canyon Sisters of Perpetual Indulgence in Arizona:

> I had a very nice opportunity where I was dressed as a Sister, it was a day event, and there were three ladies, we were in a restaurant and they were sitting and eating at the restaurant. They were like, "Oh, this is very beautiful. What are you doing?" And so I started to explain the Sisters of Perpetual Indulgence, and that I'm a twenty-first century nun, and I started explaining the process, so they started asking more in-depth questions and I didn't think twice. So I was explaining the aspirants, postulants, novitiate, and then the fully professed, and they just continued to ask questions. And I said, "Well you all are very intrigued with us." I said, "We would love for you to explore more. I mean, we would love to have you as nuns if possible." And they said, "Well, we couldn't do that because we're already part of an order." And they were actual, they were nuns. And so that was very, I mean, I probably had a look, 'cause I show my emotions on the outside. . . . But they were very complimentary on us, and one nun actually said to me that it was quite an honor to have somebody that paid attention to following the path; imitation is complimentary. And so it was very comforting to me.[58]

Heretics they may be, but for many Sisters the good regard of those they emulate is all they need; the disapproval of the Roman Catholic hierarchy combined with the beneficence of Roman Catholic nuns offers further proof of their claims to "do the work" and to hold the moral high ground relative to the official Church.

Resolving the Paradox

A comment made by an early member of the order offers an important insight into the relationship between the Sisters' seriousness and their parody with regard to Roman Catholic nuns. In the midst of a conversation between me, my partner, early Sisters Loganberry Frost and Mary Media, and the more recently professed Sister Σplace., we were discussing the claim that the order mocks nuns. Sister Mary Media reflected thoughtfully, "I think for some of the Sisters there is maybe an element of mocking. I'm not sure. I don't think for most Sisters there is, but there is an element of camping."[59] This distinction between mocking and camping is crucial, I would argue, for understanding how the Sisters' serious parody works. Like parody itself, camp does not necessarily entail a rejection of its subject; in fact, as biting as camp humor can be, it can also be downright reverential.

Camp and Serious Parody

Countless commentators have attempted to define camp, resulting in lengthy articles and lengthier rebuttals. It is neither my place nor my interest to join in this fray. Rather, I appreciate the observation of Fabio Cleto, editor of a key sourcebook on camp:

> Representational excess, heterogeneity, and *gratuitousness* of reference, in constituting a major *raison d'être* of camp's fun and exclusiveness, both signal and contribute to an overall resistance to definition, drawing the contours of an *aesthetic of (critical) failure*: the longing, in fact, for a common, constant trait (or for an intrinsic, essential, stabilizing "core") in all that has been historically ascribed to camp . . . sooner or later ends up being frustrating, challenging the critic *as such*, as it challenges the cultural imperatives that rely on the manageability of *discrete* (distinct and docile) historical and aesthetic categories.[60]

Since camp can range from the work of the Sisters to the fifty or more ticking and chiming cuckoo clocks with which a friend of mine once covered the walls of his house, it is no surprise that it evades detailed definition and is instead better understood through its practice. I would argue that camp as a practice, as a verb, is how the Sisters resolve the paradox of serious parody. In fact, from the perspective of camp, there may never have been a paradox at all.

Camp, in some of its forms, takes a traditional cultural object or practice that has become slightly antiquated, an object of nostalgic and even saccharine affection in some areas of mainstream culture, and re-invigorates it with an ironic, queer twist that can be respectfully subtle, cunningly subversive, or blatantly shocking. I have seen all three of these versions of camp performance in the Sisters, who, it must be re-membered, began wearing traditional Roman Catholic habits just over a decade after the end of the Second Vatican Council, at a time when those habits had indeed come to be regarded, for better or worse, as slightly antiquated. Some Sisters dress relatively conservatively and pick names that are funny but not sexual or religious, such as Sister Saviour Applause or Sister Maria Caffeina Mochalatte. These Sisters often tell me that they make such choices not out of any objection to the sexualized names and self-presentation of other Sisters but because their ministry extends beyond the adult queer community into places where that sexu-alization would be counterproductive.

The Australian tradition may be a particularly good example of the cunningly subversive approach: dressing so conservatively that they have been mistaken for Roman Catholic nuns on more than one occa-sion, and wearing no whiteface, this order is far closer in appearance to the figures they are camping than are Sisters from the Americas or the mainland European orders. As Sister Rowena observed above, the Australian order's closer adherence to the Roman Catholic visual tradi-tion may make their camp critique even sharper. And on the more bla-tant side, some such as The Abbey of St. Joan's Sister VixXxen pull out all the stops in emphasizing the playful sexuality of the Sisters, which is an important aspect of their safer-sex work. With the triple X in her name and a fondness for wearing corsets without much else, Sister VixXxen leaves no room for doubt that the Sisters are sex-positive pro-mulgators of joy and expiators of guilt. Drawing on the image of the drag queen as fun, sexy, sassy, and gay, and the image of the nun as a compassionate, spiritual, selfless provider of healing, education, and service to the community, the Sisters use camp to meld the two into their unique practice: the serious parody that creates twenty-first century queer nuns.

A Persona, Not a Person

A number of Sisters have pointed to an additional factor that may impact the effectiveness of the Sister image in the communities the order serves: their anonymity. This feature of the Sisters came about somewhat by accident; Sister Vish appreciated the artistic effects of whiteface makeup, and within a few years of the order's founding the San Francisco Sisters had discovered that the white makeup drew attention and cameras, both of which were useful for spreading the "good news" of joy, no guilt, and safer sex. The Australian order, founded just two years after the San Francisco house when the latter had not yet fully adopted whiteface, opted for plain faces but discovered quite quickly that the sunglasses they found necessary during most manifestations in the Australian sun also helped to protect their identities. Although such protection was valuable for many reasons (and rumor has added a few apocryphal ones),[61] the Sisters soon discovered that the people they served were more willing to listen to and talk with a Sister whose secular identity could not be determined.

Sister Mona Little-Moore's conversation with me about whiteface is illustrative here; not only is her perspective representative of what I heard from numerous Sisters, but the end of our conversation shows the connections between whiteface and the Sisters' serious parody, or camping, of the Roman Catholic ritual tradition. Sister Mona's first response to my question, "What's it like to wear whiteface?" was to talk about how many community members were drawn to its beauty, and the common response in which the Sisters turn the compliment back to the community by saying, "I'm just a reflection of the beauty in you." Then she added her own perspective on the importance of the whiteface:

> I mean, I do say "Thank you," and I am flattered by [the compliments], but that's not the reason why I put the whiteface on. I put the whiteface

on to make me more approachable, which allows me to do what I need to do. . . . You know, talk with [people]. So, like condom outreach is a really good example. As Ken, or like if I was working for CAP [Cascade AIDS Project] and just a city guy, they're just out there in their street clothes . . . no makeup or anything on. They walk up to a [bar] table, and I used to be one of those people at the table. They'd walk up to a table and say, "Are you interested in a safe sex kit" or whatever, and we'd be like, "No, we don't need it." . . . But as Sister Mona, with the whiteface, because of that anonymity I can go up there and say, "Okay, raise of hands, who's going to go home and bone?" You know, and start these conversations. So the whiteface is just another tool of the whole thing, it's part of the habit, and allows me to do the work that I want to do.

"Why is the anonymity important?" I asked. Sister Mona replied,

It's not so much important to me. Well, in some ways it is because, like I said, I can say things and do things that I wouldn't do out of habit. But I think it's really important to the community. Because, again, if I went out just as Ken and was trying to have these conversations with people I don't think that they would open up to me, or to somebody else, because that's a face, that's a person that, you know, can point to you later on and say, "Oh yeah, I talked to that person about—" Whereas as a Sister we're anonymous, pretty much, it's almost like a safety factor. So we're easier to talk to because we're not really a real person, we're just this image of whatever a Sister is. But we're not a real person that will later on go out and identify you as somebody who just tested positive, somebody who's doing meth, or whatever we're talking about. And I think that that's why it's so important, because then the community feels a little bit safer with us.

"That's really interesting," I commented, "because it makes me think about how Catholic confession works. And the anonymity of the priest." "Absolutely," she responded. "And I think that there's parallels there. Absolutely. Same thing. You're saying something to the priest, but you're not seeing him, and so it's still a little safe. And same thing with us. That whiteface is kind of that confessional wall sometimes."[62]

Serious Parody as Activism

A bit like camp, activism is hard to define. The latter term, though, is contested not so much because of its many forms but because of its positive and negative valences among different discursive communities. Social conservatives in the United States today complain of "activist judges" when they perceive a court to be overstepping the bounds of its constitutional authority; protesters who favor marches in the streets deride other approaches to social justice as not, or insufficiently, activist. For the purpose of analyzing the Sisters' ministry, I make use of a broad definition of activism as activity that aims to ameliorate injustices in a community, one's own or others'.[63] Because the Sisters' communities are many and varied—small, large, urban, rural, predominantly queer, predominantly straight, conservative, radical, and so on—and because houses also differ in the demographic makeup and priorities of their members, activism looks different in every house. The Sisters' serious parody, however, plays a role in every case.

Take fundraising, for example. While the Sisters are aware that their serious parody is not effective in all settings, they have become so well-known in many communities for their seed grant programs and their community outreach that they hold celebrity status. Their very presence at another group's fundraiser can raise the event's profile, provide an endorsement of its goals, and thereby contribute to the amount of money raised. When raising money for their own grant funds, the Sisters make use of serious parody in ways that lend a sense of campy fun and sexy playfulness to a process that by definition is often elitist. The Sisters raise money at a rate of $10 for an inseam's length of raffle tickets (and oh yes, most Sisters will measure the *entire* inseam of a *very* tight pair of jeans), rather than $200 a plate. Instead of formal speeches and polite applause in a ballroom, a Sisters fundraiser might feature lip synching to Portland musician Storm Large's campy song "Eight Miles Wide" or to popular show tunes with certain lyrics strategically removed ("I could have [bleep] all night, I could have [bleep] all night, and still have begged for more"). Or the fundraiser might be an adult-themed bingo, held in a bar with easily available drinks (good business for the bar on a slow afternoon), where the crowd roars when O-69 is called seductively, where the prizes range from princess wands to gay porn, and where every place at every table is graced by safer-sex kits and perhaps a few copies of the *Play Fair!* pamphlet. Each time a North American house is about to celebrate an anniversary, it puts out a call for grant applications. All this uproarious fun, in addition to providing a casual and lighthearted setting for educating about and encouraging safer sex and STI testing, provides thousands of dollars for organizations that offer direct services to the Sisters' communities, and to celebrate their anniversaries most houses hold a grants party at which they announce the year's recipients.

Sisters conduct bar ministry, a pub crawl with a purpose, spending fifteen to thirty minutes in each bar as they engage the patrons to raise funds, offer safer-sex supplies, provide a listening ear, dispense blessings and joy, and jump in to help those who have had a bad night or have drunk a little too much. In many regions they partner with governmental health services to make HIV testing a little less daunting or to do harm reduction outreach in areas where professional health workers would be ineffective. The Las Vegas house provides direct services through the Sisters' AIDS Drug Assistance Program. The Sisters staff gates at block parties, keep the peace, campaign against violence in their communities, dance away religious homophobes bent on shaming individual members of queer communities into sexual if not religious conversion, and intercede with police and politicians when everyone else is taking sides.

And they march. They march in Pride parades, throwing glitter or dancing like Sisterly Salomés around the papier-mâché head of a homophobic politician on a giant platter. Sisters have marched in AIDS Walks and World AIDS Day vigils, and they have been a regular presence as cyclists in habit on California's AIDS Ride from San Francisco to Los Angeles. Sisters take part in Walk a Mile in Her Shoes and Slut Walk, both marches to raise awareness of and protest violence against women. They walk in trans marches and drag marches. Some take part in Black Lives Matter protests in the United States, and Sister Mish has for years attended the annual protest against the School of the Americas, often with other Sisters in tow. In France there is a tradition of Sisters lending their efforts to support and agitate for the rights of sex workers of all genders. The Sisters' activism addresses a variety of justice issues, in a variety of ways, on a variety of levels. Always their serious parody is central to their effectiveness, whether through their sexy appeal for safer (but still hot) sex, their emotional and spiritual care for their communities, or their use of the nun image to call others to task.

A particularly striking example of the latter, and of the efficacy of the Sisters' serious parody even among those who find them—and all queer folk—abhorrent, comes from Sœur Rose of the Couvent de Paname in Paris. In 2010 Sœur Rose traveled to Warsaw with another Sister for that year's Europride. She recounted,

> The Europride was not able to start because there were two hundred fascist people blocking the parade. And the chief of the police was waiting to have the order to attack them to make them move. Of course, as it's Poland, the order was not coming. And they were like, "No, we're not allowed to do anything to move because they are here, and as long as we are not allowed to fight them, we will not be able to start." I was in face, I was with Sister Aura from Berlin. I said, "Okay, Aura, come." She was way too afraid. She stand back. And I decided to go there anyway. I passed the police line, and I just stand in front of them in the Christ position, with my coronet and everything. And the Paname coronet really looks like the Catholic one from one order [that] was really important in France, and in Poland too. So when they looked at me like this, it's really like they are coronets, Catholic ones. So, Christ position, coronets, the guys were like so afraid, they did not know who they were fighting. Is that a drag queen? A man? A woman? A new kind of nuns? The Christ? They step back. And the Europride start.[64]

Serious Parody as Ludic Activism

Applied theater scholar James Thompson has suggested that "hedonism is a bunker" for people who are sometimes quite literally under attack; he frames his work around Emma Goldman's insistence on joy in activism and on "everybody's right to beautiful, radiant things."[65] "Rather than being a distraction from radical politics," he argues, "beauty can be positioned as central" because "beauty's power to disturb is crucial and has important, rarely acknowledged, political power."[66] Sister Merry Peter seems almost to echo Thompson's perspective when she observes,

That's why we talk about promulgating joy and not promulgating happiness. Happiness is easy. It's momentary, and it's based on a sugar high or a good cup of coffee or a quick fuck. Joy is hard won. Joy is what's left in the crucible after you throw in all the tears and all the anger and all the shame and you burn it at a high temperature for five hours. And what comes out is the luster of joy.[67]

Sister Unity Divine, a formally trained theater professional working in Los Angeles, offered a related analysis of the Sisters' work. "Fun and artifice, and performative," she described it. "And in a way, that's the lure and then you hook them, and then you give them the real. And from my conversations with some of the earliest Sisters that's what they've always known: that the makeup not only delivers a message but it attracts the crowds so that you can then, you know, it's the spoonful of sugar and then you can give them the medicine." Earlier in the interview, Sister Unity explained one form that this "medicine," "the real," might take:

If you can talk to me in greasepaint, glitter, and drag, like I'm a real character, like I'm a real person, and relate to a drag nun as a real person, then in your neighborhood when a six-year-old with a penis tells you, "I'm a girl," then the doors of your mind are open enough that you might be able to say, "Well, it's nice to meet you." Period. You know what I'm saying? You may be able to accept people for who they are, *as* they are, and that is my personal mission, to make room in the world and let people know that there is room for them to be who they are, as they are. With security, freedom from guilt, joy, and abundance of gifts to give back to the community. *That's* my mission. And I think that the trick of making people accept Sister Unity as a real *thing*, as a real person, is part of the core of how we do that. It's the magic trick.[68]

Sara Warner argues that "acts of gaiety are performances of redress that transform the vicious banality of homophobia and misogyny into something fantastic and fabulous." She explains that as a "gesture of radical openness, gaiety shows us that what hurts, what causes us shame, and what we feel is wrong with the world is not necessary or inevitable, and it gives us license to unmake and remake it in other guises."[69] "Fantastic and fabulous" is exactly what the Sisters are. With the taller members quite literally larger than life in their stilettos or platform boots, eye-catching whether they are wearing traditional habits with plain faces and sunglasses or colorful dresses with whiteface and glam makeup, when a group of Sisters sweeps into a queer space, the change in the atmosphere is often palpable. In their efforts to promulgate universal joy and expiate stigmatic guilt, the Sisters offer to their communities precisely this "license to unmake" "what we feel is wrong with the world," the strength and courage and confidence in oneself and one's community to hope for and work toward change. If fabulously sexy queer nuns can exist, then perhaps anything is possible.

3

"A Sacred, Powerful Woman"

Complicating Gender

Sister VixXxen wears lingerie well. Her petite frame allows her access to a wide range of styles designed to conform physically as well as aesthetically to traditional white European standards of feminine beauty. Her clean-shaven, coyly smiling face adorned not only with smooth, white pancake makeup but with an artfully arranged assortment of colors, jewels, and glitter that marks her as an experienced member of a house closely affiliated with the imperial court system, Sister VixXxen would be an excellent candidate for glamour drag were it not for the fact that her chest remains unshaven. She is a Sister, after all, not a drag queen, and the genderfuck is never far away. All the same, The Abbey of St. Joan in Seattle has such close ties to the world of drag that two of its members retired from the order during the course of my fieldwork in order to dedicate more time to their drag careers.

Yet, as with their roles as nuns, with gender too there is something more complicated going on in the Sisters than what might at first be assumed by an outside observer, and Sister VixXxen is an excellent example. In her secular life, Sister VixXxen explained, "I identify physically as a male, but mentally, psychologically as a female. And I like the two, I like the dichotomy of it. I'm not seeking to change anything. I personally feel like being a woman housed in a man's body, in this world we're living in right now, is the luckiest thing that could have happened." Reflecting on my question toward the end of the interview about whether she considers herself a nun, Sister VixXxen mused, "I had to think on that one, but there are various different perspectives of sacred women throughout all different societies and cultures, and among my tribe I see myself as a sacred woman. And [being a Sister of Perpetual Indulgence] is just living true to that. . . . Yes, I see myself as a sacred, powerful woman."[1]

Although male-born people who identify in some way as men pre-dominate in the Sisters, the order has included cisgender women since 1983 and self-identified transgender members since at least the mid-1990s. Furthermore, the history of Sisters troubling gender norms and advocating for feminism goes back to the beginning of the order, and when the transgender rights movement was on the rise in the early 1990s, at least some of the San Francisco Sisters were already advocating fiercely for that cause as well.[2] At the same time, most of the cisgender women and trans people whom I interviewed during my research told me of struggling to find or create a space for themselves within what remains a largely cisgender and genderqueer male organization.

The struggles of cisgender women and trans people within the order echo concerns in the communities surrounding the Sisters. Some of these concerns center on the order's perceived use of drag. In the 1980s such objections frequently came from feminist groups, many of which at the time considered drag to be a patriarchal appropriation of women's lives and a simultaneous reinscription of some of the most sexist and misogynist assumptions about women; that some drag queens' performances incorporated misogyny into their patter did nothing to assuage feminist concerns. Indeed, according to Sister Soami, the Sisters' first official manifestation as a named order faced resistance in part on the basis that they were considered offensive to women.[3] While fewer feminists hold such opinions today—in part, ironically, because of the transmisogynist consequences they have had within cisgender feminism—fresh concerns about drag have been raised by some trans activists. At times these concerns focus on the open transphobia expressed by some drag queens; other activists argue that drag performance appropriates transgender cultural production or makes light of the identities and struggles of trans people.[4] The Sisters, with their simultaneous referencing of and distancing from drag and their dual history of advocating for feminism and trans rights while not always fully supporting individual cis women and trans members, find themselves at times awkwardly located within these political currents.

Gender Identities: The Sisters and the Communities They Serve

In the demographic section of the interviews, I asked members of the order how they "identify in terms of gender or gender history." I gave no options from which to choose; rather, I left the answer entirely open to the participant's own terminology. Consistent with what I observed during fieldwork, the majority of Sisters and Guards whom I interviewed over the course of this research identify as cisgender men, or more commonly simply as "men" or "males," which I take to imply the unmarked category of cisgender. Of the eighty-three interviewees who answered the question about gender, fifty-seven identified in this way. Some were even startled by the question, perhaps understanding sex and gender as conflated terms: "Gender?" queried one interviewee with a laugh. "I've always had my cock! What do you mean?"[5] Another nine interviewees described themselves as "female"; again, I read the lack of mention of gender history as an unmarked invocation of cisgender identity. Three participants identified as trans, two of whom were transmasculine and one transfeminine. The other fourteen offered a variety of terms indexing a complex and often fluid gender identity that ranged from "genderqueer" (the most common term, but invoked by only four interviewees) through "neither man nor woman" to "Berliner Hinterhof Tunte," which Mother Katharina Lætitiam Donans translated for me as "Berlin backyard drag queen," while also immediately qualifying that *Tunte* means "pansy" or "fairy" more than "drag queen" as the latter term is generally understood today.[6]

Gender diversity was evident in all of the houses whose members I interviewed except for the Sydney house; however, few conclusions of any significance can be drawn from this anomaly, since I interviewed only five members of that house and was unable to conduct fieldwork in Australia. More notable, perhaps, is that all three of the Guards whom I interviewed identified as cisgender men, a pattern that appeared more broadly during my fieldwork. Recall that the role of Guard was originally created to allow for the participation of leathermen who wanted to be involved with the order but did not wish to wear habits. While people of all genders can now be Guards, at least in the houses where the role of Guard is an option at all, the predominance in the order of people assigned male at birth, combined with the unambiguous masculinity of the Guard role, leads logically to the prediction that most Guards will be cis men, a prediction that appears to be borne out in the international order.

In all, the eighty-three Sisters and Guards who answered my question about gender made use of twenty-four different terms to describe their gender identities. Interestingly, one of those terms, which I include above under "cisgender man," was "gay male," a term used by no fewer than fourteen interviewees to describe their gender. One respondent even simply said "gay" when I asked about gender and gender history. Sister Urania elaborated on her answer by describing it as a "very, very, very old-fashioned kind of thing." Contrasting "gay" to "all the queer ideas and diversification," she reiterated, "No, gay." Then she added a particularly telling recollection. "As usual," she reflected, "as [with] most queens, I would say, there was a time when you were seventeen or eighteen, when you had the idea, would it be appropriate to get changed in some way? Is that part of the process?" "To get changed?" I asked. She replied,

> How to deal with my body. Is it the right body, and all that. You know, I think a lot of people come into that valley and walk through it. And some are going [to] that side of the hill, and others [to] the other side. So, for me, from a spiritual perspective, I just decided one day, I incarnated that way. So why should I change things? No need for that. [In the] next life, maybe. But bearing children is really not my kind of thing.[7]

She left it at that, and I moved on with the interview while continuing to ponder the decision that this Sister had faced between what scholars and activists alike now consider separate aspects of identity: gender and sexual orientation. But they were not always so separate, and the legacy of the intertwining of desire and gender shows through clearly in Sister Urania's own story of identity navigation, as it does in each of the respondents who described his gender as "gay male."

Gender in Gay Male Communities

Gay men, like people of any sexual identity or none at all, identify with many different genders. Many are cisgender; some are transgender men or transmasculine people more broadly. Others consider themselves genderqueer, gender fluid, nonbinary, or in some way feminine while also still considering themselves gay men. Cisgender identity has its own subcultures among gay men, such as the barrel-chested, hirsute, masculine bears and the equally masculine, black-clad leathermen. There are "queeny" or "swishy" men who do not identify as genderqueer or trans, there are Radical Faeries who identify as gay men and who deeply value the opportunity to express their "feminine side" at gatherings and other Faerie-sponsored events, and there are drag queens who embody a hyperfeminine persona for the stage and return to a cismasculine gender presentation after the performance ends.[8] All of this gender diversity has a history, rooted in no small part in engagements with the nineteenth-century inversion model that maintained compulsory heterosexuality by explaining "true" same-sex desire as stemming from a gender identity that was opposite to—inverted from—the gender one had been socially assigned.[9]

As the inversion model became the popular understanding of homosexuality in the late nineteenth and early twentieth centuries, some same-sex–attracted people embraced it and others rejected it, setting the stage for more than a century of tensions over gender within and between gay, lesbian, and eventually bisexual, transgender, and queer communities. In the mid-twentieth century United States, organizations in the homophile movement such as the Mattachine Society and the Daughters of Bilitis expected gender conformity from their members; the Daughters of Bilitis went so far as to encourage normatively middle-class, white feminine standards of dress in its meetings.[10] In the bars at the time, on the other hand, fairies, drag queens, and butch lesbians flourished despite the severity of police harassment and the widespread laws banning so-called cross-dressing. Gendered fault lines ran through these communities along classed and racialized channels that played an important role in the rise and evolution of the gay liberation movement in the 1970s and that still shape what are now called LGBT politics.[11] Meanwhile, at the gender clinics that began to form in the United States, gender conformity was enforced in such deep collusion with normative models of gender and with compulsory heterosexuality that many people seeking sex reassignment surgery learned to present themselves through clear, binary gender stereotypes and heteronormativity simply in order to be granted access to medical services.[12] In this milieu, it is unsurprising that the teenage man who would become Sister Urania weighed his attraction to men with his sense of inner femininity and wondered whether to get a sex change.

When the transgender movement began to gain political traction in the United States and the United Kingdom during the early 1990s and claimed for its membership all gender-variant people regardless of sexual desire or sexual identity, it put one of the final nails into the coffin of the inversion model. Yet this was not an untrammeled victory. As David Valentine pointedly remarks, despite their initially concerted resistance to including transgender people and movements in their own circles,

> mainstream gay and lesbian organizations have come to *depend* on [the concept of] transgender not simply to define themselves as a discrete set . . . but because transgender incorporates, and thereby removes from the category "gay" (and in different ways, from "lesbian"), gender-variant behavior or identities. That is, not only does transgender provide a foil against which "gay"—implicitly white, middle-class, respectable, private, dependable, and most deeply, male—can define itself but it allows any gender-variant behavior—even from those who identify *as* gay—increasingly to be moved into the category transgender. . . . It is the acceptance by both gay and lesbian *and* transgender people of the ontological distinction of their identities that reinforces the racialized and class-inflected diversity politics of mainstream gay and lesbian politics.[13]

While Valentine rightly notes that many elite, cisgender gay men have been all too happy to have any trace of gay femininity reassigned to the category of transgender, by the middle of the 2010s his argument elsewhere in the same work that "border wars" over who can claim and enact gender nonconformity have taken place only between masculine people assigned female at birth, such as butch lesbians and transgender men, no longer held true. The growing tensions between gay men and transgender women over who can claim drag—as their history, as their art form, as their politics, as offense against or appropriation of their community—indicate the presence of a newer border war over queer femininity as well.

These are the choppy historical and political waters that the Sisters, queer nuns manifested largely by cisgender and genderqueer people who were assigned male at birth, have navigated since 1979. The legacy of the invert, tensions over gender roles in gay male communities, and border wars between feminine gay men and trans women play out in the identities of cisgender and genderqueer, male-bodied Sisters in two main ways: the importance to some of a sense of inner femininity or gender complementarity, and the difficulty that others have with accepting and adopting the femininity of their roles as Sisters.

Sister Personas as Feminine Selves

When the Mattachine Society expelled its communist-leaning leadership in 1953, founder Harry Hay withdrew from public life for the better part of two decades.[14] During the rest of the 1950s and 1960s Hay continued pondering his own nature as a gay man, the natures of other gay men, and their collective purpose. While the Mattachine Society quickly came to espouse assimilationist politics and gender roles (amusingly, an old television clip shows one member reassuring the U.S. viewing public that the homophile movement would never demand something so radical as marriage or adoption rights),[15] Hay went on to explore the anthropological theory, increasingly adopted by gay and lesbian anthropologists for their own activist causes, that indigenous cultures around the world understood same-sex–attracted people to be part of a third gender. Western and particularly U.S. anthropology, it seemed to him, was proving that inversion was real, it was innate, it was widespread, and it was valued by all cultures that had not been spoiled by what he saw as the homophobia of Christianity.[16] Hay began to speak publicly about the importance of claiming one's gay nature. In one well-known turn of phrase, he exhorted attendees at the first Radical Faerie Gathering in 1979 "to tear off the ugly green frog-skin of Hetero-male imitation . . . to reveal the beautiful Fairy Prince hidden beneath"—in today's terminology, to reject the cisgender conformity of assimilationist gay culture and instead explore gender nonconformity as a part of one's natural gay being.[17] In attendance that day were Reverend Mother and Sister Hysterectoria, as well as several other men who did not yet know that they were soon to become members of a new order of nuns.

The influence of the Radical Faeries is still strong in the Sisters of Perpetual Indulgence. Regardless of their own direct involvement in the Faeries, a number of gay male Sisters also spoke to me about the importance of balancing masculinity and femininity in their lives, and the ways that gendered combination reflects their gayness. Sister VixXxen, with her sense of self as "a sacred, powerful woman," is a prime example; so is Sister Urania's lament that "there are no roles that fit here [in contemporary Western society]. . . . There is no We'wha here, there is no third gender idea."[18] In Zurich, Mother Belleza Tulips@analia and Sister Benedikta both referenced gay male femininity in association with their own identities and with their roles as Sisters. "What gay man did not at a younger age nip into his mother's or sister's makeup box and try it all on at some point?" asked Sister Benedikta rhetorically. Mother Belleza related a longer story, which she prefaced by saying, "It started with me as I was a child."

> You can imagine [living in] the country, [as a] farmer, and then I went to put on from my grandma, her dresses. On the bike, go through the neighborhood, go playing with others, and then suddenly my mother said, "I don't care if you wear the dresses, but not on the bicycle. It is too dangerous." But afterward she told me a little bit ashamed she was, so she said to me it is too dangerous because the dress can go into the spokes. But at that time I didn't know I was gay. But I felt I liked [wearing the dress]. . . . So I have always had a feeling to dress like a woman.[19]

Notice here that Mother Belleza concludes a story about childhood gender nonconformity by saying that he did not yet know that he was gay, thus implying, as Sister Benedikta did and as Sister Urania concluded after considering sex reassignment, that male femininity is a mark of gay identity and not of transgender identity.

Sister Petunia Encarnata, who was a novice when I interviewed her, offers a bridge between those Sisters who express a sense of inner femininity as a part of their gayness and those Sisters who struggle with the feminine gender expression of the Sister persona. When I asked why she had chosen to become a Sister rather than a Guard, Novice Sister Petunia reflected that

> all my life, I'd never allowed myself to express my feminine side. I believe that most of us gay males, we have homophobia instilled in us from different sources, mostly religion. In my case, it was Roman Catholics. And I never allowed myself to be a girl. You know, no women's clothes, no acting girly, nothing like that. So I saw the Sisters as a venue for me to express that internal side of me that all gay males have. And by doing so I embraced my own internal homophobia, and let it go.

Novice Sister Petunia described her early development as a Sister, "allowing myself to have fun by doing girly things," as "the first steps into myself"—by which, again, she means her gay self and not a transgender identity. Later, when I asked whether her secular self and Petunia were different, she replied,

> No. Oh, no. Petunia is just the female face of who I am. But no. No difference. I'm learning to *name* Petunia, because I'd never done it, and I'd never allowed myself to have that female aspect of me recognized, acknowledged, embraced. Now I am. I'm learning to embrace Petunia, the little flower. This little South American flower [Sister Petunia is originally from South America] that is powerful. It's not so fragile anymore.[20]

Novice Sister Petunia associated femininity with being gay by attributing a stifling of that femininity to internalized homophobia, and understood the Sisters as having allowed her the opportunity to honor and "embrace" that side of her being. She is not the only one to recall struggling with the feminine appearance that is required, at least to a certain extent, of those who manifest as Sisters rather than as Guards.

Sister Honey, BE! recalls objecting fiercely to any attribution of femininity for much of her life. "When I first came out," she told me,

> I was a little hot man. And I worked at a gay bar downtown in South Philly. And it was three floors. And all the guys were just regular gay guys, but they were more like gay-queeny. I said, "I don't like that shit." And then they [responded], "Look at what she's talking about!" And I said, "Don't refer to me as she," and they would refer to me, "Oh, here she comes!" I would butch up and say, "Don't do that shit." And one time when I came in late for work they were all up on the third floor, in the stairwell coming down. [They said,] "Oh, she's late." And I'm screaming up, "Don't call me she! Don't call me she!" And then they nicknamed me Stella. You know, from the movie [*A Streetcar Named Desire*], when he's screaming up the stairwell? Stella. That was my girl name. Now, even as I grew and matured, of course, I could be playful and everything like that. But I still couldn't stand being referred to as she or her. It annoyed me. 'Cause I was never in that role, I never understood myself in that role. I never understood myself in a *dress*! Ever! I never got dressed in drag. It never crossed my mind.

Now, as I evolve with the order, talk about stretching. And now I *can* say she. And I can be referred to as her. In the context of being a Sister. But outside of that context I'm not comfortable with it.

Later in our conversation, as she described to me the experience of learning to wear dresses as a Sister, Sister Honey, BE! joked about being careful what you wish for. "You say a prayer, and I don't know where it goes, and I don't understand it theologically, it's just a habit: 'Oh God, I need to dress in drag before I die someday.' Right? Well, who would have expected it to happen, that not only do I dress in so-called drag—" She interrupted herself to clarify. "They're our habits, not drag. So when you look at somebody's dress, I don't say, 'Oh, that's a really nice dress.' I say, 'That's a really nice habit.' That's important."[21]

These different ways of navigating gay male femininity—embracing it, considering resistance to it a sign of internalized homophobia, rejecting it except as a means to an end, considering it strictly a performance while simultaneously distinguishing it from the undesirable femininity of the drag queen—all have their roots in the tangled history of gender non-conformity and same-sex desire in nineteenth- and twentieth-century Western cultures and in debates among activists over whether to claim and reconfigure the inversion model or to reject it by firmly claiming and performing a model cisgender identity. As David Valentine and Peter Hennen have each demonstrated, both approaches have their dangers. They also have implications for the participation of cisgender and genderqueer women, and transgender people of all genders, in the order.

Cisgender and Genderqueer Women in the Sisters

Sister Maria Caffeina Mochalatte joined the activist group Queer Nation in college. Although she found "the anger and getting in people's faces to be really, really useful," she also found it draining, particularly in "that period of AIDS where you would see somebody one week, and the next week they'd be dead." She started wondering what she could do to address the suffering she saw around her more directly. She had "seen the Sisters around Capitol Hill [Seattle's gay neighborhood]," and she remembers thinking, "Oh! They're gorgeous, but, eh, another old fags' club. They probably don't accept women." Like most of the women members of the order with whom I spoke, Sister Maria had seen only male-bodied Sisters, and given the history of sexism in gay male communities, she had assumed that she would be barred from joining. A member of the original Seattle house corrected her assumption, and she joined soon thereafter.

There was a clear difference, though, between accepting women and establishing a space in which women members of the order could thrive. Sister Maria chose her words carefully in explaining this part of the history of The Abbey of St. Joan. "We did have some early issues with a certain amount of what Sister Glo [Euro N'Wei] calls 'old white gay male culture,' " she noted.

> We had a certain amount of sexism and a certain amount of misogynistic jokes and stuff that were really unkind to women's bodies. You know, a couple of people with fish jokes and stuff like that. We had a certain amount of that initially, and it drove a couple of [female] Sisters away. They were really unhappy about it. They didn't like going out and having Sisters be cruel about them and their bodies and such.[22]

Sister Maria articulates in depth two problems I heard about repeatedly from cisgender and genderqueer women members of the order: first, that women members are not particularly visible, so they had no idea that they would be eligible to join the Sisters and even as Sisters they were illegible within their communities; and second, that being a member of the order means having to navigate a legacy of sexism in cisgender gay male communities.

Cisgender and genderqueer female-born members of the order are less visible than gay men for a number of reasons. Some of these causes date back to the historic schism between lesbian and gay communities during the 1970s, when lesbians hoping to find a radical feminist revolution in gay liberation found instead yet another opportunity to make coffee and mimeographs for the men, and found their concerns for women's rights dismissed as being women's issues, not gay ones.[23] Even though many lesbian and bisexual women overcame the rift between the communities during the height of the AIDS pandemic through their support and care for the ill, the dying, and the caregivers (not always separate categories during this period) within gay male communities, lesbians and gay men continue to be separated in marked ways, from bars to residential patterns to activist concerns. Furthermore, the enactment of high femme drag by female-bodied people in queer communities has been overshadowed by the figure of the gay male drag queen. Thus, when genderfuck nuns hit the streets of a gay male neighborhood, many observers presume that everyone in the group is male-bodied and male-identified. In fact, several female Sisters told me of having their breasts eagerly grabbed by admirers who thought they were touching particularly good falsies but discovered to their horror and chagrin that they were squeezing living flesh.

Moreover, the legacy of misogyny that Sister Maria references is still, unfortunately, alive and well in some circles. Sister MaryMae Himm expressed grave concern over this problem during our conversation. "Diversity work has been really important to me," this long-standing member of the San Francisco house related,

> particularly around sexual diversity and also the intersection of race and culture, and the way in which gay men are traditionally misogynist and traditionally racist, and what is it that we can do to start to unpack that? White gay men are by and large not really [open] to examining their privilege. . . . As the AIDS crisis becomes less of a crisis, I'm noticing more and more misogyny creeping back into the community. And it breaks my heart, because I'm from the generation when I watched women jump to the forefront to take care of us and help us despite the way that they were treated in the past. . . . So for me to see younger gay men expressing this misogyny again, it just *really* pisses me off.[24]

In addition to misogyny, another factor that may be impacting the participation of cisgender and genderqueer women in the order is the fact that people assigned female at birth have a very different relationship to traditional femininity than do those assigned male at birth. Many of the former are raised with expectations that they perform femininity, and many struggle in one way or another against these expectations. Just as some cisgender gay men are reluctant to join the Sisters because of the requisite expression of femininity, so too some female-born people, queer or not, may be uninterested in manifesting the sort of femininity that characterizes the Sisters. While becoming a Guard may offer more options for such women, Guards are more in the background and do not have as many opportunities for direct service as Sisters do, so this may be a less-than-desirable resolution to the problem. There are women who serve in the order as Guards, but in my experience they are even fewer and farther between than those who serve as Sisters.

In the Australian order most female-identified people, regardless of gender history or sexual identity, become "lesbian monks" or take on other roles that are traditionally filled by cisgender men within Roman Catholicism. While Sisters in the Australian order (and still some in the United Kingdom) wear traditional habits akin to those of Roman Catholic nuns, and therefore do not appear as high femme as their counterparts on other continents, nevertheless the male roles that are the default for women in those houses may offer another space for women who are willing to engage with or ignore any misogyny that may be present in the house but would prefer to avoid the performance of high femme femininity.

Transgender People in the Sisters

Similarly complex challenges attend the inclusion of transgender people within the order. Like cisgender women, transgender people—initially transgender women, specifically—have been a part of the Sisters of Perpetual Indulgence for quite some time, but also like cis women, they have faced invisibility, active prejudice, misunderstanding, and ignorance within the order. Like cisgender and genderqueer women, transgender members of all genders also have allies within the order who work together with them in the hope of seeing the Sisters become more inclusive over time.

Sister Connie Pinko was assigned female at birth and identifies as genderqueer. Because they present as masculine in their secular life, Sister Connie faced a great deal of misunderstanding as she went through the process of becoming an FP. "When I first joined the order," Sister Connie explained to me, "there was a lot of drama around my gender. A lot of the old nuns couldn't really handle it." Senior members of the house frequently asked Connie, "'Why don't you become a Guard, because then you can have a masculine persona?' And I was like, 'I don't want a fucking masculine persona. I want to dress in drag.' . . . There was a lot of pushback around that, and . . . this assumption of what would be better for me."

In the San Francisco house, as in many houses, the process of elevation from one rank to the next involves an interview through which the senior members of the house determine the candidate's readiness for the next rank. Except in her final elevation from novice to fully professed, Sister Connie experienced more questioning about her gender during these interviews than about her work in the order. "There were a couple questions," she explained, "one or two questions about why do you want to do this and what you like about the ministry, but most of it was, 'Wait, so how do you identify? Wait, so why do want to dress like a girl?'" Sister Connie almost quit the order before going up for elevation to novice. She explained why, and why she decided in the end to stay:

> I was constantly correcting people with my pronouns, and constantly correcting people when—'cause people were always assuming that I was a dyke, and I felt like I was invisible, like people weren't listening to me, like my identity was invisible. . . . And luckily Sister Tuna [Noodle Cocktail] talked me into staying. She was like, "You've just got to keep hitting them over the head with it until they get it." And she was right. Most of them get it now. But, yeah, that was really tough.

To make matters worse, when in habit Sister Connie faces further confusion regarding her gender because of her embodiment. "The other thing that sucks," she told me, "is when community members are like, 'Oh, you're a real girl!' And I'm in this position where it's not appropriate for me to give them a Gender 101 lesson. So I always find myself going, 'Weeell, not really.'" At the same time, though, and like many cisgender and genderqueer men in the order, Connie also credits the Sisters with giving her a space in which to express the feminine aspects of her own identity: "The Sisters were an incredibly important step in my gender formation, and being a Sister is really an important way for me to express my femme identity and my femme side; it's the only way that I've found that is comfortable for me."[25]

Sister Connie is not the only member of the order to experience such challenges regarding gender identity, particularly as a postulant and a novice. Novice Sister Jen Derfukt, a transgender man who moved away from the Portland area before he could elevate to FP, pushed on the very identity of the Sisters themselves when he began to develop Novice Sister

Jen's persona, which embraces the genderfuck for which she is named. Although she felt supported by and close to the Sister who was Novice Mistress in the Order of Benevolent Bliss at the time, Novice Sister Jen also found herself in disagreement with that Sister over gendered manifestations. She remembered her Mistress of Novices saying, "'A Sister is a feminine persona and a Guard is a masculine persona.' And I was like, 'No. A Sister is a gendered persona, and my gender is not necessarily feminine.' As a Sister, I can be a Sister and a whatever-the-fuck-this-is, a pink mustache Sister."[26] Novice Sister Jen was in face during our conversation, and pointed to the pink mustache drawn over her whiteface as an example. Since then I have seen one of the cisgender women in the same house also regularly sport a drawn-on, curled mustache, as genderfuck beyond the basic combination of hairy chests with cocktail dresses has become more widely accepted within the Portland Sisters.

That members such as Novice Sister Jen, Sister Connie, and Sister Maria have been able to push the boundaries of their houses in order to create space for their own inclusion reflects well on the order's chances of building and maintaining the diversity that allies like Sister MaryMae Himm want to become integral to the Sisters of Perpetual Indulgence. However, the fact that each of these members has had to create that space first as a relatively disempowered junior member of the order leaves something to be desired. Even though as FPs Sister Maria and Sister Connie can now support and mentor junior members in their own houses who are facing similar challenges, in other houses of the order and in their own houses when they are not around, the challenges still remain. Some of these challenges stem from the ways serious parody intersects with gender, leading community members to assume that all Sisters are cisgender or genderqueer gay men and to assume that all Sisters with breasts are "girls." Other challenges stem from the Sisters' communities themselves, since the Sisters not only serve their communities but also belong to them, shaping and being shaped by the people among whom they live, work, and manifest.

Feedback Loops: Communities the Sisters Serve

Many gay male communities have bars in which women's presence is an anomaly; despite presenting as masculine and having a somewhat awkward relationship with the category of "woman," I remain interpellated as such, and so I experienced this sense of anomaly from time to time when taking part in bar ministry with the Sisters in Portland and Seattle. In Berlin, though, some bars still openly ban the presence of women. Out for an evening of bar ministry with the Erzmutterhaus Sankta Melitta Iuvenis, I saw firsthand how this German house navigates such restrictions when women and female-bodied members and friends of the order are present. I had been forewarned that some bars would allow women only in the front rooms, since the back rooms were reserved for sexual activities between the male bar patrons, and that some bars did not allow women at all. In the latter cases, I was told, when women were part of the bar ministry group, the house's policy was to skip that bar entirely for the evening. Nonetheless, those out on bar ministry that night went to each bar and asked anyway. Of the five bars we visited that evening, one was a mixed bar, although I saw only four or five women out of 100 or 150 patrons. One seemed to be patronized only by men, but had many windows and was clearly fully open to the public. Two had restricted entry but allowed my presence in the front room with the Sisters as chaperones; one would not admit me at all, and the Sisters took their free condoms and their donation cans elsewhere.[27]

Having to wait at three of these bars for word as to my admission left me feeling ambivalent. As a researcher, and one steeped in feminist ethics, I felt deeply the importance of respecting the spaces and groups in which I was conducting my research. As someone who learned from separatist feminists as an undergraduate while not ultimately embracing their perspectives or priorities, I could understand the desire and even the need for separate space. Yet, while aware of the complexities of both history and politics surrounding gender-segregated bars, I had also never before been openly and unabashedly denied entry to a bar on the basis of my assigned sex and gender. In this I am privileged, but the experience also led me to wonder what impact these refusals might have on women members of the order, and on transgender and genderqueer members of all genders and embodiments when the bans extend to them.

Any Sisterly activity requires some sort of bridge to the community in which it takes place. Without knowledge of who the Sisters are and what they do, people may find them odd or even offensive.

Communities may have members who are homophobic, or who object to the male femininity that is so widely associated with the Sisters. Many Sisters have themselves been on the receiving end of homophobic violence, and some have also experienced gendered and transphobic violence both in and out of habit. For all of these reasons, the Sisters tend to serve communities with which they are familiar. Urban houses often center on the main gay male neighborhood in the city, and many of their members live close to their main venues. Because these gay neighborhoods often house and host predominantly cisgender, white, middle- or even solely upper-class men, concerns over safety and welcome result in most houses serving predominantly cisgender, white, middle-class and elite gay men. Such houses are therefore most visible to that population, and as a result they garner most of their new members from the same demographic.

Members of the order who are actively invested in broadening the reach of their houses' ministry are also concerned to avoid the appearance of paternalism in the process. A largely gay male group that is often perceived as "drag nuns" needs to tread carefully when seeking to minister to queer women, for instance, or to trans communities. A largely white group that wears whiteface as a trademark must be thoughtful and self-aware when seeking to work with communities of color. Often a Sister or occasionally a Guard who is a member of the community in question can serve as a bridge to expanding a house's ministry, but only if that person makes it through the challenges of being part of a nondominant group within the order and facing ignorance and bias during the aspirancy, postulancy, and novitiate. These dynamics work against the broadening of the order's ministry through a positive feedback loop in which the communities that a house serves shape the house's membership, and the membership in turn shapes which communities the house serves. There are exceptions to this pattern, however, that point to possibilities for those houses that are committed to expanding their reach; one example is Sister Betti Crotcher's work with queer women in Portland, Oregon.

A queer woman herself, as a novice Sister Betti had noticed that many lesbians and queer women were less aware of safer-sex concerns than were the gay men with whom she primarily worked as a Sister. She explained to me that many "think since they're not having sex with men that they don't really need to be one hundred percent safe." In addition, the condom packs that Sisters around the world distribute are typically designed specifically for sex involving penile penetration. They lack safer-sex supplies for oral-vaginal or digital-vaginal sex, such as dental dams and gloves, and they often include lubricants that, while useful for anal sex, can be difficult to clean from vaginal areas and can damage the silicone sex toys favored by some queer women for vaginal sex. Furthermore, over the course of my fieldwork more than one male-identified Sister expressed ignorance or offered misinformation to me regarding the applicability to female bodies of the safer-sex supplies she carried. Sister Betti wanted to correct these exclusions, to direct the work of her house more toward queer women and to help those women see the Sisters as relevant to their concerns. "I think we're all in the same boat and we should work together as a team," she commented, noting her frustration at the gendered divisions among queer communities. Toward the end of June 2010 Novice Sister Betti produced her novice project: a safer-sex workshop for women, complete with wine donated by a women-owned winery, at a women-owned sex shop in Portland. She was elevated to FP shortly thereafter, and as a result of Sister Betti's efforts the Portland Sisters began to distribute "Passion Packs" containing a condom, a dental dam, a glove, lube, and inclusive safer-sex information.[28]

As Sister Betti's example shows, expanding the outreach of the Sisters often depends on both the presence of at least one member who can build bridges between the order and an underserved community, and a predominance of senior members in the house who are ready and even eager to support such work. Outreach to transgender communities in the San Francisco house has followed a similar route. As Sister Connie points out, forging new paths within the order is challenging and frustrating for junior members, who should be able simply to focus on developing as Sisters and Guards, and this is an area in which senior members can do more to support and welcome new members from groups underrepresented in the order. If they survive the process of becoming fully professed, however, and if they have the enthusiastic support of allies among the influential senior members of the order, people like Sister Connie and Sister Betti can begin to move the Sisters toward greater gender inclusion in both membership and ministry.

Nurturing Nuns and Stalwart Guards: Binary Gender Roles in the Sisters

In keeping with a common image of nuns that is popular in all of the countries where the order is active, Sisters are expected to serve their communities through fundraising, education, emotional labor, kindness, and generosity, all traditionally feminine traits that are attributed to nuns at least as much because of their gender as because of their status as vowed religious. Guards, on the other hand, are expected to be in the background—distant—and to be tough, no-nonsense, and reliable. These, of course, are all traditionally masculine stereotypes. On this reading, then, the order manifestly reinforces the most blatant stereotypes of gender, even as it challenges ideas about what kinds of bodies can carry out such roles.

Some who are drawn to the Sisters find themselves choosing a persona based precisely on the ways those traditional roles intersect with their own self-understanding. Guard Noah Shame, for instance, was invited repeatedly to join the Order of Benevolent Bliss when it first started. "I wanted to do it and I felt it speaking to me," he recalled during our conversation, "but . . . the desire to go buy bolts of fabric and spend hours in front of a sewing machine creating . . . outfits, I celebrate that, because [the Sisters] do a wonderful job, but that's not me." A member of the Portland house suggested that he could become a Guard instead. "And it was like a light shining in a room. Instantly, when I started seeing [pictures of Guards in other houses], especially the makeup, 'cause a lot of the traditional Guard appearance is typically the whiteface with black. Just like around the eyes, but it's very dramatic and usually fairly masculine, and the more I read about it [I knew], 'This is what I want.'"[29] Within a few months, he had joined the Order of Benevolent Bliss to become a Guard.

Hermana Prudencia of the Orden de San Felipe y Santiago de Montevideo likewise made it clear in our interview that she was a gay man manifesting a feminine persona. "En ningún momento de mi vida como activista yo me siento femenino, ¿verdad?" she explained to me. (At no moment of my life as an activist have I felt feminine, right?) "Yo soy gay. Ahora, asumo un personaje, en el cual es un personaje femenino, y lo interpreto de esa forma. Y ahí sí, paso a ser la Hermana XXXX."

(I am gay. Now, I assume a persona, which is a feminine persona, and I interpret it in that way. And in that, yes, I come to be Sister XXXX.)[30]

The presence of a gender binary is particularly clear in the Australian order and in those U.K. houses still influenced by that tradition, where there are two possible roles available: that of gay male nun and that of lesbian monk. Mother Inferior reminded me that "the idea of gay male nuns is there to . . . make statements about gender"—that is, about the gendered ways certain roles are closed off to men and other roles are closed to women. Yet there have been times in the Australian order when its roles have also been closed in gendered ways, for instance to lesbians in the Sydney house in the early 1990s who wished not to be lesbian monks but to be lesbian Sisters—and this despite the history of a female gay male nun in the early years of the Melbourne house.[31] Interestingly, such rules applied specifically to gender identity rather than to birth sex, as indicated by a story told to me by Mother Premonstratensia. "The Cardinal in the Adelaide house," he told me, was "formerly a Roman Catholic priest, who then transitioned to being female. When I professed the Cardinal, I actually said to her, 'Who's achieved the episcopate in spite of herself.'" Having access to the Roman Catholic priesthood through her birth sex, after transitioning this woman had access only to the same roles in the Sisters of Perpetual Indulgence by virtue of the strictly drawn gender reversal that is part of the Australian approach to genderfuck.

Genderfuck: Challenging the Binary

Lest the binary seem entirely stark here, however, it is well worth noting that Melbourne's Sister Very Maculate was only the first of many members of the Australian order who have challenged that starkness. Sister Rowena Keeper of the Holy Doiley, for instance, "was the Sister of Ceremonies for a lesbian woman who was happy to manifest as a gay male nun while she was with the order." Sister Rowena observed, "There's a double genderfuck for you."[32] Likewise, Mother Inferior told me of a cisgender, heterosexual couple who joined the Sydney house in the roles of female gay male nun and male lesbian monk.[33]

In the U.K. houses, too, the sharply drawn binaries of the Australian order have been repeatedly challenged. As I noted earlier, Brother Bimbo was expected like all women to become a Brother when she first joined the Convent of Dunn Eideann in Edinburgh. With both gender and gender politics being interrogated by progressives in the United Kingdom at the time, though, the Convent of Dunn Eideann soon "decided that there was no point to" requiring women to be Brothers, "because it was possibly emphasizing a duality with which we don't agree." As a result, all of the women in the order became Sisters—including Brother Bimbo, who only retained her old title because of the alliteration in the name.[34]

Brother Bimbo's story demonstrates the possibility for creative usage of genderfuck to resist the Sisters' own strictures, yet the possibilities for genderfuck are also woven into the strictures themselves. The structured nature of gender roles in the Australian order, and in those U.K. houses that follow its tradition, exists as a commentary on the structured nature of gender roles in the societies surrounding these houses, and particularly in the Roman Catholic Church. Likewise, the "double genderfuck" of female gay male nuns and male lesbian monks challenges that structure in its own structured way. The conscious performance of gendered roles and the attendant possibility that many members of this international order are engaged in thoughtful and intentional serious parody of gender as well as of religion therefore deserve more direct attention.

Although she struggled to find language with which to explain her observations, Sister Rhoda N'Lytenment articulated an understanding of the Sisters as challenging traditional gender roles. When she first mentioned this perspective, it seemed as though she was offering a wistfully essentialist observation about the innate nurturing abilities of women. Hesitant about that observation, about how she had phrased it, or perhaps simply about sharing it with a gender studies professor, she quickly backed away from her statement. Hoping to clarify and to encourage her, I asked, "So if service and caring and support are sort of a women's thing, what does that mean for Sisters when so many of you are men? Where does it come from?" After a lengthy, thoughtful pause, Sister Rhoda replied, "I think part of that comes from the fact that part of being a Sister is to break out of this patriarchal, binary thought process which says you have a man and a woman. And a male has his roles as a man, and a woman has her roles as a woman. And the two don't intermix." She added, "For me, manifesting as Rhoda gives my male person the right to break out of that binary framework that I've been shoved into all my life. Becoming Rhoda gives me the freedom to . . . take part in all those roles that are socially and culturally defined as female roles, as being a caregiver, as being a supporter, as being the person you go to when you need a hug."[35] Working without access to academic shorthand terms like "the social construction of gender" and "restrictive gender roles," Sister Rhoda nevertheless seemed to me to be articulating precisely such concepts, and to be arguing that the Sisters help to break down gender roles by challenging the idea that caregiving, supporting, reliability, and even hugging are somehow innate in and restricted to female embodiment and identity.

In keeping with Sister Rhoda's argument that the Sisters challenge restrictive gender roles are the many Sisters who described, either implicitly or directly, the genderfuck enacted by the order (fig. 3.1). Sœur Néfertata, for example, of the Couvent de Paris, explained that the Sisters "feel very comfortable with—" She broke off, unsure how to translate the French word *folle*, a term like the German *Tunte* that does not have an exact equivalent in English but is perhaps best rendered as "fairy" or "queen," given those terms' dual implications for both sexuality and gender. "We don't have any trouble with our gender," Sœur Néfertata explained further. "We can be masculine, feminine, we can play, and it's okay for us."[36] Nearly five thousand miles away but only two months later, Sister Katie Kizum named that dynamic directly. "One of the really cool things about the Sisters," she related, "is what we call genderfuck, which is where you're doing drag, but you're not doing female drag. I'm not trying to look like a woman when I go out as a Sister."[37]

Many Sisters find this gender fluidity freeing, and Sisters of varying gender identities and gender histories noted this aspect of their work with the order. Sister Connie found in the Sisters the only way to express what she called her "femme side" as a genderqueer, masculine-presenting person. Mother Belleza of the Swiss order contrasted the Sisters to "drag queens" and "transvestites," describing the former in nongendered terms as "an institution." But it was Sister Ohna Fuckin' Tirade, a cisgender woman in her secular life, who specifically described the Sisters as "freeing" in terms of gender. "One of the things that drew me to wanting to be a Sister," she related, "was that freedom of expression. I never wore makeup, ever, before I became a Sister, but now I do when I'm not in face. And I've become such a girl." She laughed. "I have

Figure 3.1. Genderfuck among two members of the Grand Canyon Sisters of Perpetual Indulgence and Sister Shomi D. Goods of the Order of Benevolent Bliss in Portland, Oregon (*right*), at the Friday night festivities during the 2014 celebration of the thirty-fifth anniversary of the order in San Francisco. Photo by Nicole Pitsavas. Reproduced by permission.

so much pink stuff it's ridiculous. It's kind of a signature, but it's also just really freeing. I really enjoy being able to express myself in so many different ways."[38] Many male-born Sisters have described to me the value of having an opportunity in the order to express the traditional femininity from which they were often banned or discouraged as children. Many Sisters of all genders also noted the freedom of sexual expression that can come with the habit, in that some people who rarely flirt or speak suggestively to others in public will do so avidly once in face. Sisters who struggle with body image or are shy about their bodies for other reasons also find in their Sister personas the freedom to claim their own physical attractiveness; as Sister Krissy Fiction is fond of saying, "No matter what you look like, someone thinks it's hot, so work what you've got!"[39] Given this background, it is unsurprising that a cisgender woman could experience the Sisterhood as liberating in terms of gender expression.

Beyond the Binary

Some Sisters claim that "Sister" is a third gender or that Sister personas are genderless. In some cases the claim to a third gender evokes indirect and sometimes direct connections to Harry Hay's ideas about the spiritual leadership for which third-gender, same-sex–attracted men are destined. Others, though, expressed the Sisters' gender variance in strikingly different ways. Some, for instance, linked gender to sexual activity, arguing that because Sisters are generally expected not to have sex while in habit they are therefore genderless.[40]

No fewer than four members of the Order of Benevolent Bliss mentioned, in different ways, the complexities of gender that the order manifests. Sister Maya Poonani responded to my question about gender and gender identity by saying, "Female, when I'm Cheryl. When I'm Maya, I'm just a nun. I obviously look like a woman, but I don't identify that way." "Okay," I replied, trying to understand this aspect of the order during one of the very first interviews I conducted, "so nun is different from male or female." "I think so," Sister Maya answered. "Obviously, when people first see me out, they look down at my breasts and are like, 'Oh my God, you're a woman,' and I'm like, 'I'm not a woman, I'm a nun.' That's my general response to people."[41] Maya's fellow Sister, Krissy Fiction, shared a similar approach with me during another interview on the same day. "When I'm Krissy," she explained, "I'm a Sister." Although Sister Krissy identifies as a cisgender man in secular life, she explained that her habit is "not really drag; I'm not trying to be a woman or look like a woman. Nobody's ever going to mistake me for a woman. It's just kind of a blurring of the lines. . . . I think there's something kind of profound in that." I told her, "Maya said, not man, not woman, just nun." "Yeah," Sister

Krissy replied. "It's weird because people say 'you guys' when we're out. 'You guys' or 'hey, ladies.' Neither of them feel appropriate. We're really Sisters. When they say, 'Hey, Sisters,' we're our own kind of category."[42]

In keeping with the concept of performativity within gender theory, then, enacting genderfuck has significance for the gendered self within and in some cases beyond that enactment.[43] While some Sisters mark this significance through the use of feminine pronouns, other mark it by insisting that "Sister" is the only appropriate term and that no pronouns should be used for a Sister of Perpetual Indulgence. "I don't think Sisters have gender," explained Sister MaryMae Himm. "I think that's part of what makes it work, and the magic of it, is that the Sisters don't have gender." Sister added, "When I'm working in government agencies, one of my favorite things to do is to make people just call me Sister, because it upsets the power balance a little bit, and particularly with government agencies it's fun to do that. And important."[44]

Policing Gay Masculinity

Perhaps the clearest indications that the Sisters of Perpetual Indulgence are doing more than simply reinforcing the established gender binary are the negative responses they receive from some cisgender gay men. Many interviewees, particularly those who themselves identify as cisgender gay men, told me of these reactions. Notably, I heard such tales from both Sisters and Guards, though the Guards were generally describing reactions toward Sisters in the order. I was most likely to evoke stories of these experiences when I asked whether there are any disadvantages to being a member of the order. One of the most common answers I received was that glitter never comes out of grout, advice that I surely will find useful one day; the other was that Sisters have a tough time getting laid. Sister Babylon Anon had a particularly pointed response to this problem. "If they're identified bear or leather," she explained, "or on that old clone butch thing, some men won't have sex with you or be attracted to you if they've seen you in women's attire. Which I think is *so* fucking shallow. Please." A member of a long-term trio, she added archly, "And, you know, with two at home, what the hell do I care?"[45]

Sister Babylon's fellow Sister, Sister Rhoda N'Lytenment, told a more poignant version of the same story:

I have three [things] that I have to put out there [when I first start seeing someone], which can be a deal breaker at any time. And so I kind of do them in order of escalating [risk of rejection]. "Okay, [for] all intents and purposes I consider myself to be a meth addict. I would never use, but I'm an addict. Bottom line, I will always be." Once they've had time to process that, process that, process that, "I'm HIV-positive." Processing, processing, processing. "Oh, you're still here. I'm a Sister." Gone. And it's like, "Okay, you accepted the fact that I'm a meth addict. You accepted the fact that I'm HIV-positive. But you have a problem with the fact that I wear a dress." Does not compute to me at all![46]

Ironically and perhaps unsurprisingly, both cisgender and genderqueer gay male Sisters seem to be on the receiving end of the same gender biases that they are also accused of enacting, at times directly in their words and their ministry and at times indirectly through their performance of gender. That is to say, the same biases that lead gay men to reject men who are Sisters also drive transmisogyny in gay communities, and sometimes in the order itself. Even as these men who have always been the mainstay of the Sisters struggle to embrace and fully include trans members of all genders, female members of all gender histories, and nonbinary or agender members, they too are targets of the same prejudices. In this way, and in part because of its serious parody, the order has become a lightning rod for tensions around gender in queer communities as a whole, and even in the larger communities of which they are a part.

The Virgin and the Whore: Genderfuck Meets Religionfuck

From the beginning of my fieldwork, the members of the order whom I met knew that I was interested in religion in the Sisters. Trying to sort out attitudes toward Roman Catholicism in the order, and to learn of members' experiences with the reactions of Roman Catholics, I also asked in every interview about the order's and the individual member's relationships with the Roman Catholic Church. Three types of response quickly became commonplace: claims to be on the Vatican's official list of heretics; stories about the goodwill of Roman Catholic nuns toward the Sisters; and stories about two Sisters in San Francisco who took communion at a Roman Catholic Mass and ignited a media firestorm. The third story had two variants. In one version, the Sisters were activists enacting intentional sacrilege in order to stick it to the Catholic hierarchy, a sort of Sisterly version of the Stop the Church protest at St. Patrick's Cathedral in New York City. In the other version, the two Sisters who took communion were themselves Roman Catholics, attending Mass as any practicing Catholic might do. Since they were also expected at the Castro Street Fair that day, they had no time for secular clothing; thus, they had no choice but to attend in face. According to the only one of these two Sisters whom I was able to interview, neither version is accurate.

Sister Σplace. came up with the idea of attending Mass on that October Sunday in 2007. According to this Sister, whom I interviewed several years after the incident, the impetus for attending was the visit of San Francisco's relatively new archbishop, George Niederauer, to Most Holy Redeemer Church. Located in the heart of the Castro, this parish has struggled for decades to navigate between the demands of LGBTQ people for inclusion and the exclusionary mandates of the Vatican. Although Sister Σplace. has "always been very, very spiritual," and had some childhood exposure to both Protestant and Roman Catholic Christianity, the Sister's contemporary practices center more on Taoism and the Sōtō school of Zen Buddhism. But the archbishop's visit to Most Holy Redeemer was being closely watched by conservative Catholics. Sister Σplace. recalls seeing a notice online that asked the question, "What is the archbishop going to say to this predominantly gay, homosexual church in the Castro?"[47] The Sister told me,

> I read that question and I was like, "You know what? That is a really good question. I have that same question myself! And you know what? As a nun, as a Sister of Perpetual Indulgence, I owe it not only to myself but to my community to go and listen to what the archbishop is going to say tomorrow, so that I can represent and I can speak the truth to what he says. And to what happens."

Sister Σplace. sent an email to the San Francisco Sisters' list, notifying them of the event and of the Sister's intent to attend. "I said, 'If anyone's in with me, I'm feeling called to really sit presently. So if you're in, let me know. If not, it's probably going to go down, so don't be surprised if you hear about it.' No intention of anything coming from it, only the intention of bearing witness to what the archbishop was going to say at Most Holy Redeemer."[48] Sister Delta Goodhand, a practicing Catholic, replied to the email and expressed interest in coming along.

That Sunday morning, both Sisters dressed conservatively. Photos and video footage from the event, all readily available from homophobic Christian websites, show Sister Delta Goodhand in the San Francisco house's traditional black-and-white habit and Sister Σplace. with a long, loose black top over a nearly ankle-length print skirt.[49] Sister Σplace. wore a circlet of silk roses atop the traditional coronet, woven together with a rainbow feather boa whose ends trailed down the black veil along with white and lavender panels of fabric. Sister Delta wore a string of pearls, and had fastened her veil to her wimple and coronet with three medium-sized brooches. Both Sisters wore whiteface with muted makeup. As Sister Σplace. tells it, they were enthusiastically welcomed by the assembled congregants. "We go to the front door, and we are surrounded by this love and welcoming, and the place goes *electric*. 'The Sisters are here, the Sisters are here! We have Sisters of Perpetual Indulgence at the door.' They hand us the program, we go in, we're seated, and the place just, like, lights up."

Their experience in the Mass was also extremely positive. They participated fully in the service, and Sister Σplace. recalls that "the homily that morning from the archbishop was *beautiful*. I still have it at home. He talked about brotherly love, and he talked about how Jesus [said] thou shalt not judge, and really loving one another and really not hating but just coming together. And it was a very beautiful message for him to deliver at that church." The two Sisters had discussed briefly whether or not to take communion; in the end, according to the Sister, it was Σplace. who decided that they should do so, both out of a sense that their experience of the Mass would otherwise be incomplete and out of that Sister's misunderstanding about how to participate respectfully in a Roman Catholic service. As Sister Σplace. put it,

> If you're going to go to a Sōtō Zen ceremony and not stand up when other folks do, or do the processional form with other folks, you're not really getting that full ceremony. And part of that is tea, often. If you're not going to take the tea and eat the cookie, wow, that's kind of disrespectful.

Isn't it? So, if you're going to go to a Mass and not do the full thing, I feel like you'd be disrespectful.[50]

Indeed, the video of the service shows both Sisters partaking respectfully in communion. Archbishop Niederauer places a wafer in each Sister's hand; each Sister then consumes it. Sister Delta crosses herself after placing the wafer in her mouth. Footage apparently taken following the service shows the two Sisters mingling with other congregants, and shows one man approaching them and clearly saying, "Thank you for being here." All, it would seem, was well. Sister Delta even sent a note of thanks to the parish for the lovely service.

But just as the Sisters had come to observe the archbishop's response to the parishioners in the Castro, so too had the conservatives, and their idea of respect was somewhat different from the Sisters' understanding. One of these attendees filmed the Sisters taking communion and posted the video online; it quickly went viral, and the story soon received coverage from major news media sources both in the United States and internationally. Conservatives deemed the Sisters' actions a "hate crime," "blasphemy," and "desecration";[51] fans of the Sisters lionized Sister Σplace. and Sister Delta as gutsy activists who had taken on the Roman Catholic Church. Neither side seemed to know or to care what the two Sisters' actual motivations had been.

The story of the Mass at Most Holy Redeemer is an important example of the powerful reactions that the Sisters can evoke. Without any knowledge of the individual Sisters who took communion, without any sense for their religious backgrounds, current practices, or intentions in attending the service, observers have persistently cast them as engaging in a politically radical act. Whether one decries or lauds the act depends not on a deeper or shallower understanding of these two Sisters, but on one's opinion of the Church. That is to say, commentators on the Most Holy Redeemer incident from across the political spectrum have all made the same assumption about the Sisters who attended Mass and took communion that day: that they intentionally committed sacrilege and made a political statement.[52] But on closer examination, it is entirely unclear precisely what aspect of the Sisters' actions that day constituted sacrilege. One clue to the puzzle, though, lies in the experiences of Sisters who manifest a masculine persona.

Male Sister Personas

With the exception of the gender-structured (or perhaps genderfuck-structured) roles of the Australian order and some of its U.K. descendants, there are only two fully professed roles available in the Sisters of Perpetual Indulgence: that of Sister and that of Guard. A Sister, however, may also develop a secondary persona modeled after a traditionally male role within the Roman Catholic Church (fig. 3.2). Such

Figure 3.2. Pope Dementia the Last, one of the earlier members of the order to manifest a masculine persona, at the thirtieth anniversary party in San Francisco on Easter 2009. Photo by Bill Weaver. Reproduced by permission.

roles are different from those of Sisters like Brother Bimbo and Father Oh, Mary! because the latter understand themselves as Sisters who simply have masculine names and sometimes manifest in masculine ways. Male personas also differ from Guards both in that they reference religious figures and in that they play the same roles within the order as Sisters do. Or at least they *try* to play the same roles as Sisters do, and herein lies the importance of male personas for the questions at hand, for Sisters who have a male persona generally report that few members of the public interact with him.

Sister Daya Reckoning, for example, manifested once or twice a year as Cardinal Carnal Cravings during the time of my fieldwork with The Abbey of St. Joan. "You get a very, very different reaction from the community when you're out in male nun drag, so to speak," she explained to me. "The few times I've actually done it, it's almost like you're a fly on the wall within the Sisters." One of the first times she manifested as the Cardinal, she recalled,

> we went to C.C.'s [C.C. Attle's, a bear bar] for an outreach, and I had condoms. But I had whiteface and a masculine version of my Sister face on, with my red robe, my Cardinal nametag, and I had a very mixed reaction. Some people totally ignored me, which was interesting. I sat in the background a lot. People, once I told them that I can manifest however I want and I could be a male persona or whatever, I got this, "Oh, okay." And then they'd start talking to a Sister.[53]

Sister Daya had been forewarned by her mother in the order to pay attention to public reactions should she ever manifest a male persona, so she was prepared for this difference, but nevertheless she did not enjoy it and she felt that it hindered her work. These drawbacks are responsible for the rarity with which Cardinal Carnal Cravings manifests.

Sister Daya was far from the only Sister to tell me of negative or ambivalent public reactions to male personas.[54] When compared to the delight or, at the very least, bemused fascination with which Sisters are often met, these reactions present a stark contrast. Furthermore, most Sisters who manifest a male persona are themselves male-bodied, and generally are not transgender men. While this pattern may simply reflect the demographic makeup of the order—most Sisters are cisgender men, and few Sisters have male personas, so the few male personas are quite likely to be male-bodied as well—the one female Sister whom I know to have manifested a male persona did not mention this sort of negative reaction. Then again, I did not know at the time to ask about her experiences in this regard.[55] It is therefore possible that reactions to male personas also have to do with their perceptibly male embodiment, and the consequent loss of genderfuck and perhaps also of serious parody.

What seems clearest about the reactions to the two Sisters who took communion and to male personas within the order is that they have little to do with the intentions or self-perceptions of the Sisters involved. Instead, these images and personas seem to be functioning as symbols, or better yet as forms of symbolic discourse in and of themselves. What is most important, then, to understanding both their acclaim and their denigration is not what the authors of these images and personas thought they were doing, but what those reacting to them thought they saw. And what they thought they saw seems to have a lot to do with sex.

Sexualized Sisters

It is widely recognized that those inhabiting the unmarked, dominant categories of social power, particularly elite, white, heterosexual, cisgender, and temporarily able-bodied men, are represented as both subject and ideal, with all others being measured against this standard and inevitably falling short. These dynamics pertain as well to representations of certain bodies as appropriately or inappropriately sexual. Some othered and abjected groups are cast as failed sexual subjects, insufficiently in control of their desires or lacking them altogether, while others are cast not as subjects at all but as objects, and still others fall outside this economy of desires entirely. Much of one's placement within this system has to do with embodiment and its perception, as well as one's position within what Jasbir Puar terms the "assemblage" of power.[56] Imputed gender and imputed gender conformity seem to play a pivotal role in the assignment of sexualized, hypersexualized, and desexualized status to certain bodies and classes of bodies. Gay men, following the model of the invert, have traditionally been cast as both feminine and hypersexual.

In addition, gay men in particular have long been represented as predatory, and because of the gendered basis of the invert model, this representation has tied gender nonconformity tightly to predatory sexuality. With the shift that Valentine notes toward assigning gender nonconformity solely to transgender people, the decade of the 2010s has seen a sharp ratcheting up of representations of transgender people, and especially transgender women, as heterosexual predators. On both sides of this historic change, gender nonconformity functions as a marker of pathology; however, as the attribution of nonconformity has shifted, so too has the attribution of pathology. In the older model, gender nonconformity indexed the presumed pathology of same-sex desire; in the newer one, gender nonconformity indexes a pathological form of predatory and pedophilic heterosexuality.[57] One key, therefore, to disentangling the reactions to the Sisters at Most Holy Redeemer and to masculine personas like Cardinal Carnal Cravings is to sort out how presumptions of gender, desire, and sexualization work together in these cases.

The common assumption that all Sisters are gay men places external understandings of the order within the older model of gender nonconformity, associating the Sisters' femininity with same-sex desire rather than with predatory heterosexuality. This association, in turn, connects the Sisters to the hypersexualization of gay male bodies, even those that are white, cisgender, and male. For conservatives of any gender or sexual identity, this hypersexualized image of gay male sexuality also assimilates it to illness, both the ontologically gendered, psychological illness to which some social conservatives still attribute same-sex desire and the equally sinister linkage of gay men to AIDS that has proven impossible to undo since the disease was dubbed Gay Related Immune Deficiency in the early 1980s. Hypersexualized, ill, and literally defiled, gay male bodies of all classes and races become in this representational system the epitome of impurity, with the Sisters an example par excellence.

The Sisters' gender presentation, regardless of their actual dress, in combination with the embodiment ascribed to them by many observers, makes them irrevocably sexualized in the popular imaginary. In this they are like women, and particularly women from nondominant groups; this argument is borne out in disturbing ways by the sexual assault that several members of the Sydney house experienced during an early manifestation in a local gay bar.[58] However, this inevitable sexualization is routed not simply through the Sisters' feminine appearance but more precisely through the gender inversion and accompanying same-sex desire that this symbolic system infers from the combination of feminine appearance with presumed male embodiment. From such a perspective even a traditional nun's habit cannot remove, but rather heightens, the sexualization because it represents femininity on an apparently male body. As presumptive gay men who wear garments usually restricted to those women whom Roman Catholics and many others consider to have attained the greatest purity possible for human women other than the Virgin Mary, the Sisters appear to conservative audiences literally as whores in virgins' clothing, importing psychological and physical illness and the sinful nature of their sex into the purest possible human space. For gay men to claim the virgin's pedestal as their own appears to be nothing short of defilement and sacrilege from within this particular symbolic system.

Some within LGBT communities see the Sisters through the same sacrilegious lens, or see them as keeping alive a harmful and false gendered stereotype of gay men. The Sisters disrupt the gay and lesbian assimilationist tactic of attributing all gender nonconformity to transgender communities and thereby divorcing gender nonconformity (and, importantly, transgender people) from assimilationist gay and lesbian politics. In this the order is indeed, as Sister Vish recalls early assimilationists objecting in San Francisco, "ruining it for everyone."[59] But for those transgender activists who object to gay men's continued claim to gender nonconformity as a part of gay rather than transgender history and culture, and for those feminists who object to gay men's continued claim on femininity, the Sisters present a problem precisely because of the intertwined assumptions within which the order has positioned itself, whether intentionally or otherwise.

This tangled set of gendered, sexualized, and religious images and assumptions also helps to explain why male personas receive such a lukewarm welcome from the Sisters' otherwise adoring public. Men, even when they belong to dominant sexual, racial, and class groups, are widely presumed within many Western cultures to be innately incapable of celibacy; indeed, such assumptions underlay the widespread Protestant allegations of priestly sexual abuse that led repeatedly to anti-Catholic violence in the nineteenth-century United States.[60] In the twenty-first century, in light of the sexual abuse scandals that have implicated a horrifying number of Roman Catholic priests in the sexual abuse of children of all genders, and the Vatican's repeated attempts, particularly during the papacy of Pope Benedict XVI, to pin the blame on "homosexual priests," a public that is delighted by an order of explicitly sexualized gay nuns may be disturbed by an order of explicitly sexualized gay priests. Clear support for this argument, in fact, is evident in a meme that appeared in several related versions in the spring of 2016 as a response to the widening prevalence of transphobic laws in the United States. "Men wearing dresses and molesting our children?" one version reads. "The word you're looking for is clergy, not transgender."[61]

In addition to their potentially disturbing symbolic import, male Sister personas may also experience less engagement from their "gathered faithful" for simpler gendered reasons. Feminine people are expected to provide community service and to perform emotional labor, whereas masculine people are not. Throughout the century and a half since the invention of the inversion model, gay men have been assigned a variety of positively and negatively valenced stereotypes that are typically associated with cisgender women. Those feminine-identified gay men who embody not the negative stereotypes of the drag queen but the positive stereotypes of the self-sacrificing vowed woman religious are thus culturally coherent from two angles: as playfully sexual figures and as emotional laborers. They are therefore eminently approachable within the queer communities they serve, and sometimes within the larger community as well. Masculine-presenting men who embody the burly and distant masculinity expected of cisgender men of all sexualities—male-bodied Guards—are also culturally coherent; they do not expect to be approached and they generally are not, although there certainly are some exceptions to this rule. The vowed male religious figure, although he embodies neither of these forms, is assimilated in important ways to normative masculinity. Male personas within the Sisters, then, are treated ambivalently by their communities not only because of the impact of the child sex abuse scandals in the Roman Catholic Church but also because the Sisters can challenge gender only so much. Even queer communities still expect feminine figures to nurture and masculine ones to lead, and this presumption is only strengthened when those figures present themselves within traditional religious roles.

In challenging restrictive gender roles, in reclaiming positive images of femininity for gay men, and in clearing space within the order for women of all genders and gender histories, trans people of all genders, and agender and nonbinary people, the Sisters both forge new paths and reinforce old ones. They challenge who can nurture, but not the gender associated with nurturance. They advocate for feminism and transgender rights, but transgender people and cisgender and gender-queer women struggle to find space within the order and to mobilize concerted and lasting outreach to their communities. They find themselves on the giving and the receiving end of transmisogyny, sometimes simultaneously. They both disrupt and reinscribe norms and assumptions about gender, embodiment, and sexuality. Lauded by queer activists, castigated by conservatives, the Sisters find themselves entangled within a complicated gender politics. As any Foucauldian will affirm, there is no exterior to power, no citadel of pure privilege to which to lay siege from the grounds below. The only route to resistance, from this perspective, is through subversion, and serious parody is one particularly effective source of such subversion. But because power is so tangled, is routed through assemblage in Puar's formulation, one must always be careful what one subverts and how, lest resistance in one area simply reinforce privilege in another.

4

"Sister Outsiders"

Navigating Whiteness

On May 13, 2014, San Francisco Sister Baba Ganesh posted a blog entry entitled "Sisters Outsider," an apparent reference to a well-known collection of works by the late black lesbian author Audre Lorde.[1] Subtitled "A Love Letter to Sisters of Color on Race + 2043," the blog post expresses Sister Baba's passionate commitment to the Sisterhood along with her simultaneous longing for a more racially inclusive order and for closer connections to other Sisters of color. "I'm reaching out," she writes in the introduction, "because I'm feeling called to connect with you precious + few + Beauty Full brown, black, golden + multi-hued Sisters across the country + across the globe. While you will all ways be precious, I hope we Sisters of Color will not always be 'The Few.'"[2]

The frame for Sister Baba's reflections is a U.S. Census Bureau prediction that in 2043 the country will become "a majority-minority nation."[3] In light of this prediction, Sister Baba explains, "I hope to start a dialogue on race + class + difference, all within + not outside of our tradition. I think our Present-Future depends on it." She goes on to explain her perspective:

> I am a Brown Sister in a House that is majority white in a city that is 31% Asian + Pacific Islander, 14% Latin@ + .07% Native + 14% mixed race.[4] To be clear, I will always love my House + MY SF Sisters, but they don't + can't always go where I need to go. Where I have to go. Also I get kind of lonely. Yes, I connect with the few other Sisters of Color in the House along with a handful of other non-SOC allies but I need more. Moreover, with our Majority-White House, I wonder about our relevance + ability to connect in a Present-Future that is increasingly more hybrid + diverse.

Sister Baba poses the question of why the San Francisco house is so white. Raising a few possibilities, she ultimately concludes that answering such questions and developing strategies for making houses more inclusive is a collective task, one in which she wishes to engage together with the Sisters of color who she hopes will read the post. "In my five years of Sistering," she reflects, "I've experienced countless Queer joys + continue to grow + be sustained as a Queer Ministrant. I've also been subject to + hurt by blatant racism + microaggressions on the regular." A poet, editor, and art director with decades of organizing experience, particularly in Asian American and Pacific Islander queer communities, Sister Baba cuts to the chase: "Racism + White supremacy are systemic + pervasive in our culture + we Sisters, all of us, are not exempt."

Turning to subtler questions of inclusion and visibility in the order, Sister Baba asks, "Sister . . . what's your take on whiteface?" She posts several pictures of herself sporting various versions of a stunningly intricate, lacelike pattern of white makeup that reveals her skin beneath (figure 6 of the color insert). "This is me in my signature lattice face," she writes. "I don't easily mask this honey-brown deliciousness under white anything. It's no disrespect to our WhiteFace tradition. It's actually an hominaje, a tribute to the Originals, many of whom wore fresh face." An accompanying archival picture from the early days of the order, in which a few Sisters were in whiteface but most were not, illustrates her point. Calling for a gathering—maybe even a Conclave—of Sisters of color, Sister Baba reiterates, "I am not calling for separatism. I am seeking empathy + safe space within our House with hopes for full support + buy-in from our non-SOC allies. We all need each other but I need more than simply defaulting to majority monoculture."[5] Closing with a thank-you in Tagalog ("Maraming Salamats!"), she offers specific thanks to founder Sister Vish, to white ally Sister MaryMae Himm, and to Latina Sister Lupita Fajita Buffet.

Sister Baba's initial post seems to have been well received by both Sisters of color and white allies in the order. Just six days later it was followed by another post, now under the slightly altered title of "Sister Outsiders," which features reflections from Atlanta's Sister Chiquieata Banenea, a multiracial Sister raised by her Colombian mother in Panama and Colombia. Sister Baba's introduction to Sister Chiquieata's comments announces enthusiastically, "Since posting Sister Outsider: A Love Letter to Sisters of Color on Race + 2043, I'd heard from . . . Sisters of Color from around the world expressing excitement + thanks for addressing race + difference issues of our global Sister culture." She adds that "Non-Sisters of Color" had also expressed support and had asked "how they can be NOT allies but accomplices" in antiracist work within the order and the surrounding communities, and she specifically mentions that "Beloved Mothers Vish + Mish" had taken up the cause, letting other Sisters know of the work Baba was doing.[6] Another post, detailing the life and experiences of Sister Leigh Viticus, a cisgender woman of Anglo and Mexican heritage who grew up in Guam, followed twelve days later.[7] There were no further Sister Outsider features until early December.

"So a Transgender Sister + a Brown Sister walk into a Vietnamese restaurant," begins the post from December 4, 2014. This opening is illustrated by a selfie of Sister Baba and Sister Connie Pinko. The post continues, "A good bit of what we discussed was how we might reconnect back to our House that is collectively (not individuals, per se) challenged by a lack of diversity in our membership. We are the Founding House," Sister Baba reiterates,

> whose membership holds strong at majority white gay cis-males in 2014 in a city and world that is undeniably diverse. The very mention of this fact offends some of my Sisters, tantamount to treason but with all due respect it's true. And the guilt/defensive or push back to outright hostility we get from *some* of our beloved cismale Gen X and older Sisters, is the painful confusing bullshit that keeps Sisters like me and Connie at bay. A consciousness shift toward a radical celebration of difference is in order for this Order.

Ever hopeful, Sister Baba offers three "concrete strategies" that houses might use to develop greater openness to and support of "the radical celebration of difference."[8]

The final entry in this series on *Baba's Blog* is an extended interview with Sister Freida Peoples, the first black member of the order. While Sister Baba's passion for preserving the history of the order merges here with her passion for highlighting the contributions and expanding the membership of Sisters of color, it seems clear from her introduction that white and cis male Sisters have in general not responded well to her activist efforts. "During this past year of very difficult conversations with non-Sisters of Color about my call for diversity," she recounts, "I was often reminded about how 'diverse' the Order is by citing . . . that we had Sr. Freida AND Sr. Mystie (a bio cis-female)." Sister Baba flatly labeled these responses "insulting tokenism."[9] Indeed, the presence of a single black (male) Sister and a single (white) cis female Sister in the early history of the San Francisco house is hardly evidence for the order's inclusiveness. If anything, the persistent references to these two Sisters prove the opposite: in being constantly invoked to demonstrate the order's inclusiveness along the lines of race and gender, Sister Freida and Sister Mystie become the exceptions that prove the rule. Despite the excitement that Sister Baba's ideas generated in the spring of 2014, in the end it seems that the resistance of cisgender white men in the order weighed more heavily. There are no more Sister Outsider posts, and after three subsequent posts on other topics the blog falls silent for over a year, resuming in April 2016 with posts unrelated to the Sisters.

Sister Baba's blog entries encapsulate much of what I observed and learned from other Sisters and Guards. Two events from my fieldwork, one less than a year into my research and the other at the very end of it, illustrate some of the challenges facing Sisters of color and their allies. In July 2010, at an anniversary brunch for Sisters and Saints of The Abbey of St. Joan, I was in conversation with an FP and two junior members of the house. At one point the two junior members, both of whom are Latina, conversed briefly in Spanish. Later in the event the FP, who identifies as white, and one of the same junior members were in conversation with another white, senior member of the order. The FP complained teasingly that she had not been able to understand the two junior members earlier, because "they were speaking Mexican." Taken aback by her remark, I looked over at the junior member and observed that she did not seem to know quite how to respond. I suspected that her status as a novice in the presence of two FPs had at least something to do with her silence.[10] A similarly racist incident took place at the very end of my fieldwork, during the Easter in the Park celebration for the thirty-fifth anniversary of the San Francisco house and therefore of the order as a whole. While thousands of people, most of them white, enjoyed a warm and sunny Easter Sunday with the Sisters in Golden Gate Park, taking in the Hunky Jesus and Foxy Mary contests along with the queerest Easter bonnet competition I have ever seen, a white member of the San Francisco house made an offhand remark about "BBCs" from the stage, over the microphone. A familiar reference in gay communities to the time-worn racist stereotype that African American men have larger-than-average genitalia, this comment caught me so much off guard that I have no recollection of the reactions from the rest of the audience. I think some people shouted their approval; I remember no apparent attention to the racism of the remark. In that moment, there on the rolling lawn of San Francisco's famous park, I thought of the many queer artists of color—essayists, poets, filmmakers, musicians—who have castigated the whiteness and the racism of the Castro District. That whiteness and racism, I saw especially clearly that day, were literally incarnated within the San Francisco house.

With race and settler colonialism as with gender, the Sisters' serious parody lands them within a fraught history and a tangled network of power. Chuck Kleinhaus's observation regarding camp and cultural subversion is apropos here: "Camp, like any particular subcultural attitude in our society, operates within the larger boundaries of a racist, patriarchal, bourgeois culture. That it defines itself in difference from the dominant culture does not automatically construct Camp as radically oppositional. Only an audience and the work's exhibition context can complete that subversion."[11] Sisters of color, Native and non-Native, navigate these complicities and tensions as they come up through the ranks of the order and as they strive to serve all of the communities that they consider their own, and they navigate them differently depending on the varying importance of race, ethnicity, and skin color as sources of social identity and division in their own communities and countries. Also as with gender, in the context of race and settler colonialism the Sisters are again engaged in a feedback loop in which the order serves predominantly white communities, recruits as a consequence largely white participants, and in turn finds itself called and qualified to serve largely white communities. These dynamics not only maintain the whiteness of the order and those whom it serves; they also make it exceedingly difficult for Sisters of color and their allies—or "accomplices," in Sister Baba's wording—to push back against implicit and explicit racism and colonialism in their houses.

Moreover, the advocacy by some Sisters of the third-gender model of gay maleness, when combined with the rarity of Native members of the order and the rarity of the order's work with Native communities, places them in a position of complicity in the ongoing process of settler colonialism. As Scott Lauria Morgensen explains in a study of other non-Native, largely white queer activist groups, notably including the Radical Faeries, "embracing a primitive sexual nature linked to roots within Native culture articulate[s] the defense of modern sexual minorities with normative assertions of settler citizenship."[12] Yet Sisters of all races and ethnicities reflect on the order's genderfuck and its use of white facial makeup in complex and thoughtful ways as they navigate the symbolic and literal whiteness of the order. As they signify on a practice developed partly through happenstance, partly in a very particular cultural moment with a very particular cultural history, members of the order who use makeup and those who do not both rely on the artificial whiteness of many Sisters' faces as a point of entry into larger questions around race, colonialism, and the meaning, purpose, ancestry, and legacy of their order.

Navigating Whiteness

Like Sister Baba, other Sisters of color also note the whiteness of their order. For some, this is not a problematic state of affairs; others share Baba's longing for a larger community of Sisters of color. In her remarks on Sister Baba's blog, Sister Freida says to "the Sisters of today" that "I am glad to see the immense diversity you express and though I'm told there are many more Sisters-of-color than were when I 'entered', I'd sure like to see more of you."[13] Sister Chiquieata relates, "For a long time I thought I was alone."[14] And in the middle of a conversation about whiteface during the 2011 international Conclave, Sister Jonbennet Gesserit commented to me, "I haven't met very many Sisters of color." "I've not either," I responded, already nearly two years into my fieldwork. Sister Jonbennet continued, "I think I've met—" She paused to count. "Three."[15] Sister Baba even joked during our interview that when other members of the San Francisco house ask her about her lattice face she always replies, "You're welcome! Because you could use the P.R."[16] White members of the order around the world have also criticized not only whiteness but also racism in the Sisters. Mother Inferior, for example, one of the founders of the Australian order, told me flat-out that "some nuns are racist and sexist. We can't have that in a Sister of Perpetual Indulgence."[17]

To put a few numbers to the patterns I describe herein: of the ninety-one Sisters whom I interviewed, seventy-six were asked and answered my question about racial and ethnic identification. Of these, two replied that they do not identify racially. Two more found the question problematic—one even called it offensive—but both reluctantly described themselves as having white European heritage. Including the latter two Sisters, a total of sixty-one—over four-fifths—of those who answered this question identified themselves as solely white and/or European in ancestry. Seven interview participants identified as multiracial, having among them white, Latino, Native American (one Nez Perce and the other two unspecified), black, South Asian, Filipino, and Chinese ancestry. Three considered themselves Latino, Hispanic, or Chicano, two identified as Native American (one Morongo and one Cherokee), and one identified as black. Because I had the opportunity to interview a number of Sisters with whom I did not conduct field-work, these demographics are if anything less white and less non-Native than those I saw when attending Sister events in the United States and Europe.

Five of the Sisters who identify as white also described an ancestry similar to that described by the Sisters who consider themselves multiracial. All had some white ancestry and generally felt that they were perceived as white by those around them, which impacted their decision to identify as white. In addition, one participant had Pacific Islander ancestry, one had Chinese ancestry, and two had Latin American ancestry.[18] The fifth Sister who identifies as white but whose ancestry and racial identity relate in complex ways is both white and Cherokee; her story contrasts with that of another Sister of similar heritage, and this pair of stories reflects tellingly on the complexities of race, settler colonialism, and identity in the contemporary United States. Novice Sister Spinna DeVinyl of Portland's Order of Benevolent Bliss told me that her heritage is both white and Cherokee, and that she has sufficient Cherokee ancestry to allow her to register with the tribe. However, she explained, "I do not [choose to register], based on the fact that I am, complexion-wise, so white. I don't want to be stepping in and taking away benefits from other people of the Nation that deserve [them]. So I identify as white."[19] Like Novice Sister Spinna, Sister Kali Vagilistic X.P. Aladocious of the Asylum of the Tortured Heart in San Diego, California, has been told that she has both white and "Kentucky Cherokee" ancestry. Being adopted, though, she does not have any documentation of her Cherokee heritage and is not registered with the tribe. She therefore often indicates her race as white, "depending on what I'm filling out," she told me. In terms of her own sense of self, though, when we spoke, Sister Kali told me that she had recently begun identifying as Native American.[20]

The communities served by the Sisters reflect the racial demographics of the order itself, and vice versa. Numerous studies of gay male neighborhoods have indicated their class and racial segregation, with the well-known "gayborhood" in any city nearly always being overwhelmingly inhabited and often even visited by middle-class and elite white men.[21] In Portland, Oregon, which has no clearly identifiable gay neighborhood, even a queer-oriented party held in a warehouse district can be overwhelmingly white. At that city's 2010 Red Dress Party, a community fundraiser held in multiple U.S. cities at which all participants must wear a red dress regardless of gender, I noted approximately a thousand attendees and estimated in my fieldnotes that "I saw maybe five African Americans, ten Asian Americans, and five Latinos" during the entire evening.[22] Even given that city's largely white population—over 72 percent non-Hispanic white in 2010, according to that year's census—and the gap between self-identification and the admittedly dubious practice of racial assignment by an observer, this is still a disproportionately low number of people of color.[23]

These demographics indicate the whiteness of the Sisters themselves and of the communities in which they generally minister. That Sisters of color are often isolated in their houses seems clear; that they face similar challenges to those faced by cisgender and genderqueer women and transgender people when coming up through the ranks of the order is also clear. Such situations are even more difficult for Sisters of color who are also women and/or transgender. Novice Sister Jen Derfukt, manifested by a transgender man who faced difficulties in being the first trans member of the Portland house, also noted the challenges involved in being a Sister of color. During our conversation, Novice Sister Jen noted the "powerlessness" that attended her rank, and her concern that "identifying with a lot of different minority communities as a Sister can be difficult in that I'm never quite sure if what I've said is being heard in the way that I want it to be heard."[24] In addition, the reluctance or outright refusal of some white Sisters to identify themselves in terms of race suggests a commitment to "color blindness" or "race blindness" that is also cause for concern. In a society that is still deeply racist, to refuse to "see" race can render one incapable of or resistant to perceiving racism, a phenomenon that Eduardo Bonilla-Silva has dubbed "color-blind racism."[25] On the other hand, some Sisters, both Sisters of color and white allies in many different houses, believe that the order should be reaching out more broadly in terms of its membership and the communities it serves, and many are working actively to make that vision a reality.

Sister Odora Flatulotta D'Pew, herself a white Sister and one of the founders of the Grand Canyon Sisters of Perpetual Indulgence in Arizona, was particularly concerned with outreach to Latinx and Native communities, especially given that her order is not focused within a specific city but rather tries to serve all of the state. "We try to get a Spanish-speaking Sister at most of our events," she explained, "because we go to events where we have Spanish speakers." Sister Odora's initial name was also intended in part as an outreach to Spanish speakers: Heidi Osmio is a playful rendering of the Spanish exclamation ¡Ay, Dios mío! (Oh, my God!). Sister Odora related, though, that her house met with some misunderstanding and suspicion among the Latinx communities with which they attempted to work in Arizona—not queer Latinx communities, specifically, but communities of all sexualities and genders in which many people were deeply committed Roman Catholics and were unaccustomed to the sort of campy self-presentation engaged in by the Sisters. Likewise, according to Sister Odora, a Navajo member of their house, Sister Navi Ho, encountered resistance when she showed up in Indian Country in face. "When she started going back to her community on the Navajo reservation," Sister Odora recounted, "a lot of the older Navajos were actually scared of her. And scared of us. And what it was related to was that we looked like living Katsinas that come from the Hopi tribe. And so they were like, 'We know that you're who you are and what you do, but you're really scaring us because this is what our traditions, our culture, told us about.'"[26]

Outreach to queer communities of color and to communities of color as a whole in large cities equally demands respect for, awareness of, and sensitivity to the needs of each community. Those like Sister Chiquieata Banenea in Atlanta and Sister Mary-Kohn in Los Angeles are committed to building bridges between their orders and local Latinx communities; in her comments on Sister Baba's blog, Sister Chiquieata remarked, "I try to give this message [of racial inclusivity] out in English and in Spanish. I would like to minister in Spanish more."[27] And in San Francisco, while Sister Baba makes clear that racism is alive and well in her house, Sisters of color and white allies are also working to broaden the house's outreach to communities of color. In response to a question from me in 2013 regarding the house's focus on white communities, white Sister MaryMae Himm reflected that "I still see predominantly white faces and predominantly male faces, but I'm seeing where we're starting to examine why that is. And the Sisters who have joined who have those commitments [to communities of color, trans communities, and cisgender women's communities] are starting to push back a little bit, which I think is also really valuable." As an example, Sister MaryMae Himm explained that "I can think of at least two or three [Sisters] that I know who particularly work in the Tenderloin [an area of the city with high rates of poverty and homelessness] and areas like that, [promoting] harm reduction and working with communities of color and young people."[28]

Likewise, Sister Merry Peter told me several stories about the broadening of her house's ministry beyond white communities. "You can't just show up in someone's neighborhood, 'cause that's an insult. Right?" she asked rhetorically. But when an apartment building was destroyed by fire in the poor, largely black community of Hunter's Point, the few Sisters who lived in that neighborhood brought in other members of the house to help. Sister Merry Peter recounted,

> And [the] same day, through our social network, we started to get clothes and blankets together. And then a bunch of Sisters, not wearing face but wearing our name badges only and then just regular clothes, showed up and organized the relief before even the Red Cross got to it. And that started conversations. And then they start more conversations about, well, what's happening in your neighborhood? And how can we help? I think that's where those conversations get started with a deep sense of

respect. And then, what slowly starts to happen is kids in that community start to bubble up, and sometimes they join [the Sisters] or sometimes we're just supporting them.

Likewise, she explained, the San Francisco house's sizeable grant program had in recent years begun reaching out to organizations for queer youth of color and trans youth, hoping to encourage grant applications from those groups. Such proactive yet respectful approaches seem to have met with success in the San Francisco house: "seed money is starting to flow that way," reported Sister Merry Peter. "[There's a] lot more to do. I mean, there's always more to do, but I think that's a good beginning. And over-due."[29] With some senior members of the house still unable to hear, much less respond to, concerns such as those raised by Sister Baba Ganesh, it appears that outreach work carried out by white allies, "accomplices" who are educated in and sensitive to the complex dynamics of doing antira-cist work as white people in a white racist culture, can have a significant impact not only on the surrounding communities but also on Sisters of color at this stage in the house's and the larger order's history. The current presence of such allies and the work described above offer the possibil-ity that the order can indeed become more inclusive in its membership and its ministry if and as such inclusiveness becomes an organizational priority, and if and as white allies attend closely to the perspectives and experiences of Sisters and Guards of color.

Navigating Whiteface

The San Francisco Sisters' archives contains numerous newspaper clip-pings about the house, along with an original habit, coronets from various orders around the world, posters from years past, and pieces by some of the many artists whose work has captured the Sisters over the years. One clipping in particular stood out to me when I visited. Taken from a late August or early September 1980 issue of the *San Fran-cisco Sentinel*, the clipping includes a front-page teaser image headlined "Neo-Nuns Rout Neo-Christians," as well as a short article written by Reverend Mother about the Sisters' resistance to the evangelical Chris-tian SOS (Save Our Souls) campaign.[30] The subject of the story, however, is hardly the most notable aspect of the newspaper clipping. Rather, it is

Figure 4.1. A rare photo of Sister Hydrangea, Reverend Mother's blackface alter ego, from the *San Francisco Sentinel*, ca. August 1980. Sister Hydrangea is accompanied by Sister Hysterectoria (*left*), Sister Missionary Position (*right*), an unknown Sister, and an unknown member of the community.

the appearance of the Sisters themselves. One of the four pictured in the photo has black ovals edged with white makeup around her eyes, while another sports minstrel-style blackface (fig. 4.1).

According to both Sister Soami and Sister Hysterectoria, the Sister in blackface here is Reverend Mother. One of those who passed away fairly early in the order's history, Reverend Mother can no longer enlighten us about his decision as a white man to manifest this alternate persona that Sister Soami recalls as "Sister Hydrangea"; instead, all that remain are the recollections of his fellow Sisters.[31] However, the fact that a founding member of the order wore blackface from time to time is important enough to justify relying on those Sisters' memories for a little more context, albeit with caution as they are of necessity secondhand reports.

Sister Hysterectoria connected Reverend Mother's use of blackface to his fondness for Africa. Mentioning the makeup more in passing than as a specific point of conversation, Sister Hysterectoria told me that "we made another appearance, the four founders, and we were all dressed quite differently." "Quite differently meaning some in habits and some not?" I asked. "No," he replied, "it was our version of habit. Like, Reverend Mother did blackface and had been in Africa, or had all these African, authentic things. So he put it on, all this African—" At this point the Sister's roommate walked in, and after the interruption we did not have the time to return to the topic.[32] Suffice it to say, though, that Sister Hysterectoria understands Reverend Mother's use of blackface to have more to do with an attraction to African cultures than with the history of racism in the United States.

Sister Soami offered another angle on the story. Recalling that Sister Hydrangea had indeed manifested during the Sisters' response to the SOS campaign, he explained that "Reverend Mother was a very evolved nun. I probably was a little horrified when she came to those first routings of the Christians, when she chose to come in blackface and be Sister Hydrangea." Upon reflection, though, Sister Soami recalls, "I realized the range of what that allowed her to do. I mean, some of these people were coming from the South. It really became a big shock-value kind of thing. And I think it's good for us to figure that out."[33] Sister Soami resolved his horror at Reverend Mother/Sister Hydrangea's use of blackface by considering the context. A group of white Christians from the South, he reasoned, might see the parallels between the grotesqueness of racism and that of homophobia. Given the whiteness not only of the missionaries but also of the Castro community they were attempting to convert, there may be a certain logic to this argument. However, the Castro was not then, and never was, entirely white; neither was the readership of the gay press. The impact of Reverend Mother's blackface experiment, therefore, likely went far beyond the small group of evangelists and activists who were present that August day in 1980.

Sister Vish, ever into visual experimentation, also has a history with black makeup, but not in the same minstrel style as that used by Reverend Mother. In fact, when I wrote to ask about her occasional use of black pancake makeup, she replied that "it was intentionally NOT 'minstrel black face' that white people wore in the 19th & 20th centuries impersonating African Americans on stage."[34] An image from the Sisters' 1984 exorcism of Jerry Falwell and Phyllis Schlafly shows Sister Vish in her then-signature veil with a striated border, studded collar, and bare chest, with solid black makeup over her entire face save for a white stripe running over her nose and across her cheekbones (fig. 4.2).[35] Both

Figure 4.2. Sister Vicious Power Hungry Bitch wearing black makeup at the 1984 exorcism of Jerry Falwell and Phyllis Schlafly. Reproduced by permission.

she and Sister Soami recall her using similar makeup on a few other occasions. "I wore this makeup as a declaration of cultural war on our bigoted religious enemies," Sister Vish explained.[36] Sister Soami, for his part, has considered the possibility that still today Sisters of all races might find in the "enlightened and principled" use of blackface a tool for political protest with productive shock value. Considering the ongoing presence of racism in the order, though, he has "pulled back from that, because . . . it could end up [with] Sisters being like the blackface Al Jolsons of the past."[37]

Unsurprisingly, no Sisters of color whom I have met have ever found the idea of the resistant use of blackface at all appealing; in fact, in response to my questions about their experiences with whiteface, two of them specifically told me that although they do not consider whiteface to be racist, wearing blackface certainly would be.[38] But even the use of whiteface is navigated differently by Sisters of color than it is by white sisters in the context of a largely white order serving largely white communities.

White Sisters Navigating Whiteface

Efforts among white Sisters to articulate the meaning of whiteface go back to the early days of the order. An apocryphal story, circulating among the Sisters since the release of a 2009 documentary on the order and that film's accompanying trailer, claims that many of the early members were sex workers who wore whiteface to disguise themselves from their clients.[39] In fact, the use of white pancake makeup began with Sister Adhanarisvara's artistic interests and caught on in the larger order when other Sisters realized how striking it appeared in black-and-white newspaper photos. Certainly the anonymity provided by the whiteface was just as useful in those early years for Sisters seeking dates in an insistently masculine gay culture as it remains today, but "it was never done for prostitution, to hide from the johns," Sister Vish stressed to me. "That was not it at all." Instead, she explained,

> what is true is, as I've described, the attitude of the community in the '70s, which bled into the early '80s, was one of conformity and hypersexuality. So if you didn't get laid every other day, oh my God, something's wrong with you. And hypermasculinity. So if you were known to do drag, your sexual prospects went way down. It was very drag-phobic. So, hiding under the makeup you were incognito. And no one would know that you had done drag because of all the heavy makeup. It was very rare that people would spot you out of drag. And to this day that is true, too.[40]

In other words, in a transmisogynist gay culture that also scorns men who do drag, the anonymity offered by the whiteface allows Sisters to avoid immediate rejection by potential sex partners when they are out of face. Given that gay slang of the 1970s and 1980s used the term "trick" to refer to a partner in casual, unremunerated sex, it is possible that the misunderstanding spread so widely by the documentary is rooted in confusion over terms, since "turning tricks" is in such common usage today as a reference to prostitution.

Sister Hysterectoria, who was in his own words "*horrified*" by the wide reach of the apocryphal story about early members being sex workers, added that the Sisters came to appreciate the anonymity provided by the whiteface because it enabled their community to interact with them as

Sisters. "When we were not Sisters," he recalled, "once we started doing whiteface, nobody knew who we were. And we kind of liked that. And we didn't care if people remembered our name, because that wasn't important to us. We were an order of nuns, we were a Sister of Perpetual Indulgence. That's all we were asking people to remember. And we would tell people our names, but it was more like a comedy. And we saw ourselves as clones."[41]

Fully appreciative of the irony inherent in calling a group of gay male nuns "clones" at the height of the hypermasculine "Castro clone" era, Sister Hysterectoria also points to one of the central understandings of whiteface that still prevails, at least among white Sisters, today. For many such Sisters, the makeup changes their secular self into their Sister self, creating a barrier between the two that offers protection, anonymity, freedom, and a great deal more.

Hoping to evoke interviewees' varied perspectives on whiteface without leading them into a specific focus that might not be relevant to their own experience, I kept my initial question about the makeup broad. "What's it like to wear whiteface?" I asked. For some people, the physical experience of wearing pancake makeup was the first aspect that came to mind. Whiteface is hot, sticky, itchy, and sometimes hard to manage. It cracks easily and must be sealed with professional makeup sealant or, for those on tighter budgets, with a generous amount of cheap hairspray. It runs when it should not, such as when someone cries or has a cold, and many Sisters carry cotton swabs to stanch drippy nostrils and fans to dry tears before they fall. It also stubbornly refuses to come off when it should, especially when one has forgotten to restock the baby oil or other effective makeup remover, and it leaves some with raw or irritated skin. Depending on which Sister one asks, whiteface can either take twenty years off of one's age or highlight every single wrinkle on one's skin.

Some Sisters and Guards thought of the artistic aspects of whiteface. Several called it a "blank canvas," often meaning not only a physical canvas on which a Sister face might be designed but also a more symbolic one, a "blank slate" as other Sisters said. For Sister Angelpopstitute and Mother Belleza Tulips@analia, the plain white with which a Sister face begins symbolizes death—death from AIDS, death from homophobia and transphobia—upon which the Sisters then build life or rebirth

as they add colors and jewels to their faces.[42] Hermana Prudencia
Ernestina Simona Cruciphija Cienfuegos recognized a liminal moment
in the whiteface, explaining to me that "es como un aislamiento, como
una cosa entre lo divino y lo profano" (it's like a setting apart, like a thing
between the divine and the profane).[43] Some Sisters have a ritual process
for putting on their whiteface, beginning by painting a white cross, dove,
or other symbolically significant image on their faces and meditating on
that before filling in the rest.

Linked to this sense of symbolic and ritual import are those Sisters
who thought first of the experience of whiteface as an honor or a privilege because of the ministry they undertake when wearing it and the
legacy in which they take part. Hermana Dolores Raimunda offered a
particularly powerful explanation of this perspective:

> El uso del maquillaje acompaña a los hábitos por una tradición y también
> por un respeto a las Hermanas del mundo . . . para militar y para llevar
> a cabo el activismo en homenaje a otras Hermanas que sufrían ciertas
> estigmatizaciones, ¿bien? Eso se respeta y eso se lleva a cabo como el resto
> de las Hermanas del mundo, el pintarse la cara. Me parece que eso es cor-
> rectísimo y es un homenaje a los orígenes de la formación de las Herma-
> nas en el mundo. . . . También nos pintamos de blanco la cara como señal
> de reconocimiento histórico [de] aquellas Hermanas, aquellas primeras
> Hermanas fundadoras en el mundo, aquellas primeras luchadoras del
> SIDA, en sus orígenes. Esos años tan difíciles . . . esos años que se con-
> ocía muy poco, que nos daba tanto miedo, tanto terror, y tanta angustia
> y soledad. Por eso es de reconocer a esa labor histórica y en el momento
> histórico en que nacen las Hermanas de la Perpetua Indulgencia, un mo-
> mento muy difícil, de mucha homofobia, y también de lo que fue el fla-
> gelo, de los orígenes del SIDA, ¿bien? Y eso no hay que olvidarlo.

> (The use of the makeup accompanies the habits by tradition and also
> out of respect for the Sisters around the world . . . to fight and to carry
> out activism in homage to other Sisters who suffered certain forms of
> stigmatization, right? That is respected and that is carried out like the
> rest of the Sisters around the world, the face painting. I feel that this is
> absolutely [the] correct [thing to do] and it is an homage to the origins
> of the formation of the Sisters around the world. . . . We also paint our

faces white as a sign of historical recognition [of] those Sisters, those first founding Sisters around the world, those first fighters against AIDS, in their origins. Those years that were so difficult . . . those years when very little was known, that gave us such fear, such terror, and such anguish and loneliness. For that reason it is to recognize this historic labor and in the historic moment in which the Sisters of Perpetual Indulgence were born, a very difficult moment, of much homophobia, and also of what was the scourge, of the origins of AIDS, right? And this must not be forgotten.)[44]

By far the most common perspectives on whiteface, though, were those that reflected the function of the makeup—or, in the Australian order and its descendants, the large sunglasses that are often worn in lieu of whiteface—in creating a persona. A person's Sister or Guard persona is always in some way separate from that person's secular persona, even though the two may converge over the years. The evocation of the former through the masking of the latter via whiteface or sunglasses amounts, for many, to a shift in both character and personality and a signal of membership in a movement larger than the individual self. Sister Saviour Applause and Sister Dominé Trix told me independently of each other that the whiteface and habit constitute a "superhero costume";[45] for others, they offer anonymity that protects both the privacy of the secular persona and the confidentiality of community members.

The anonymity of the Sisterhood, particularly that provided by whiteface, can also allow some Sisters to overcome certain forms of discrimination and personal challenges in connecting with their communities. Sister GreezElda GreedLay, for example, who was sixty-four at the time of our interview, is deeply and actively engaged in battling ageism in the gay community. He explained to me just how powerful the whiteface can be: "I cannot do what GreezElda can do," he said bluntly, referring to his secular self. "Because it would not be accepted. I mean, I would be an 'old troll,' a 'nasty old man,' and get thrown out of the bar." He reiterated, with emphasis: "If *I* did what GreezElda does, I would be tossed out of the bar."[46] Similarly, Novice Sister D'Wanna DeWitt, a Sister who has autism spectrum disorder, spoke of the whiteface as a "conduit to the world" that helps her to connect with her community.[47]

Anonymity, though, is neither neutral nor innocent. Sister Nova Aggra explained that once in whiteface, "we're not white or black or gay or straight, we're a nun."[48] And this is true, to an extent. But just as many outside observers presume a gender identity they can neither see nor confirm when they encounter the Sisters, so too with race. In a society where race is highly salient and where white people are socially and culturally dominant, and in equally white-dominated queer communities, a racially unmarked Sister is not in fact raceless or racially neutral; she is presumed to be white. In this context, the concerns about whiteface raised by Sister Baba Ganesh and others become particularly apposite. If Sisters are assumed to be white in the absence of explicit countervailing evidence, and if Sisters are, as many claim, "mirrors" for their community, then as Sister MaryMae Himm pointed out to me, their very anonymity can further alienate communities of color. "A lot of what the Sisters do is about reflecting," Sister explained to me. "And if you can't see yourself in what's in front of you, if you can't see yourself in me, part of that is my responsibility, 'cause it means I'm not seeing you fully. Right? But also there is something about, you need to be able to see yourself in what the Sisters do, and so there are people who think that the whiteface is racist."[49] While none of the Sisters of color with whom I spoke considered whiteface to be racist in and of itself, many found its use to have racial significance, whereas very few white Sisters spontaneously associated whiteface with race in any way.

Sisters of Color Navigating Whiteface

To be sure, some Sisters of color also viewed whiteface as a part of creating a persona, as a canvas or a mirror, and potentially as a source of anonymity. Most of them noted, though, that these functions were differently inflected for them than for white members of the order. Sister Pure Heart, for instance, appreciated the anonymity offered by the whiteface but noted that it was hard for her to attain. "I try to fool people," she told me with a chuckle, "but I can't because I'm a little dark skinned."[50] In a largely white house, showing even a little skin can give away the secular identity of a Sister of color whose friends know that she is part of the order. For two of the Sisters with whom I spoke, though, the literal whitewashing of their identity and their tendency to pass involuntarily as white when in habit were precisely the source of their concern. "It's a difficult position," explained Novice Sister Jen Derfukt, "because we're branded on the whiteface. So the whiteface gives you the visibility" as a Sister. But the whiteface makes a person of color invisible. Novice Sister Jen pointed out, "Portland, in my view, is a very white city. There are a lot of white people, a lot of white gay people, and it's assumed, almost, that if you're gay you're white." Other people of color, she noted, make the same assumption. She related a conversation with a friend, another person of color who "know[s] my politics" and who asked about the use of whiteface. Novice Sister Jen explained that "almost everybody's white, so it's not a big deal [to them]." Her friend replied insightfully, "Yeah, because people of color just see that and they're like, 'No, I don't want to put on whiteface, I don't want to, that's not me, sorry.'" Although Novice Sister Jen left Portland before she could elevate to FP, when she spoke with me she was looking forward eagerly to the time when she had the seniority to make her own makeup choices. "I'm not going to wear whiteface ever again after that," she vowed.[51]

Sister Jonbennet Gesserit faced a similar concern with power dynamics in her own struggle with whiteface. "Jonbennet doesn't wear whiteface," she explained to me at a time when I had not yet seen her in habit. "Jonbennet is a colored Sister. And, for me, that's also representing the diversity within the Sisterhood itself. I've wrestled with the idea of adopting a white face when I am not a white person, and fully accepting the color of who I am to shine through my Sisterhood as well." But Sister Jonbennet, like Novice Sister Jen, also had to grapple with balancing her desire not to be whitewashed with her desire, as an independently or "rogue" veiled Sister, to become part of a house. Because Sisters who have been independently veiled by other members of the order have not come up through any house's training process, established houses often refuse to honor their rank and ask them to enter the house as aspirants. Having recently moved to Portland, Sister Jonbennet worried that "being so new to the organization, and not exactly in a secure standing at all, I don't want to rock the boat too much. . . . I'll admit I am a little afraid if I actually speak my truth about that and don't wear the whiteface, will I be accepted as a Sister?"[52] With Novice Sister Jen having already left town, and Portland's sole founding Sister of color in retirement, Sister Jonbennet had to rely primarily on the support of white allies in the house.

Just as most Sisters of color thought about the ways wearing whiteface hid their racial identity, they also considered various responses to this state of affairs. Novice Sister Jen's response was her plan to abjure white-face entirely once she was elevated to FP, following the established al-beit alternative tradition in the whiteface houses of manifesting in what many members of the order call "Mish-face" and Sister Baba terms "fresh face." Sister Jonbennet had considered a "middle ground" that involved using pancake makeup of a darker shade than stark white—perhaps, she thought, something between her own skin tone and the color of white-face. Sister Baba developed her lattice face, but as an artist of Filipino and Chinese descent she also honored the connection between white-face and what she called classical "Asian arts," such as the makeup art-istry of the geisha.[53] Sister Mary-Kohn, turning to her Mexican heritage, saw in the whiteface the skulls of el Día de los Muertos. For her, the stark white of the makeup offered an opening to the sacred and a canvas on which to build representations of her Chicanx community. Between the visual references on her face to Día de los Muertos and her sly choice of name that punned on the Spanish equivalent of "faggot," she hoped that community members—particularly those who were Latinx—would recognize her as a Chicanx Sister and see themselves mirrored in the order in ways they otherwise might not. In a city like Los Angeles, Sister Mary-Kohn found such outreach particularly important.[54]

Finally, some of the Sisters of color with whom I spoke found subver-sive opportunities in the whitewashing enacted by whiteface makeup. Sister Pure Heart implied as much when she told me that she tries to "fool people" but cannot because of the color of her skin. The obvious solution to this difficulty, of course, is to cover all of one's skin, and other Sisters found promise in precisely this approach. Sister Baba, as one might expect, had thought it all through. "Blackface and whiteface are not equal," she asserted when I asked whether she saw "potential racial dynamics" in the use of whiteface. "I don't assign a lot of racial coding to it, other than it's an opportunity for me. I'm brown and they see the whiteface or the tradition of whiteface as something [that] makes us uniform, which I think there's power in, but it's the ways you slip in your distinction and your messaging, that's where the brown arrives for me." Sister Baba's lattice face is one form in which her "distinction" and "messaging" come, but she also pointed to an effective way of trou-bling or subverting the whitewashing effect that is very much in line with what Marvin McAllister calls the "cultural work of whiting up" in the history of African American performance and the "seriously subversive cross-racial play" for which McAllister calls.[55] "What's interesting," Sister Baba explained,

> is there's also a running joke, 'cause I look at Sisters and I'm like—in whiteface—she's Asian, she's Asian, she's Asian, she can come with me to that event. But [with the whiteface] off, they'll identify as Latino, they'll identify as Croatian, whatever. One Sister who's Russian, Viva, when she's manifested, her and Billie, who's Native and Latino, she manifests, we can go to an Asian thing, and you'd think there were Asian Sisters. You know what I mean? Something really happens in the masking, and there's some interesting things that happen with the layers of perception, reality, and how one identifies.

Throughout my interview with Sister Baba I appreciated the combination of artistic and theoretical training that allowed her to see such connections; she was an especially important interlocutor for me when it came to race and whiteface, and I was not in the least surprised to hear from her a subversive and performative approach to both. She was not the only one to see such opportunity, however.

Sista' Anita Lynchin', a founding member of the same house in which Novice Sister Jen struggled against whiteface, and a black gay man in a very white city and if anything an even whiter gay community, took advantage of the whitewashing enacted by whiteface in a way that, intentionally or not, underlined and subverted the presumptions of whiteness in her community. When I asked her what it was like to wear whiteface, Sista' Anita laughed. "Interesting," she replied. "Real interesting." She explained that "when I first started I would cover up the arms, I would wear gloves, and with our headgear and everything . . . you wouldn't know that I was black. I also wore color contacts, so I either had blue eyes, green eyes, whatever. . . . I don't even recognize myself half the time." Passing as white simply because of the false neutrality of the whiteface, "I could walk up on so many people, and it'll still take them two to three minutes to catch on who I am."

As is evident from Sista' Anita's name, habits and whiteface are not the only way she takes on the topic of race in a white-dominant gay community. When I asked my usual interview question about how she had chosen her name, Sista' Anita told me that her initial choice of name had been Cialis Woody. Most people she encountered, though, did not understand the reference to erections and erectile dysfunction, "and I was like, nah, I need something catchier." The inspiration came from her mother's response to learning about her participation in the Sisters. Having been raised Catholic, and "not having the full concept" of the Sisters' work, "her first comment was, 'Nigger, someone oughta hang your ass.'" "Wow," I replied, raising my eyebrows. "Yeah," Sista' Anita agreed.

> And it wasn't as harsh as it sounds because, as you know, we can use the n-word for us and everything. So it was almost like, "Boy, you know better." But something stuck with me after that, and when I came back here to Oregon I told one of my other friends, and he had about the same response. He's like, "Ooh." "Well, she didn't mean in that way," I said, "but I kinda like it in a way." And he's like, "Hmm." And he's like, "How about," and he basically came up with the rest of it. He's like, "How about, you need to be hung, it's like you need a lynchin'." And I was like, "I need a lynchin'," and [he]'s like, "But say it like Anita." And I was like, "Oh, I like that!" Also, the second part to that would be, okay, being the gay male and everything, and most people would assume that we all like this, so I like 'em well hung. . . . So when people ask, and they have that look on their face, then I quickly interject with that: "Yes, I need a lynchin' because I like 'em well hung."

Although Sista' Anita claimed that her name was "not about the racial context," she then immediately went on to contextualize it by saying, "especially being a black Sister, you know, and then the second part of that is, I'm known as the Queen of Spades."[56] Perhaps she meant that she did not consider her name to be racist; it seems clear that through the use of strategic passing, her name, her explanation of it, and her tag line, Sista' Anita was keenly aware of the dynamics of and assumptions about race in her community and was engaged in performatively subverting and critiquing them.

Sisters of color generally regard whiteface in ways that both align with and differ from the perceptions of white members of the order. The challenges and opportunities they see in the makeup and the habits depend in part on the inclinations, perspectives, and politics of the individual Sister; they also depend on that Sister's ancestry and the ways white pancake makeup can or cannot serve as a link to that heritage and a mirror to those communities. Sister Baba saw in whiteface the legacy of Asian artistic traditions, and Sister Mary-Kohn saw Día de los Muertos skulls; other Sisters, such as Anita, Jonbennet, Pure Heart, and Jen, saw racial erasure, and responded to that erasure in a variety of ways that reflected their own politics and also their respective statuses and ranks within their houses. The quest to connect the Sisterhood to a longer and older tradition—a quest that frequently attends searches for meaning and significance in new religious movements and queer communities alike—has occupied many members of the order. Some Sisters of color see links to their own cultural heritage; some Sisters and Guards, both those who are people of color and those who are white, connect the Sisters to earlier European performance traditions such as mimes, court jesters, and clowns; and still others follow the Radical Faeries' lead toward an indigenous, sacred, third-gender nature, likening the Sisters to the anthropological construct of the berdache or, in a possibly more productive approach, describing the Sisters as sacred clowns.

Berdache and Sacred Clowns: Navigating Settler Colonialism

Sister Unity Divine has a YouTube channel. Sorted into such topics as "Spirituality," "Gay Rights/Equal Rights," and "Hinduism" (Sister Unity is part of a Hindu-based new religious movement), the more than one hundred videos on the channel feature the Sister telling stories, singing, or even silently holding up cards with text on them. Some are serious; some, like my personal favorite about having a Bear (the two-legged kind) in her bed, are funny and silly.[57] A few, featuring her alter ego Sister Crap, mobilize absurdity for political ends. She has an "It Gets Better" video, and other videos for LGBT people facing homophobia or considering suicide. One video included in both the "Spirituality" and "Gay Rights/Equal Rights" playlists is entitled "Berdache, The Holy Gay."[58] With over 20,000 views, over 200 likes and only a few dislikes, and scores of positive comments over the years mixed with a few virulently homophobic ones, this seems to be one of the Sister's more popular videos. Indeed, it was no doubt in part because of this video that other members of the order told me for years that I absolutely must interview Sister Unity.

With Samuel Barber's ethereal *Agnus Dei* playing in the background, Sister Unity frames her roughly five-minute video by explaining in measured tones, "I want to talk to you about what it is that there are gay people in the world." In the next sentence, though, her focus turns to gender:

> We have all been taught that there are two genders, male and female, that there is this yin and yang, this black and white. And yet if you look at a yin and yang symbol, you will notice that in the greatest part of each color . . . there is a small dot of the opposite. There is always a little of the opposite, a minority of the opposite, in the midst of the majority. This is what the Native Americans used to call, in people, Two Spirit. When the French first came to North America, they met Two Spirit people, gay Native Americans, men who dressed like women. And they called them berdache, which is a seventeenth-century French equivalent to faggot. But in this day and age, berdache is what they call a reclaimed word, which means that people in academia use it to refer to this cross-gendered social role. And it is remarkable to note, as noted in the book *The Other Face of Love*,[59] that each early urban or pre-urban civilization in the world has had cross-gendered or gay men performing the specific role of spiritual functionary in their society.

Sister Unity goes on to explain that early Spanish invaders in the Americas found such a spiritual functionary in "every village they rode" into; they labeled them heretics and killed them. A similar fate met the same figures in "pre-Christian Europe." "What happened to all of these people?" Sister Unity asks. "Why did it change so much?" She answers:

> Well, there was a concerted effort. When Christianity came to Europe, it came associated with political power, and there was a great change in the religious structure, political structure, and social structure of society in Europe. In short, most of these cross-gendered shamans were burned, or otherwise killed, or suppressed for what was supposed to be their heresy. But again, it's important to remember: *They were there*. Since the dawn of human history, gay men have occupied an important social role.

"The reason why gay people will not go away," Sister Unity concludes at the end of the video, "is because we're part of nature."[60]

The story of the berdache has captivated Western, non-Native, LGBTQ people for decades. In the face of both intimate and societal brutalities—police entrapment and assault, federal investigations, emotional and physical torture masquerading as medicine and psychology, religious condemnation, familial rejection, and the intra-community and self-inflicted violence that always accompany such widespread oppression—the berdache story places very real suffering in a context that promises, "It wasn't always like this." If you, and people like you, are not a symptom of the degeneracy of modern society, not a delusion of Satan, but instead a fact of nature that has existed for all time, then you are therefore a natural and innocent part of humanity. If your presence in the past can be verified through your presence in so-called cultural vestiges of the past—that is, by a social Darwinist evolutionary logic, in contemporary indigenous cultures around the world—and if indigenous cultures, as stand-ins for ancient human cultures everywhere, revere people like you, then it is your oppression and not your existence that is the mark of social degeneracy. Imagining a past in which they were consistently honored as "spiritual functionaries" rather than consistently excoriated as spiritual failures, gay men and some lesbians, mostly non-Native, have found the strength to imagine a future in which they are treasured by their own societies rather than ejected from them.

Because of its power, the berdache story has been retold by numerous popular gay authors, most of them white.[61] Its intersections with separatist and lesbian feminist stories of ancient matriarchy and with neopagan stories of the Burning Times, both of which explain the European and North American witch trials as Christian persecution of wise women and practitioners of indigenous European religions, have led to versions of the berdache story making their way into lesbian communities and queer or queer-friendly pagan communities, and the clear theme of gender diversity in the story has led transgender activists to claim it for themselves as well.[62] Gay men who have an interest in the Radical Faeries have often heard the story through that group or through the writings of its co-founder Harry Hay; indeed, the berdache story provided a key foundation for the Faeries, and continues to do so today.[63] Sister Unity, in fact, cites "the writings and talks with Harry

Hay" first among the sources for her video, adding to Hay's corpus only the aforementioned book, *The Other Face of Love*, and Mark Thompson's Radical Faerie–influenced book, *Gay Spirit*.[64]

Sister Urania learned the berdache story through Judy Grahn's popular work *Another Mother Tongue*.[65] Given that Sister Urania had considered having a sex change as a teen before deciding that gender nonconformity was a part of being gay, it comes as no surprise that this was a powerful narrative for her. "My perspective," she told me, "[is that] when you come from an incarnation of being a keeper for many years—in mortal years it would be thousands and thousands and thousands and thousands of years back, back to the Deluge—you remember quite well what your job [is. But] you have no clear idea about it"; that is, you have no clear idea what that job looks like in present-day Western cultures, which have no established spiritual leadership role for feminine, same-sex–attracted men. "And then suddenly there comes this funny thing around Sisters." Reading about the San Francisco house in Mark Thompson's *Gay Spirit*—the same book cited by Sister Unity—Sister Urania knew exactly how to carry out her aeons-old role.[66]

Despite its power, though, the berdache story is not true. Many sacred stories are not empirically verifiable, and this lack of verifiability matters not at all to those for whom those stories are world-making; this may be true for many of the people who rely on the berdache story and its various offshoots for strength, sustenance, validation, and hope for the future. Because this story captured the imaginations not only of mid-twentieth-century anthropologists but of gay and lesbian anthropologists as they began to be open about their sexuality and to organize politically in the 1970s and 1980s, and because it therefore gained the (non-Native) academic imprimatur during that time, it has had enormous staying power despite being protested for decades by Native queer and Two Spirit people and discarded in the 1990s by many anthropologists, both Native and non-Native. The term "berdache" is by no means a reclaimed term, as Sister Unity suggests that it is. A French word that seems to have meant something akin to "boy prostitute," it has never been an accurate reflection of Native genders or sexualities but has instead been used to justify colonial activities, including both cultural and physical genocide, especially but not solely in North America. The only people who can be said to have "reclaimed" the word *berdache*, therefore, are those non-Native queer people for whom it functions as a world-making story.[67]

The Sisters' relationship to the berdache story is complex. Even Sister Unity, in an interview with me that took place almost exactly six years after she posted the berdache video, suggested a more strategic approach to the concept for the order. "We're very conscious of the historical berdache," she explained, clearly still adhering to the veracity of the tale, "that the role of cross-gendering men in history was to be the intermediary between the secular and the divine; we're the ones in between." She added, though, that the Sisters "are wary of codifying" that role, out of a concern for becoming dogmatic. On the one hand, the berdache story has a powerful function for the order: "We codify it in certain ways, and we'd love to jump on it, because it's another feather in our cap. 'A-ha! We've got *this* superpower!' It makes us legitimate." On the other hand, she explained, the concern to avoid what she saw as the Christian and particularly Roman Catholic error of dogmatism prevented the order from insisting on any particular understanding of ultimate truth—beyond, perhaps, talks posted on YouTube by individual members.[68]

While few Sisters or Guards used the term "berdache" in conversations with me, the concept of an innate gay femininity linked to certain kinds of spirituality was definitely persuasive for a number of those with whom I worked. This linkage ties back to the berdache story, for many Sisters, because of the order's close historical (and in some houses current) ties to the Radical Faeries. But it also serves a broader effort to make sense of who the Sisters are and what precisely they are doing. They only became queer nuns, after all, through a series of developments: the presence of those three habits in Ken Bunch's closet on the day when he and his two friends got bored; the sense they had that there was a certain power in the responses they received on that first day and their interest in investigating what was happening; Agnes's insight that lots of men dress up as nuns but none of them claim to actually be nuns, so *being* an order of nuns would be an interesting innovation; the descriptive intent of the order's first constitution that named (and thereby performatively created) them as "an order of gay male nuns"; and the order's eventual decisions to admit members of all genders, gender histories, and sexual identities. Since there has never before been an order of gay male or queer nuns, at least not as far as anyone knows, Sisters had and still have the challenge of figuring out, alongside their communities, what exactly queer nuns are and what preexisting roles, in addition to that of vowed women religious, they might resemble.

Sister Hysterectoria remembers that the early Sisters often considered themselves clowns, and that this self-understanding made the use of makeup called "Clown White" seem perfectly logical when whiteface began to gain popularity within the San Francisco house.[69] During fieldwork and interviews with Sisters and Guards, I heard a number of different comparisons as people reached for ways to explain who the Sisters are and what they do. Sister MaryMae Himm suggested that they are like the old European court jesters, "act[ing] as the lightning rod" for cultural tensions.[70] Sister Benedikta rejected the idea that the Sisters are court jesters, but she said that they are as colorful as jesters, and that they often play the role of clowns.[71] Sister Angelpopstitute was among those Sisters who likened the order to Japanese Noh theater, and Sister Trystina T. Rhume, who works in theater herself, saw many different parallels in the whiteface alone: Japanese Kabuki theater, classic French mimes, French Pierrot clowns, and the U.S. clowning tradition.[72] Not surprisingly, for many Sisters the prominence of the berdache story, combined with the use of whiteface, the historical understanding of the Sisters as clowns, and their own sense that their work with the order is spiritual, led them to explain the Sisters as sacred clowns. Although this analogy also draws upon anthropological renderings of Native traditions, it may ultimately prove more useful than the berdache story.

Scholarship on the use of parody, humor, and absurdity in ritual and political settings has drawn together many of the European traditions referenced by the Sisters, such as the court jester, the mime, the clown, and the fool, with examples of related modes of performance in numerous contemporary and historical cultures, often under the comparative concept of the clown or, in ritual contexts specifically, the ritual or sacred clown. While there are significant aspects of cultural specificity in clowning that must be recognized in any attempt at comparative study, a strikingly consistent observation links not only studies of various clowning traditions but also other modes of performance that are related to but not always considered a part of clowning. It appears that the creation of a recognizable role or persona, when combined with the performative

use of parody, buffoonery, irony, and/or humor, can provide a powerful source of social commentary through transgression. It also appears
that this performative mode of commentary, protest, or even subversion
is particularly accessible to nondominant groups. Serious parody, then,
might be one subset of this broader mode of subversive performance,
and this alignment would explain the associations made by many members of the Sisters between their order and these other transgressive
personae.

Consider, for instance, the original source of the Sisters' whiteface.
Several months after reading an initial draft of chapter 1 of this book,
Sister Vish emailed me to share an insight. Having recently spent time
with her roommate from the mid-1970s, she had recalled during the
visit that when they were rooming together he insisted that they watch
Bob Fosse's 1972 film *Cabaret*. "I remembered," she wrote to me, "having run around for a whole year saying 'divine decadence' and flash-
ing my painted nails, it had such a strong influence on me. I believe
my inspiration for first wearing whiteface makeup . . . came from that
film. I think I started wearing whiteface because of the film *Cabaret*."[73]
This is a striking revelation, because while aesthetics seem to be the sole
causal link between Joel Grey's Emcee character and the eventual adoption of whiteface by the order, some scholarship on *Cabaret* has aligned
the Emcee with a tradition of political commentary in the cabarets of
Weimar-era Berlin. Mitchell Morris notes, for instance, that the Emcee
"is identifiably queer in the most inclusive sense, with his makeup and
apparel recalling the epicene nineteenth-century figure of the Dandy. . . .
His performance style is a wonder of brittle artifice, such that there is
no character outside the mannerisms of his performance. He cannot be
fixed, and this is the source of his fascination as well as of his danger."[74]
Writing a few years later and drawing on Morris's work, Steven Belletto
expands on the political function of this queer figure. "The Emcee's ambiguity," he argues,

> is actually the source of his most powerful political commentary, for as
> fascist aesthetics seek to subsume ambiguity and difference under the sign
> of a stridently political message, the Emcee's songs operate through vari-
> ous registers of irony that always invite viewers to ask "whether" he means
> this or that. If the audience is indeed left to wonder, as Morris does, what

exactly to make of the Emcee, then this confusion, rooted as it is in ambiguity and irony, is how the film generates its antifascist critique.[75]

Belletto goes on to suggest that *Cabaret*'s "Kit Kat Klub can be understood as the aesthetic descendant of the real-life Weimar 'Kabarett mit
K' that used these characteristics [of ambiguity and irony] to generate
political critique."[76] Drawing on Theodor Adorno's analyses of Brecht
and other artists contemporary with these political cabarets, Belletto
suggests that the Emcee's performances in Fosse's film constitute a form
of Adorno's "committed art."[77]

The white pancake makeup used by Joel Grey's Emcee is not what
makes him either queer or committed in Adorno's sense; it is, though,
both a historical and a symbolic link between this figure and the Sisters
of Perpetual Indulgence. Causality and makeup aside, the Emcee and the
Sisters share several crucial traits. Both are personas, living in some ways
beyond the performance but not existing in tangible form in between
manifestations. Both make use of this ephemeral nature, and of a certain
illegibility—"ambiguity" in Belletto's terms, "queerness" broadly writ as
Morris describes it—to enact sharp social and political commentary.
Sœur Rose in her "Christ position" facing homophobic protesters comes
to mind here, as do public protests throughout the history of the order.
And if, to reiterate Belletto's words, "the Emcee's songs operate through
various registers of irony that always invite viewers to ask 'whether' he
means this or that," the Sisters' manifestations always invite viewers to
ask whether they are nuns or drag queens, whether they are men or
women, whether they are white people or people of color, whether they
are sacred or sacrilegious. Perhaps one might speak, then, of "committed
performance" as a subset of "committed art," and of serious parody as a
subset of committed performance.

Yet these connections, as noted in Belletto's comparison of the Kit Kat
Klub with real-life Weimar cabarets and in Adorno's work on Brecht and
his contemporaries, also extend beyond the realm of the queer, at least
if one restricts that term to its meanings regarding sexuality and gender.
Consider this remark from Eric Lott's classic study of blackface in the
United States, regarding "a feature of American blackface masking that
critics have been slow to recognize: an unstable or indeed contradictory
power, linked to social and political conflicts, that issues from the weak,

the uncanny, the outside."[78] Marvin McAllister likewise sees "percep-
tive appropriations and deconstructions of whiteness" as possibilities
in African American whiteface performances.[79] A report on modern
"clown politics" notes that such performances are alive and well internationally, and Fletcher's work on the Clandestine Insurgent Rebel Clown
Army (CIRCA) demonstrates the same viability in a specific U.S. case.[80]
José Esteban Muñoz finds subversion along sexual, racial, and gendered
lines in the disidentificatory performances of queer people of color, perhaps the most striking of which in this context is Vaginal Creme Davis's
whiteface performance as Clarence.[81] Furthermore, in the context of
Native North American uses of humor and buffoonery, and those figures who first bore the moniker of "sacred clowns," Robert Brightman
has also argued for the importance of "performative transgression" as a
source of social subversion.[82]

Brightman sees ambiguity not only in the messages of clowning performances but also in their effects, and he locates much of that ambiguity in the varied relationships between audience members and the
social structures the clown critiques or subverts. "Subversive clowns,"
he suggests, "possess the Janus-faced capacity to point both towards the
naturalization and towards the deconstruction of received convention.
And while functional naturalization and critical deconstruction have
sometimes been conceived as oppositive and successional, they may
better be conceived as virtually fusional—with a commensurate diversity of potential effect on people's conduct and dispositions."[83] Context
and social location are critical to Brightman's argument, as they are
to Kleinhaus's analysis of camp discussed above. Acknowledging that
"there exist well-founded objections to characterizations of the ritual
clown as cultural critic or revolutionary architect," Brightman draws
on William Mitchell's argument that clowning can be understood as
"conservative" or "subversive" only "in terms of specific cases."[84] In the
context of historic Northwestern Maidu clowning as reconstructed from
the reports of non-Native observers, Brightman notes the critical importance of social stratification as a backdrop to interpreting the impact of
ritual clowns in this setting. "Whatever the cultural forms in question,"
he argues, "subversive clowning can engender a critical perspective on
their veridical 'naturalness' relative to the existential verities."[85] People in
different positions within the social hierarchy may interpret the clown's

performance in different ways; conservative and subversive effects may coexist within the same audience. "Where ideology has successfully assimilated custom to nature," Brightman concludes, "'license' becomes only a respite from a human condition objectively given. The meaning of 'license' changes, however, in proportion as social constraints are apprehended as artificial disciplines that people, consensually or not, practice upon themselves or each other."[86] In Brightman's view, social location can impact such apprehension.

Ambiguity, therefore, may be the key to subversion. The ambiguity of both blackface and African American whiteface performance may drive their complex roles in reflecting and shaping the history of race in the United States. The ambiguity of the Emcee in *Cabaret* may be what allows him to be such a powerful character. In the same vein, the ambiguity of the Sisters—their genderfuck, the racial ambiguity enacted by the use of whiteface, even their religionfuck—not only aligns them with these other subversive, "committed" performances but also provides the source of their effectiveness in certain contexts and the source of their ineffectiveness in others. The Sisters are clowns to some, court jesters and fools to others, and always nuns. Because of the religious camp at their roots, as well as the way the Sisters serve as a source of spiritual expression for certain of their members, some also see in the Sisters sacred or ritual clowns. All of these comparisons lead to the conclusion that the Sisters, though perhaps properly understood as none of these figures, are still a part of a larger family of subversive, committed performers that encompass all of them. While some Sisters may see in the order a kind of sacred clown, perhaps their own queer brand of subversion introduces ambiguity even into the concept of the sacred itself, for within this order of serious, parodic, joyful, expiatory, sexualized, earthy, glittery drag nuns, it becomes quite difficult indeed to locate the place where the sacred edges over into the profane and vice versa—and this may be precisely the point.

Figure 1. Mother Lateral Thinking (Max Clarke), Sister 69 (Tony Collins), and Sister Very Maculate (Margaret Taylor), Sisters of Perpetual Indulgence, Melbourne, November 1986. Photo by Jay Watchorn. City Rhythm collection, Australian Lesbian and Gay Archives (ALGA). Reproduced by permission.

Figure 2. *Top*: The cover of the 1982 *Play Fair!* pamphlet. *Bottom*: Contemporary "Condom Savior" condom packs from The Abbey of St. Joan. Art by Donna Barr (Madonna image) and Kendal Tull Esterbrook (unicorn and lion image). Reproduced by permission.

Figure 3. Campaign poster from Sister Boom Boom's run for San Francisco city supervisor in 1982, featuring photography by Nina Glaser.

Figure 4. First manifestation of the Sisters' Paris house at Notre-Dame Cathedral, September 11, 1990. *Left to right*: Sister Psychadelia, Sister X, and Sister Vicious (San Francisco house), Sœur Rita, Sœur Thérèse, and Sœur Plat-du-Jour (Paris house). Les Sœurs de la Perpétuelle Indulgence, Couvent de Paris © 1990. Note the golden condom held by Sœur Rita; these were also distributed at the 1987 Mass against Papal Bigotry in San Francisco.

Figure 5. Images from the Mass against Papal Bigotry, September 17, 1987.
Top, left to right: Michael Hare (spelling unknown) as Pope John Paul II;
self-titled Fag Nun Assunta Femia, forebear of the order and Sister Missionary
Position's "mother in religious life"; Sister Vicious Power Hungry Bitch.
Bottom, left to right: Sister Lily White, Rick Stores in the role of acolyte, Sister
Vicious Power Hungry Bitch, Sister Luscious Lashes, Sister Mysteria of the
Order of the Broken Hymen. Photos by John Entwistle. Reproduced by
permission of Soami Archive.

Figure 6. Sister Baba Ganesh in lattice face. Reproduced by permission of Joël Barraquiel Tan.

Figure 7. *Golden Calf*, © 2016 by the Orthodox Calendar, www.orthodox-calendar.com. Reproduced by permission.

Figure 8. Serious parody on the catwalk: Sister Destiny LeFemme on the catwalk in Project Nunway 2014 in Los Angeles, wearing a habit made of a (literally) deconstructed Bible. Photo by Troy Tackett. Reproduced by permission.

5

"A Secular Nun"

Serious Parody and the Sacred

Sister Cuminja Wrasse and I were talking about the common accusation that the Sisters of Perpetual Indulgence mock Roman Catholic nuns. "What's your response?" I asked. "I say, 'You're absolutely right,'" Sister Cuminja told me. "You're absolutely right, but ask yourselves why we're doing it. . . . The Catholic Church's stance on contraception, on LGBT rights, on a hundred and one other things, is actually offensive, and offensive to far more people than I'm going to upset by trolling down the streets in a habit."

I was in London for a conference, at which I had just presented a paper on the concept of serious parody I was developing. Sister Cuminja was a graduate student interested in social and performance theory, so I couldn't resist sharing some of my ideas. "This is one of the things that fascinates me about the Sisters," I told her enthusiastically, "that you're enacting parody; for some of you, you are at some level mocking; and yet you *are* a nun, and that's a very serious thing." "Ah yes," Sister Cuminja replied, "but I'm a secular nun, not a religious nun." "Sounds like that makes all the difference," I mused. "I think it does make all the difference," she agreed. Our conversation left at least one glaring question, though: What precisely *is* a secular nun?

"Secular" may be too simple a description even for Sister Cuminja herself, although she feels that it describes her role as a Sister well. At one point in his life, the person who became Sister Cuminja was headed for the Roman Catholic priesthood. Raised by parents whom she described as "strict Anglicans," he "converted to Catholicism at university." "At the time," Sister Cuminja explained to me, "I'd have given you a hundred and one very good theological reasons for why I was doing this. If I'm absolutely honest, I think more it was to do with—converting, anyway—it was to do with the fact that if I went and converted into a Catholic priest I couldn't have sex with anybody, so the question of my sexuality as a late teenager wouldn't be an issue." Today, she told me, "the older I get, the less agnostic I become and the more atheistic. . . . I'm not necessarily saying that I would subscribe to everything that Richard Dawkins says, but I have a sympathy with a lot of what he has to say."

Does this comment explain what a secular nun is? Does "secular" here mean, simply, the opposite of religious? In the ensuing conversation, Sister Cuminja complicated any idea I might have had about what a secular nun in fact was. After describing her sympathy with Richard Dawkins, Sister Cuminja continued, "That's not to say that I don't think human beings are spiritual, or have an intense spirituality about them. But I think that organized religions have caused more damage than good, because the bottom line is, they have always been a mode of control as much as anything else." I wanted to be sure that I understood correctly. "Would you consider yourself spiritual as well as atheistic," I asked, "or can those two go together?" "I'm not sure I can answer that question, honestly," she replied, "because I think the bottom line is, I don't know. And friends will tell me they think I'm quite a spiritual person, but I'm not quite sure what they mean by that."

The Sister went on to explain that she envies "people of faith" to a certain extent, and recalls with some nostalgia the certainty of belief and the reassurance that her teenage self possessed. Some Christians, she added, "are very, very good people who live their beliefs in a very positive way." Indeed, she had told me earlier of both Catholic and Anglican priests in London who worked closely with her house. "I don't have a problem with the sweet," she explained metaphorically.

> It's the way it's wrapped up. It doesn't work for me, it works for other people. I would always respect someone's religious beliefs like I'd respect anybody's views, as long as it wasn't hurtful to someone. I mean, I'm quite prepared to accept that people are not comfortable with the fact I'm gay, the fact that I'm a nun. I can't make you change what you believe if you don't want to, I'm not even going to say that your belief is wrong, but it's not the same as mine. You have a right to believe it, I just don't have to agree and like it.

"Does that perspective feed into your work as a Sister?" I asked. "I think so," she responded. "The person that's underneath Cuminja has certain values, and that makes them partly Cuminja's as well. And I just think you should treat people properly."[1]

Sister Cuminja's perspectives resonate profoundly with many of the themes that have captivated scholars of contemporary religion, particularly in Europe and its settler colonies. The very idea that a "secular nun" could exist taps into the debates over secularization and post-secularism, and the Sister's distaste for religion as "a mode of control," paired with her openness to "faith" and "spirituality," echo what Paul Heelas and Linda Woodhead have dubbed the "subjective turn" in contemporary religious belief and practice.[2] As a now-sizeable body of literature has demonstrated, people claiming no religious affiliation, referred to colloquially by scholars as "nones," are not in fact uniformly irreligious but rather are likely to hold a variety of religious beliefs and to take part in a variety of religious practices, often though not always under the self-description of "spirituality."[3] Furthermore, it has been extensively documented that "nones" and the "spiritual but not religious" in Western cultures are particularly well represented among LGBTQ populations, whose members often have more reasons than their cisgender and straight friends and family members to question and abandon organized religion.[4] Finally, Sister Cuminja's focus on freedom of belief also echoes discussions within religious studies over the Protestant and colonial roots of a field that has for over a century participated in the reduction of religion to the cognitive, and it gestures toward rising tensions in the United States and elsewhere over the meaning of religious freedom and whether that freedom does or should preempt other state protections against discrimination.[5] But while Sister Cuminja's story touches on all of these different themes, it is hardly unique among those Sisters and Guards whom I interviewed. As with other study participants with whom I have worked in the past, these "none nuns" offer another example of the ways queer communities serve as exemplary cases for the study of Heelas and Woodhead's "subjective-life spirituality"—an approach to religious belief and practice that is often eclectic, stressing individual interpretation and innovation while also often engaging in communal practice.[6]

Spiritual Nones: Spirituality among the Sisters

Members of the order knew from the beginning of my work with them that I was a religious studies scholar and that I was interested in religion among the Sisters. Those who volunteered for interviews, therefore, likely included disproportionate numbers of people who wanted to discuss the topic of religion, particularly those who held favorable views of religion or at least of spirituality. When advertising for interview participants in a particular house or at a particular event, I always stressed that I wanted to talk to anyone with opinions on religion and/or spirituality, whether those opinions were positive or negative, and that I was just as interested in talking with atheist members of the order as I was in speaking with those who considered themselves spiritual or religious. It is nevertheless likely that the level of current engagement with religion on the part of those who participated in interviews is higher than that in the order as a whole, perhaps particularly in Western Europe, where scholars have noted for quite some time a sharp decline in the participation of whites in traditional religious practices and membership.[7] That said, the religious backgrounds of interview participants are nevertheless fairly unremarkable relative to the larger societies in which they were raised.

Religious Upbringing and Its Aftermath

Given that most Sisters belong to the majority racial and/or ethnic group in their country, it is unsurprising that they also largely belong, or used to belong, to majority religious groups. Of the eighty-four participants who discussed their religious upbringing with me, sixty-eight, or 81 percent, were raised with significant childhood and/or youth exposure to some form of Christianity. Fourteen, or 17 percent, were raised with no religion, and one each reported being raised as spiritual and as Unitarian Universalist. Two participants mentioned having mothers who were Jewish, but both were raised Christian, one because of an agreement between his mother and his Roman Catholic father and the other because of the lack of a Jewish community in his hometown. Of those who were raised with significant exposure to Christianity, twenty-nine received at least part of that exposure within Catholicism.

Thus, among the Sisters and Guards who volunteered for interviews and who answered the question about religious upbringing, 35 percent had some significant exposure to Catholicism as children and/or as youth. Although those I interviewed were almost entirely from Christian or nonreligious backgrounds, it is well known and often celebrated within the order that there are members from other religions as well. There are important Jewish figures in the order's early history, for instance, and much is often made of the more recent involvement of Sister Hyde N. Sikh, a now-resigned founder of the Vancouver, British Columbia, house, whose Sister name is said to reference her religious background. The fact that most members of the order are white, however, also makes it less likely that any significant number of members would hail from religions other than Christianity or Judaism.

Given their widespread and generally unremarkable childhood exposure to Christianity, it is worth asking what happened with religion as these members of the order reached adulthood. The U.S. pattern of leaving the religion of one's upbringing in the late teenage years is well established, as is the tendency of queer women, at least, to stay away once they have left.[8] Where do Guards and Sisters fit within this picture? While a very small number of interview participants remained with the Christianity of their childhoods, and a few more remained Christian but switched to more LGBTQ-friendly denominations, the vast majority left Christianity far behind.

LEAVING CHRISTIANITY: HOMOPHOBIA

Quite a few among those I interviewed who were raised Christian left that religion because of homophobia and transphobia, and no small number of those were shunned as a consequence by their church leaders, their religious communities, and sometimes even their families. In response to homophobia in her church, Sista' Anita Lynchin' took matters into her own hands in no uncertain terms. Growing up with a Roman Catholic mother and Baptist grandparents, Sista' Anita "always had a choice" when it came to religion, or at least to denomination. "I started off as Baptist," she told me. "I went to Methodist, and I ended up as a holy roller, Church of God in Christ." "Oh my," I replied, thinking of that church's stance on same-sex eroticism. "Yes," she said, laughing. "Choir director, the whole nine yards." It became a bit of a family business, with several cousins serving as choir directors in other COGIC congregations nearby. But Sista' Anita made clear that her attitudes toward religion have changed significantly since those days. So I asked, "What led you out of the Church of God in Christ? Was that sort of the last stop on the religion train?" "Yes, yes," she laughed. "Oh yes, it was. The straw that broke the camel's back" was a sermon on homosexuality.

> I can remember sitting in church, the back pew, on a Sunday. In the choir stand. Had just got through doing a number. And sat down, and when we sat down, I can remember my pastor getting up, and his sermon for the day was about homosexuals. And I can remember looking down the back aisle of the tenors, the baritones, and the basses, us guys, and remembering that night before, that Saturday night, there were about six people in that back row with me that were all at the same bar with me. And when I looked down, and they kind of looked at me, and then they looked down, you know. And the pastor was going on about how sinful, how condemned, and everything. I stood up, unzipped my robe, dropped it, waved to everybody, and I walked out. And that was the last anyone saw of me at that church.

It was also the last he would see of anyone from the church. "No one said anything, they knew the purpose why I walked out and everything. No one did any outreach or anything, not even the pastor himself." In walking out during a sermon on homosexuality, he had broken not only church etiquette but also what some term the "glass closet" of the sexually conservative black churches. Apparently his congregation saw no other option but to cut him off.[9]

"I look back on that," Sista' Anita reflected about her involvement in religion as a whole, "and I'm glad I went through that, but my views have changed so much on religion, or how religion still views people, or how they treat people. I'm not comfortable with their teachings now. Then I was growing up, now I know. I feel like I can achieve the same thing in my life without being part of that organized setup." Her experiences carry over to her work as a Sister, because she wants the queer community to see the Sisters as approachable even when their own religious traditions are not.[10]

LEAVING CHRISTIANITY: HYPOCRISY, SKEPTICISM, AND GUILT

Those who were raised in Christianity and left it but who did not experience direct or sustained homophobia offered a range of other reasons for leaving; most common among these were their perception that church members and sometimes leaders were hypocritical, their skepticism of church teachings, and their rejection of what they saw as a focus on guilt in their churches. Perhaps no one has a clearer view of the goings-on behind the scenes of a church than the child of a minister, and Sister Nadia Ahnwilda had precisely this experience. "We . . . got to see the crappy part of organized religion," she explained, "of people sitting there really pious on Sunday, and acting like total shits the rest of the week." Seeing such hypocrisy drove not only Sister Nadia, but her siblings as well, out of the church. "The feeling of camaraderie and stuff on Sunday became very hollow and shallow when you grow up seeing some of the crappier stuff," she explained. All of them, though, continue to consider themselves spiritual.[11]

Several people recalled being unconvinced by the teachings of their church, and ceasing to attend as soon as their parents offered them the choice, sometimes to great parental disappointment. Others began asking questions later in life, such as Sister Trystina T. Rhume, a son from a long line of Methodist ministers who was kicked out of the house at sixteen for being gay; notably, she was not the only one among my interviewees to have had this experience. "Of course I stopped going to church," she said. "But I've always had a relationship with God, as I was taught God was." Over a decade later, when he was living in Chicago, he decided to return to church and found a theologically liberal Methodist congregation. "I was astounded at how open and accepting they were," Sister Trystina told me. With his sexuality no longer an issue, he was free to reflect more deeply on other aspects of Christianity, and those reflections led to deeper questions.

Like . . . at the very beginning of the Bible, when it says God created the heavens and the earth, there's a "we" in there. And I asked who the "we" is. . . . I can't even remember what answer to that my pastor gave me, but I remember that it wasn't good enough. And so then I started questioning, questioning, questioning, and in that questioning I left that church. Left all church, and just tried to find answers to things like, if God is omnipresent, then why is it a he? . . . If God is everywhere, then why am I to believe that I am a hole in that everywhere and that God is not *inside* me? And that's kind of how it branched out.

Now most strongly identified with Nichiren Buddhism, this fourth-generation minister sees the Methodist church of her ancestors and her upbringing as her elementary religious education: "I say Jesus was my kindergarten teacher," she explained.[12]

Several people mentioned being put off by the guilt that they believed was inculcated by their inherited religious traditions; since the order's mission includes the "expiation of stigmatic guilt," these participants often linked their theological disagreements with Christianity to their work in the order. Sister Sorenda 'da Booty, for example, was deeply involved in Roman Catholicism while growing up but left it behind when she departed her home town for the somewhat more liberal setting of Guerneville, California, the location of the Russian River house. She began to explore Wicca, and when we spoke she told me, "I consider myself a born-again pagan." She still attends church with her parents when she visits them, but

the last couple of times I'm like, "Eh, no, I think I'll bow out." 'Cause *every single time* I go to church with them, I'm like, *guilt!* This place, it's *just ridden in guilt.* . . . I know for a fact I'm not going to burn in hell if I choose to practice something other than Catholicism. And sorry, but you cannot guilt me into going back.[13]

Other reasons that participants gave for leaving their religious upbringing behind ranged from family changes such as the divorce of their parents to changes in the religion itself, religious complicity in political oppression, and crises of faith resulting from a positive HIV diagnosis.

CHANGING DENOMINATIONS

Several participants remained within Christianity but switched to different denominations from those in which they had been raised. Sister Ophelia Nutz, for instance, was brought up in the Jehovah's Witnesses by a mother who was at one time baptized in the LDS Church, making

Sister Ophelia also recognized by the latter. Both traditions are quite conservative overall, and do not consider same-sex eroticism acceptable, but rather than leave Christianity entirely in response to this stance, Sister Ophelia sought and received ordination in the more liberal United Church of Christ.[14] A few participants who were raised as Roman Catholics followed a well-trodden queer path from that church to the Anglican tradition, which is particularly liberal in the United States, and some who live in areas with a significant evangelical presence have even converted from Roman Catholicism to evangelical Christianity. "I became a born-again Christian when I first got sober," explained Sister Gloria-Areola all over Gluttony of Las Vegas. "I love my Savior, I know my position, I know where my faith and my rock is. . . . I *know* where my rock is." Her fellow Sin Sity Sister, Mother Loosy Lust Bea Lady, who was also raised Roman Catholic, agreed: "I know that Jesus Christ is my Savior."[15]

FINDING RELIGION

A final group of participants were raised without religion but found value in one or more religious traditions in adulthood. Here, the story of Sister Unity Divine is particularly instructive. Although the "Divine" in her name is an homage to the famed drag queen rather than a reference to a sacred being, and although she originally wore orange not as a religious reference but because the house was picking colors of the rainbow and she was one of the last to choose, Sister Unity takes her first name from one given to Bennett (her "boy name") by a spiritual teacher. As she told me by way of introduction when I first met her many years ago, "I'm a Hindu."

Raised as a secular humanist, Sister Unity described her family's approach to life as "bullshit cutters. We're like, 'Yeah, that's bullshit. Yeah, that's bullshit.' But we want to know, 'Okay, what the fuck's going on? What is going on?'" That approach led to a combination of curiosity and empiricism, wherein spirituality is less about belief than it is about verifiable results. She explained to me,

> *My* faith is like, "Well, I poked at it with a stick, I kicked the tires, I
> stepped on it, and it bit me, so I know it's there, so as much as I know is
> there—the part with the teeth—I believe in that. And I'm going to keep

doing these [things] 'cause I hear tell there's more. I'll go check that out. But even if it's not there, what it's given me so far is worth perpetuating."

This empirical approach to religion and spirituality led Bennett to explore comparative religions with a friend as a young adult. They found numerological and geometrical patterns in the traditions they studied, and they were intrigued by their discoveries. This sense of pattern, meaning, perhaps even serendipity, threaded throughout Sister Unity's narrative.

A few months after he moved to Los Angeles, Bennett needed paint for a project and walked to a neighbor's apartment to ask whether she had any that he could use. "And she says, 'I have no paint, but I'm going to the meditation center tonight if you'd like to go.' . . . So I'm like, 'Well, yeah, I like Indian culture, let's . . . check it out.'" His friend was a practitioner of a Hindu-based new religious movement; Sister Unity has requested that I not reveal which one. At first, Bennett was drawn to the exoticism of the practice—exotic, that is, for a white secular humanist from the United States. "I'm like, 'Oh my god, this is *so* très chic. How many of my friends are chanting in Sanskrit right now in New York? None!'" He was put off, though, by the idea of bowing to the image of the guru at the front of the room. "I'm like, 'What the hell is that?' Americans do not bow to anyone." His friend explained the background as she understood it:

> "Well . . . it's a guru . . . the teacher, and you have to understand that in Hinduism the guru is you, you are the guru, your toilet is the guru, you are your toilet, you know, it's all one consciousness." And the mantra of this particular lineage is explained to me that it's translated as, "I bow to my own inner self. I bow to God who exists within me as me." And that takes it for me . . . to "Yes, there's God. Guess what? It's you, the kitchen table, and your sock drawer. And the President." And I'm like, "That's new. I can totally get behind that."

Three months later the guru visited Los Angeles, and Bennett had a life-changing experience.

The event was held at a large auditorium in the city, and Bennett was one among many in the audience. When the guru first walked out on stage, Sister Unity told me, "there was this '*Bam!*' feeling of recognition in my head." Feeling first "this weird sort of gentle breeze" and goose bumps, he then experienced a "bubbling up sensation" and began sobbing for no apparent reason. "And then this little chorus on the side of the stage starts to sing 'You Are the Wind beneath My Wings.' And they're all dressed in white . . . and it was so tacky that I burst into laughter. And I laughed long and hard, and finally it all subsided." Later, Sister Unity told me, he came to see "that this had been my *shaktipat* moment. *Shaktipat*, the descent of grace, when *kundalini* awakens." After the talk, Bennett waited in line for the *darshan*, in this tradition meaning a brief one-on-one encounter with the guru. She brushed his face with a bundle of peacock feathers, and he was again transported by her presence. "It was an extraordinary experience," Sister Unity told me, "and it gave me the key in the ignition of, there's something else going on." Roughly eight months later, Bennett left Los Angeles to spend six months in an ashram in India; the following summer would find him in a U.S. ashram run by the same religious movement.

Settling back into Los Angeles after his sojourns, Bennett found himself struggling with anxiety as he worked to find a job. He added psychotherapy to his meditation practice, and a few years later he became involved in a "gay men's performance art workshop" led by director Tim Miller, in which several of the participants were Radical Faeries. "And so I started going to Faerie Gatherings. And I was just like, 'Yes, yes, yes, been looking for you for years, been doing this for years, yes, yes, yes.'" Close on the heels of these experiences came Bennett's involvement in the Fabulous Monsters, which he describes as "a gay, Radical Faerie–themed theater company." Several of the men who would become founding members of the Los Angeles house of the Sisters saw him perform with this company, and after getting to know him through a charity drag show, they asked him to join them in starting the house. For Sister Unity, then, there is a complex but solid connection from secular humanism and empiricism, to comparative religion and a kind of empirically based mysticism, to deep involvement in a Hindu-based meditation movement, to the Radical Faeries, to theater, to the Sisters—and all of these facets are often apparent in her ministry.[16] Although Sister Unity's story is particularly complex, a number of other members of the order found their way as adults from an irreligious or actively atheist upbringing to a chosen set of practices and beliefs that aligned with their own sense of self and understanding of the world, and with their ministry within the order.

Current Religious Perspectives and Practices

As the preceding section indicates, the Sisters and Guards whom I interviewed have a much wider range of approaches to religion today than they did as children and youth. Of the eighty-seven interviewees who spoke with me about their current religious identities, practices, and beliefs, thirty-eight, or 44 percent, gave answers that fell within the realm of spiritual only or spiritual but not religious. Another ten, or 11 percent, were neopagan, and the same number said they had no religion and/or were atheists. Eight, or 9 percent, still identify as Christian, many in different denominations from those of their childhood, and six, or 7 percent, drew from a number of different religions to create their own beliefs and practices. Other answers to this question, each of which had between one and three proponents, included agnostic, Buddhist, the Sisters as religion, belief in a higher being, belief in humanity and the Golden Rule, both spiritual and religious, Taoist, Hindu, the Center for Spiritual Living, "confused," and "prophet."[17] Five of the interview participants also hold formal religious ordination, including two ministers in the United Church of Christ (Sister Ophelia Nutz and Sister Krissy Fiction), a priest in the Independent Catholic Church (Sister Honey, BE!), a Zen Buddhist priest (Sister MaryMae Himm), and a Wiccan priest in the Feri tradition (Sister Kali Vagilistic X.P. Aladocious). One other interviewee, Sister Merry Peter, has a master of divinity degree, and one, Novice Sister Petunia Encarnata, was studying for the Anglican lay ministry at the time of our interview.

Many Guards and Sisters explained their definitions of religion and spirituality to me, often at my request. Regardless of the value they placed on each concept, most participants understood religion to be institutional, organized, and structured, whereas they considered spirituality to be individual, experiential, and spontaneous. The small number who saw religion in a positive light usually thought of it as a framework for spirituality, providing not only specific beliefs and practices through which that spirituality might be structured and experienced but also spaces, resources, and communities for spiritual development. By contrast, those who expressed an aversion to religion generally saw a deeply negative side to the structure, including authoritarianism, institutional corruption, careless or sinister wielding of power, and neglect of individual rights, freedoms, or even "true" spiritual development. For the many participants who held a positive view of spirituality, that term carried connotations of personal growth, intimate connection with the sacred, and ethical action. To those few who decried spirituality along with religion, on the other hand, the former term implied self-absorption, egotism, a separation from community, credulousness, and irrationality. Predictably, Sisters' and Guards' understandings of these two terms were closely connected to the language they used to describe themselves.

NEITHER SPIRITUAL NOR RELIGIOUS

Among those I interviewed who consider themselves neither spiritual nor religious, quite a few mentioned a belief in something, or a desire to believe. None of these participants identified this often vague belief with religion, a term they generally associated with negative connotations, nor would they consider it a form of spirituality—a word that was also negative to some, and to others simply indicated a deeper and more thorough involvement than they had with such issues. As Sister Polly Amorous, a self-declared atheist, told me, "There's a higher power, maybe. . . . Do I believe that there is somebody out there maybe listening? Probably. But it's not something that is in my life."[18]

Other Sisters stressed the wonder and the sense of the miraculous they found in the natural world, pitting scientific "facts" against religious "beliefs" and finding the former more credible as well as more inspiring. Sister Prudence Improper paired this perspective with a sense of awe and mystery with regard to natural processes:

> I watch a lot of science programs, and I hear about all of the really wonderful and miraculous stuff that's out there in the universe, and I'm just in such awe of the beauty that is in the universe. That's enough to sustain me. I don't need any labels, I don't need "God," in quotes. I don't need anyone to tell me how to live, or why I should do this or not do that. I don't need any of that, because I am made of stardust. Everyone is made of stardust. . . . It's all from the same place, so there's nothing to connect to. Because we're all already completely connected in every way.[19]

Drawing on the language of values, as well as that of miracles, many of those who rejected religion and spirituality explained to me that they find in nature and science precisely the characteristics that others attribute solely to the realm of the spirit.

QUEERING TRADITIONAL RELIGIONS

Whether the term "queering" is taken to mean a kind of "add queers and stir" approach—simply a demographic alteration—or a deeper change based on the ways some queer communities challenge and rework traditional approaches to religion, spirituality, ethics, and ritual, it can be argued that there is a small subset of Sisters who queer traditional religions. Because of the vast predominance of Christianity in the religious backgrounds of those whom I interviewed, it is Christianity in this case that is being queered. Mother Inferior, one of the founders of the Sydney house, offers an excellent example. Early on in our interview, he was discussing his fondness for clothes and his sense that his own story could be told, in part, through the clothes he has worn at different times in his life. A lifelong Christian, first Roman Catholic and now Anglican, Mother Inferior turned eventually to talking about clothes in a church context and told me of going to church in drag with several of his friends. "[On] New Year's Eve, the Anglicans have what's called the Watchnight Eucharist, which is a Eucharist specifically at midnight of the new year," he explained. "We were all at an Anglican gay party, and I was dressed in my mother's black cocktail frock, and so I just put a mantilla on and I was very pious!" He laughed. There were "about half a dozen people in the congregation, and they all—" He made a noise of distaste.

> And then they said, at the greeting of peace, "Oh, thank you for coming. Lovely that you came." And then the minister . . . he came out at the end [and] he said, . . . "Oh, good! I was wondering, I thought it might have been you. Oh, that's lovely, and you brought them all here," and there're all these men in frocks and hats, and girls in boy clothes.

The Sisters, Mother Inferior thought, have challenged him to examine what he really believes and how the different aspects of his life come together. "And now," he told me, the way I say it, Melissa, is: "Well, I am." If people say, "You can't be an Anglican and a Sister of Perpetual Indulgence!" "Well, I am." . . . "Were you involved with dipping a rubber dildo into . . . amyl nitrite and blessing a congregation with it?" I said, "Probably." "Well, how can you do that?" "Well, I did!" . . . It could be intellectual laziness in saying that, but I don't think so. I just think, "Well, I am. That's the way I am. I'm homosexual and Anglican." "Well, you can't be!" "Well, I'm homosexual and Anglican *and* a gay male nun." "Well, you can't be!" "Well, I *am*! What are you going to do about it? It's up to *you*. You're the one who's trying to define what a legitimate Anglican is."[20]

SPIRITUAL BUT NOT RELIGIOUS

Being "spiritual but not religious" is by far the most common approach to religious belief and practice among those Sisters and Guards whom I interviewed, not just in the United States but in fact everywhere except among those few members of the Australian order with whom I spoke, most of whom identify with Christianity. A handful of the participants who place themselves in the "spiritual but not religious" category adhere primarily or exclusively to a single tradition, including some of those who identify as Christian, and several others are seekers, sorting through the worldviews and practices offered by different religious groups and teachers in the hope of finding something that appeals to, "works for," and "feeds" them spiritually. Most, though, often through this very process of seeking, have hit upon a "bricolage" spirituality, in which one draws the most appealing or effective aspects from several different traditions and combines them to create a tailor-made whole (fig. 5.1).[21]

This bricolage approach has been given several culinary names by scholars and other observers of culture over the years, among them "à la carte" and "buffet."[22] The Sisters have their own ways of understanding their bricolage spirituality, also often through gustatory metaphors. Sister Stella Standing, for instance, calls herself a grazer, Sister Golden Hair Surprise terms her spirituality a fondue, and Sister Nadia Ahnwilda prefers to liken hers to granola.[23] For some people the blending is mostly of beliefs, with little connection to day-to-day practice; others combine both. Sister Golden Hair Surprise, or Goldee, leans mostly toward combining practices. "I do my chants," she explained.

Figure 5.1. The home altar of Mother Katharina Lætitiam Donans, who describes herself as "spiritual, in a broader sense, *and* Christian." Photo by the author.

> I burn my candles, let my blood out every now and then, I cry at the moon, I do my solstice stuff, the equinox stuff. . . . I have my Buddhist moments, I have my Seventh-day Adventist moments, I have my agnostic moments. Oh my god, my atheist moments, you know? Depends on what day it is. You never know with me. And I think that's how it should be. Don't rely on one thing.

Although more spiritual than religious, Sister Goldee, who has a Seventh-day Adventist father, does appreciate the ethical guidelines offered by religious traditions. "Thou shalt not kill" is certainly a guideline she approves of but, she smirked, "I will definitely covet my neighbor's husband."[24]

Some Sisters seek in their bricolage a least common denominator among different religious traditions. For some this is a higher truth, be it a sacred being or force or a belief that humanity and the universe are greater than the sum of their parts; for others (and these are not mutually exclusive categories) the least common denominator is a version of the Golden Rule. Several of those I interviewed who drew on such perspectives have been powerfully influenced by twelve-step movements such as Alcoholics Anonymous and Al-Anon; others came to their views through different routes.

Sisters across the world told me that their spirituality comes down to some version of "do unto others as you would have them do unto you." In Montevideo, Hermana Prudencia answered my question about being religious or spiritual by offering another term instead: *creyente*, or "believing." She explained that she believes in the teachings of many different religions without attending any religious rituals, because "la base de todas las religiones es el amor en sí y el amor al prójimo" (the foundation of all religions is love in itself and love for one's neighbor).[25] "In the end," noted Sister Urania, seemingly echoing Hermana Prudencia, religion "comes [down] to worldwide ideas of how human beings should behave and should interact with each other. What to do, what not [to do]. What crimes not to commit. What good to do. It doesn't matter which religion it is."[26] And Mother Belleza, one of the founders of the Zurich house, remarked that "what you do to people or do with people, you can get back. Or you could give back. Or they could give back to you. If I treat them [as] somebody, then I expect that they will treat me [that way] too."[27] Other Sisters shared a similar sense of a religious or spiritual bottom line, particularly in the Pacific Northwest, which is widely known as a stronghold of the "spiritual but not religious" perspective.[28]

SPIRITUAL AND RELIGIOUS

Those few among the people I interviewed who consider themselves both spiritual and religious certainly could cite examples of spirituality and religion taking forms that resonated with the negative connotations described earlier. All of them, though, subscribed to positive interpretations of both words, and they understood their own spirituality and religion as resonating with those positive aspects. Sister Krissy Fiction, an ex-ex-gay man ordained in the United Church of Christ who was pursuing an interfaith master's degree in applied theology at the time of our interview, is a clear example of this pattern.

Kurt, who eventually became Sister Krissy, was raised with little exposure to religion by a lesbian mother who came out to him when he was fourteen. Shortly after he had come out as gay himself, attending religious services with a college friend whose father was a minister in the strictly conservative Wisconsin Synod Lutheran Church led him to conclude that homosexuality was sinful. He joined the now-defunct ex-gay organization Exodus International, and pursued a call to ministry by becoming a youth minister with the Wisconsin Synod Lutherans. He was eventually forced out of his position because his superiors became aware of his struggles with same-sex desire. In response he decided to begin accepting his sexuality; he moved to Portland, Oregon, to start over. Still quite theologically conservative on issues other than homosexuality at the time of the move, he chose to attend the United Church of Christ because of its welcoming stance toward LGBTQ people but also made certain that his church did not have a female pastor. "I just remember sitting back there and crying in the back pew," Sister Krissy told me of that initial church service in the Portland area. But remaining in Christianity was just too painful at first. He explored Wicca, became involved in a Unitarian Universalist congregation, and developed an interest in Gnostic Christianity that led him back to the UCC, where he returned to his work as a youth minister in a denomination that accepted him as an out gay man. Through all of this exploration, he has come to see religion as being "like language . . . it gives us a vocabulary to speak about something which we ultimately can't describe." If religion is like language, Sister Krissy is a polyglot.

When I asked her whether she considered herself religious, spiritual, both, or neither, Sister Krissy had a ready answer. "Yes. Both," she responded. Then I asked how she would describe her religion and her spirituality, and whether the two descriptions were different. "I've struggled quite a bit with the whole labeling thing and how to describe [myself]," she explained.

> I joke and I say I'm a spiritual slut. It's pretty accurate. . . . Nowadays, . . . depending on who I'm talking to, I'll say I'm a Christian, sometimes I'll say I'm a Gnostic Christian. . . . I'm still a member of the United Church of Christ. And I am fine with that, I love it. I usually attend a Gnostic church. It's part of the Ecclesia Gnostica, which is classical Gnosticism. I also take part in the Antinous stuff, which is more pagan reconstructionist. . . . I haven't been real active, but I am technically

kind of part of a coven; I was initiated in the first degree [within the] Alexandrian [tradition]. But I don't carry the Wiccan label too much, although I carry a lot of the nature-based, earth-based stuff with me.

Returning to her language metaphor, Sister Krissy added, "so I say I'm fluent in Christianity and fluent in neopaganism, [and] I can kind of ask where the bathroom is in Buddhism."

With years of Christian theological training, experience and initiation in pagan and gnostic traditions, and graduate work in comparative theology under her belt, Sister Krissy had access to a rich vocabulary to describe her theological perspectives. "Sometimes I feel like I'm an atheist almost," she ventured,

and on the other end of the spectrum I believe in everything. But I'm kind of a monotheist too. I'm a nondualist. So it's really complicated for me sometimes. A lot of times I say my theology is really like Jewish mysticism, Kabbalah, Gnosticism, like those kind of esoteric—that describes my theology really well. I'm a panentheist. My mythology is really tied in with Christianity, the whole dying, resurrecting God-man, . . . Antinous is kind of the dying resurrecting God-man also. And then my practice is very earthy, nature-based, ceremonial magic to some degree.

"I don't know if any of this is making sense," she concluded. "Yeah, it does," I replied. "Absolutely. . . . You don't have the two-word explanation." "Yeah," she agreed. "I mean, ultimately I do—I'm a panentheist—but most people don't know what that means."

Complicating matters even further is the fact that in 2009 Sister Krissy had begun to develop her own religious path as a Sister, which was intimately connected to but different from Kurt's. Several months before our interview, Sister Krissy had attended—in face, as the Sister—the Spring Mysteries, a reenactment of the ancient Greek Eleusinian Mysteries hosted by a pagan reconstructionist temple in Seattle. During the event, she told me, "I went to Aphrodite's temple and dedicated to Aphrodite." Reflecting on this turn of events, she explained that "a lot of what I do as Krissy, I feel, is Aphrodite's work. . . . Aphrodite has different levels. She has the sexual base level, but there's also that higher level, too, of Aphrodite, where the universal love is there. So I feel like she really encapsulates a lot of what it means to be a Sister."[29] In the ensuing years since that interview, Kurt has become involved in a shamanic movement known (somewhat ironically) as the Unnamed Path and has continued to be interested in the contemporary reverence of Antinous, the deified lover of the Roman emperor Hadrian. In 2015 Sister Krissy was elected to be one of three Magistrates of the Ekklesia Antinoou, an organization that maintains contemporary Antinouan worship.[30] But while Sister Krissy is unique to my knowledge in having her own religious practice, separate from although interwoven with Kurt's, she is far from being the only one among the Sisters and Guards to see her spirituality as deeply intertwined with her work in the order.

Spiritual Nuns: Spirituality in the Sisters

Although they function in many ways like one, the Sisters are not a self-identified religion; this may have been part of Sister Cuminja's point in calling them "secular nuns." The order has no religious affiliation, and it neither offers nor requires any specific religious belief; in the words of many Sisters who adhere to the negative definition of religion, the order has no dogma.[31] On the other hand, as Sister Soami reflected, "when you put on the habits of nuns, you're entering into the territory of spirit and spirituality. So Sisters, by taking on the habit, have to deal with what that means." A significant part of the meaning, for him, is "the empowerment [the founders] took on with taking on the habits of old dead nuns," which leads to "letting really deep traditions, that go prior to Catholicism, manifest in the world and come forward."[32] So while the Sisters, not being a religion or even necessarily an officially designated religious or spiritual space, fully embrace their members who are neither religious nor spiritual and who do not consider their work with the Sisters to have anything to do with spirituality, others see their work with the order as profoundly spiritual. The order, for them, can be an expression or application of their spirituality, a source of spiritual enrichment, a spirituality or even a religion in itself, and a ritual space. Understanding these connections—and the lack thereof for other Sisters and Guards—can further clarify the workings of serious parody as the Sisters enact it.

The Sisters as Spiritual Expression or Application

For Sister Trystina T. Rhume and Sister Kali Vagilistic X.P. Aladocious, as for many others with whom I spoke, being a Sister is connected to spirituality in deep and meaningful ways. "I honestly feel that I was born to be a Sister," affirmed Sister Kali, adding that the role is an "expression of the Goddess within me. . . . I felt that it was a natural expression of what's inside of me, in a lot of ways a destiny." As discussed above, Sister Trystina "also had that calling," expressed in language that reflected her religious heritage.[33] Other members of the order with widely differing religious perspectives nonetheless share with these two Sisters and with each other the sense that their spirituality contributes to and even fundamentally shapes their ministry.

The language in which Christian Sisters speak of their work with the order is striking. Abbey of St. Joan founder Sister Maria Caffeina Mochalatte left Christianity in her youth, but eventually returned to Roman Catholicism to focus on what she called "the red letters of the Bible": the words of Jesus. While she has many differences of opinion with official Church doctrine, Sister Maria remains a Catholic, albeit in her own words a "heretical" one, in part because of those red letters. As one might predict, then, it is also the words of Jesus that partly inspire her ministry as a Sister. In talking with me about her work on sexual health, for instance, Sister Maria explained,

I'm trying to move the whole conversation away from clean, dirty, et cetera. . . . I look at the example of Jesus, I see that work of accepting people where they are, no matter what. Instead of jumping on the woman caught in adultery, saying, "Well, go and do better. Go do better next time." . . . We're trying to do the same thing. "Here's a condom. Go do better next time. We're here for you."

The story of the adulterous woman was not the only part of Jesus's ministry that served as a model for Sister Maria. Her ministry as a Sister, she told me,

seems so consonant with . . . this person whose highly mythologized persona I emulate. I look at him, and he's not judging. . . . And the whole concept of *all* children of God, whether God exists or not, . . . that we all contain holiness. . . . And not being unkind, and not bringing down shame on people. . . . If Jesus as this person, as this individual existed, and if all of these things are in fact true, I don't think that Jesus would be into that at all. He wouldn't be into people being shamed for who they are, shamed for who they love.

Sister Maria concluded her explanation of the connections between her Catholicism and the Sisters by reflecting, "I almost feel guilty because it's so *easy*."[34]

Some Sisters not only see their work as an expression of their spirituality, but they also say they apply their spirituality within their ministry. Novice Sister Spinna DeVinyl, for instance, told me that she had "never really thought about what the connection would be" between her spirituality and the Sisters. "I mean," she added, "I do interject my spirituality into it, but that comes with stepping forward." As she thought more about my question, Novice Sister Spinna, who is a professional D.J., explained that she is also a Reiki master. "I do healing work as I'm DJing," she reflected,

but I use that same Reiki healing as a Sister. I step forward, putting out love and whatever healing needs to happen, and some people will immediately trigger me to do whatever type of healing, whether they know it or not. I just step forward in that. So that way when you're in the presence of a healer, whether you're conscious of it or not, it takes effect, and so, it just makes people feel a lot better.[35]

Others cited aspects of their spirituality such as strength, grounding, and wise teachings that they remember having an important impact at key moments.

For several Sisters, there is no clear line at all between spirituality and their work with the order. Although she explained that most French Sisters do not see spirituality in their ministry, and although she formally separated herself as an adult from the Roman Catholic Church in which she was baptized, nevertheless, Sœur Néfertata told me, "I think . . . one of the reasons I became a Sister [was that it] was a way to be both gay and spiritual."[36] "I promise my spirituality to my Sister work," said Sœur Rose from the other Paris house, the Paname Couvent des Sœurs.[37] And Sister Σplace. made no bones about the issue: "When I do hospice, when I do health, when I do clinical things, when I go to hospitals, when I march down the street carrying a sign, when I block traffic, when I get arrested, it's the spirit that's driving me."[38] The Sisters, then, can be not only an expression or an application of one's spirituality, but also a source of spiritual development.

The Sisters as Spiritual Enrichment

The Sisters and Guards I interviewed who found their involvement with the order to be spiritually enriching felt variously that the Sisters deepened or reinforced their existing spirituality, that the order supported positive values, that it advanced their spiritual development, that it gave them what traditional religion could not or even helped them to heal spiritually from the damage caused by homophobia in traditional religion, and that it was a source of spiritual experience in itself.

When I asked Sydney's Sister Mary Arse Licked and Old Lace whether he considers himself a nun, he explained his affirmative answer by saying that the order "gave me a vehicle, I think, to be able to be caring and kind whether I was in habit or out of habit." He added, "I try to . . . become more Christian. . . . Which is interesting, 'cause I never thought, and never in my wildest dreams would think, that that was going to be an end result of it all."[39] By contrast, the Sisters became central to Sister Babylon Anon's spirituality long before she even joined the order. Raised in San Jose, just an hour south of San Francisco, he came to the Castro on weekends as a teenager in the 1980s and moved there as soon as he could get out of his parents' house. The Sisters watched over him and his friends as they all rode out the devastating waves of AIDS deaths and coped as best they could. Sister Babylon recalls that "early on, if I had any kind of official sponsor [in the order] it would have been Sister Loganberry Frost." She continued, "She was very dear to me. She taught me about TM meditation, centering yourself, trying to turn your positive side out. And really made me look deeply at my spirituality, which I had rejected up until then. Because as a young man, spirituality and religion were the same thing. . . . So I rejected it, and she opened my eyes to that."

Today a member of The Abbey of St. Joan, Sister Babylon finds that she gains spiritually from her fellow Sisters in Seattle as well. Her involvement in the house "keeps me centered," she explained. "And there's so many Sisters whose presence just centers me and fills me with such a feeling of peace and grace that I could just let out any of that darkness and just shine. And when they're not around I miss them." Earlier in our conversation, Sister Babylon indicated that the order was also more than a source of spiritual insight for her. "For somebody like me who's against organized religion," she explained, "this is as close as you could get without the dogma. It's like trying to take all the dogma out of it, and all the rules, and all the judgment, and just spread the universal message of love that permeates all religions."[40] For some people, then, although the Sisters have no religious affiliation and are not a religious order, they are indeed a spirituality and even, in some cases, a religion.

The Sisters as Spirituality and as Religion

Sister Babylon's fellow member of The Abbey of St. Joan, Sister Stella Standing, shares her attitudes toward religion, spirituality, and the Sisters. "I have such an aversion to religion," she told me. "Now, personally, I don't care what anybody does or whatever they enjoy. Whatever brings them happiness. But my whole thing is, don't push your shit on me. You know, whatever your security blanket is, I don't need to cuddle with it. It's got your slobber on it, it's yours." Spirituality is a much more positive term for her; she practices bricolage, and her spirituality is deeply tied up with the order. "As you put that donut on," she told me, referring to the Abbey's circular coronet, "you feel the world. It almost feels like a giant satellite dish, and I felt like I became connected with the world around me and the community, and I just felt really tapped in to feeling energies more . . . As some might say, it opened up my chakras and just really allowed me to feel." When I asked specifically about connections between her spirituality and her work with the order, Sister Stella replied, "Oh, god. It's been the most spiritual experience of my life. I mean, it feeds my soul more than anything anybody could ever do." As she reflected further, she added, "You know, it's funny. It's coming to me now, with these questions and everything, I guess my religion would have to be the Sisters. . . . The closest thing to my religion is being a Sister."[41]

Despite the objections to religion that she expressed earlier in the interview, in this passage Sister Stella appears to shift from a negative definition of religion as irrational and controlling to a positive one of religion as an organized space in which to experience spirituality. Other Sisters who understood the order as a spirituality or a religion also associated it with positive concepts within their own religious or spiritual experiences. Sister Σplace. and Sister Mary Media, for instance, both Buddhist practitioners, called the order a *sangha*—a Buddhist community. Noting that the "*sangha* in Buddhism is one of the three refuges," Sister Σplace. described what it meant to take refuge in the Sisters as a *sangha*: "stepping behind [the order], in the belief that if I succumb and if I step out into these things, it's going to sustain me in my practice."[42]

Perhaps unsurprisingly, given the Sisters' emulation of Roman Catholic nuns, a number of members of the order described the Sisters as spiritual ministrants; in fact, at least ten of the ninety-one people with whom I conducted formal interviews thought of the Sisters in this way, and many more casually used the term "ministry" in conversations with me during my fieldwork. For Sister Merry Peter, this ministry was a response to a calling that initially manifested, much to his teachers' surprise, in childhood. "There was a multiple choice career preference test that school counselors were good at giving you," she explained. I nodded and interjected with a wry grin, "I was supposed to be a landscape architect." Sister Merry Peter bested me. "I was supposed to be a nun!" We laughed hard for a moment, and then Sister Merry Peter continued. "I got called up to Sister Clarence's office after the test results came back," she recounted. Sister Clarence demanded, "'Mister . . . , what have you done to screw with the test?' . . . They reread everything, and I had filled out male and done all the right questions, but my number one career preference came back as nun. So I think it's been working itself out for a while."

Years later, he would find himself a graduate student in a Jesuit school in Toronto, trying to hold together his activist and religious commitments. "My university president, a Jesuit priest [and] very good friend, knew I was struggling," Sister Merry Peter recalled.

I was putting on these great AIDS mass spectacles and protesting the lack of women's ordination every time he turned around, and he could see this was not an easy fit. At one point he sat me down and said, "You know, I marvel at you. Because the gift is so apparent." He said, "But what I keep asking myself is, when I look at you, I see a preacher without a church. And I see a doctor without a hospital. And I see a teacher without a school. Why are you fighting so hard to get back in the building? Why don't you just embrace who you are and stand on the street corner, because that's where everybody who needs to be reached is living?" . . . That was *really* just a *gift*, a free gift! I left school, I left the Church.

He soon hit the streets, as his Jesuit friend had advised him to do, in a form the college president might not have expected: as Sister Merry Peter, missionary to Toronto. As we wrapped up the interview, Sister Merry Peter reflected laughingly on some of the opportunities for ministry that the Sisters had opened to her. "Can you imagine a Jesuit priest throwing glitter from the altar?" she asked. "Well, I *can*, but that's why I would get in trouble. That's why they don't invite me for dinner." The Sisters offer her not only a plethora of opportunities for glittery ministration, but also the freedom to follow her own activist path and still get invited to dinner, glitter and all.[43]

Ritual in the Sisters

Religious or not, spiritual or not, many Sisters are familiar with the use of ritual in their own or others' houses. Ritual is sometimes a public part of the Sisters' activism; at other times it is conducted privately and focused on the members of the house themselves. Private ritual can take a form as intimate a lighting a candle for other Sisters, locally or around the world. For many Sisters, the process of manifesting is also a private ritual, conducted by oneself in meditation and prayer or with other members of the house, bringing the house itself into being as a sacred presence in advance of their ministry for that day.

Bridging public and private ritual are the vows that Sisters and Guards take, particularly vows of full profession. Not all members of the order consider their vows to be spiritual, or even to be a ritual at all, but many speak of them as deeply moving. Because houses differ so widely in how they carry out vows of full profession, Sisters' and Guards' experiences with them also vary. The setting of one's vows can have an impact as well;

Sister Maya Poonani, for example, was stunned to be called up to take her vows during a group photo shoot on the steps of Mission Dolores in San Francisco during the thirtieth anniversary celebration of the order, with more than fifty other members of the order looking on. "It was Sister Jezabelle from San Francisco that was next to me, holding the bullhorn mike," she recalled, "and I just kept looking at her like, 'What? Can you repeat what's being said to me?' 'Cause I'm just having an out-of-body experience at that point. It was amazing. And tears . . . oh my god, unbelievable."[44]

Sister rituals that not only take place in public but also are directed at the community range from blessings to protests to memorials. Two forms that are particularly well-known in the order are the "darshans" of the San Francisco house and the Veil of Shame, a darshan developed by a San Francisco Sister that has since been adopted by other houses. "Several years ago," Sister Constance Lee Craving explained to me in 2012,

> Sister Merry Peter started talking to us about the term *darshan*, which is a Sanskrit word [that] loosely translates to having sight. So we've taken that term and we've made it into an actual ritual that can cover almost anything, but it's a way to have sight to within ourselves, or encouraging others to see each other as they are. We've done many darshans. Some of them have been around understanding the origin of HIV. . . . I think one of them was the Twenty-Fifth Anniversary of the First Reported AIDS Cases Darshan.[45]

Because combatting shame is an important function of both the Sisters as a whole and San Francisco's darshans in particular, it is not surprising that the ritual known as the Veil of Shame has its roots in a darshan, at least according to Sister Constance. As she explained to me,

> One of the things that I had done in the past was I created this darshan where I had cotton t-shirts, and either our volunteers would wear the cotton t-shirts, or Sisters can wear them as veils, and I had magic markers, handed them out to people on the streets, and just said, "Please, anything you've ever had told to you that has just made you feel less than human, any hurtful thing, anything that's ever made you feel really terrible, write

that on the t-shirt, leave it with us, we'll take care of it and get rid of it for you." . . . We ended up burning the t-shirts in a ritual.

Recognizing in her description a ritual I had seen the Portland Sisters do during their bar ministry on World AIDS Day (figs. 5.2, 5.3), I asked, "So this is the origin of the Veil of Shame that other houses do, then?" "I don't know!" said Sister Constance, surprised. "They have a Veil of

Figure 5.2. Sister Maya Poonani of the Order of Benevolent Bliss in Portland, Oregon, wearing the Veil of Shame during bar ministry on World AIDS Day, December 1, 2009. Photo by the author.

Figure 5.3. Sister Polly Amorous sets the Veil of Shame ablaze while Postulant Helen Baak looks on. Order of Benevolent Bliss, Portland, Oregon, December 1, 2009. Photo by the author.

Shame?" I explained to her the ritual in which I had taken part with the Portland house, and told her that I had heard that The Abbey of St. Joan in Seattle also did something similar; the likely connection between the two, I thought, was that the Abbey had been the mentor house for the Order of Benevolent Bliss. Sister Constance filled in the rest of my guesswork with some of her own. "Sister Glo stole that from me!" she exclaimed with a smile, referencing Sister Glo Euro N'Wei, who works professionally in HIV care and prevention just as Sister Constance does.

"My first time I did it, I did it in Philadelphia and Sister Glo was there. Wow! I had no idea! I've birthed something. That's really cool!"[46]

From their earliest years, the Sisters have had to face death in the order. While HIV-related deaths have dropped precipitously in communities whose members can afford the newest and best medications, gay men—like all queer and trans people—still die from violence, from the various side effects of rampant cultural homophobia, biphobia, and transphobia, from the effects of other forms of systemic oppression that intersect with these social ills, such as racism, misogyny and transmisogyny, and poverty, and from diseases that strike without regard to social location. Echoing the power of ACT UP's political funerals,[47] the Sisters sometimes have blended memorials with social justice advocacy; one recent memorial illustrates this long-standing practice.

I interviewed Sœur Rose just two months after her best friend died of AIDS, and during the course of our conversation she told me about carrying out his last wishes. "He wanted two things for his funerals," she told me. "He wanted a political funeral made by ACT UP, and he wanted just a funeral led by the Sisters." The Sister funeral, over which Sœur Rose presided, was a clear enactment of the order's religious serious parody; it was modeled on a communion service. Her friend, she said, ate a great deal of yogurt, "so we were like, 'Drink this, this is my—well, you know,'" she ended suggestively. Envisioning the color and texture of yogurt, I surmised that this was a semen reference. And, Sœur Rose continued,

> as he was a huge drug user, I light five joints at the same time, and really strong ones, and we were like, "Smoke this, this is my hair." That was fucking hilarious! . . . And at the same time that was so amazing because, you know, that could be just smoking joints and giving joints to people, but no, for the people [who] were here, that was really important and they were not smoking joints; they were smoking his hair.[48]

Clearly, the Sisters' relationship to religion and spirituality is far from simple. In fact, it may be their serious parody that enables this complexity. While the Sisters often enact seriousness and parody simultaneously, as with the communion-service-meets-AIDS-funeral that Sœur Rose led, at different moments one or the other may come to the fore. Within any given house there are likely to be Sisters who lean toward the serious side of this twinned approach and those who lean toward the parodic, as well as those who move between the two depending on occasion, mood, or moment. Likewise, there are those who lean toward the serious approach to religion, those whose preferences lie with parody, and those who mobilize the two in complementary ways. Both seem always to be in evidence, though, and the flexibility introduced by their combination appears to be a key factor in the ability of the order to include the wide range of opinions about and approaches to religion and spirituality that has been the focus of this chapter. Such flexibility does not answer the question of whether the Sisters are secular nuns, though, or even what exactly a secular nun might be. For that inquiry, it may be useful to return to scholarly conversations about contemporary religion.

Secular Nuns or None Nuns? The Sisters and Contemporary Religion

Meredith McGuire has pointed out that individualized religious practices and beliefs are not unique to either Western cultures or the contemporary period; they did not suddenly arise in the 1960s in order to flaunt millennia of consistent communalism and tradition.[49] Nor is religious bricolage anything new; the histories of many different cultures indicate that people have been creatively combining religions for millennia. But it may be the context of globalization, in its particular contemporary form, that gives Heelas and Woodhead's "subjective-life spirituality" its unique qualities, and the language that many scholars and practitioners use to describe contemporary understandings of spirituality highlights this connection. At the heart of subjective-life spirituality is the importance of choice, be it the ability to choose which aspects of a single religious tradition to accept and which to reject or the ability to select from specific aspects of a wide variety of traditions to create one's own personal religion. The focus on individual *choice* rather than individual practice or belief per se (for, as Heelas and Woodhead point out, subjective-life spirituality can be practiced in both solitary and communal ways)[50] may be precisely what distinguishes subjective-life spirituality from the historical forms of spirituality and religious individualism noted by McGuire and others. This connection to the contemporary era is also evidenced by the wide range of economic metaphors used by scholars and other commentators to describe its practice. Wade Clark Roof titled a book on this phenomenon *Spiritual Marketplace*; others have used terms such as "pick 'n' mix," connoting a store display from which shoppers can select a mélange of items for a single flat price, "buffet" or "smorgasbord," connoting a restaurant service with the same properties, and "à la carte," connoting a set of independent options with separate prices from which one may choose any or all, be they foods or airline services.[51] All of these metaphors of free choice are driven by a capitalist model wherein consumers attain "freedom" through the functions of the market. The language, in other words, is that of neoliberalism.[52]

In 2005 Jeremy Carrette and Richard King made the link between neoliberalism and spirituality glaringly explicit. Writing of a "corporate takeover of religion" that has stripped religion of its potential for social critique and has made it instead both a commodity and a tool for corporate management, Carrette and King depict spirituality as a neoliberal opiate of the masses. "Alongside TVs, hi-fi systems, washing machines, IKEA furniture and designer clothes," they write, "you can also have your very own spirituality, with or without crystals! . . . You can now buy it wholesale and ignore the corporate links to poverty and injustice."[53] While the argument for a link between contemporary spirituality and neoliberalism is clear and defensible, the tone of Carrette and King's argument is at times reminiscent of the subtle and occasionally blatant scorn and panic that circulated around the story of the pseudonymous Sheila Larson, the original religious individualist extraordinaire, after the publication of *Habits of the Heart* in the mid-1980s.[54] Indeed, François Gauthier, Tuomas Martikainen, and Linda Woodhead insightfully comment that "not only nostalgia for past forms of real or imagined community, but perhaps for more traditional gender relations, is very near the surface in such laments [as Carrette and King's], since consumerism, 'shopping,' and 'shallow' spirituality tend to be coded as feminine, whilst production and the 'solid' values of more rational forms of historic religion tend to be coded as masculine."[55] Nonetheless, these authors argue, the ties between neoliberalism and contemporary forms of religion are real, complex, and deserving of greater study. "What [our] approach stresses," they explain, "is how the present situation in societies across the world and how the development of transnational and global realities have been shaped through the growing impact of economic factors on social life, above all through the coupling of intensified consumerism as a dominant cultural ethos . . . with neoliberalism as a cultural and political ideology."[56] One of the key tools of neoliberalism, in the economic sphere but also, as a growing number of social theorists argue, in the political sphere, is privatization.

The neoliberal doctrine of privatization refers most directly to the relocation of public goods and service provision from the hands of the state to private, usually corporate, control. But queer theorists since the late 1990s have been documenting the leaching of this more strictly economic application of privatization into a broader political sphere. Although they do not specifically reference neoliberalism, for instance, Lauren Berlant and Michael Warner clearly indict consumer and corporate capitalism in their landmark, scathing analysis of the privatization of queer sex.[57] A few years later, Lisa Duggan placed neoliberalism at the center of her argument that a new gay and lesbian politics, which she termed "homonormativity," had emerged in the United States. Basing its argument for rights on imputed economic power—the so-called gay dollar—and a promise to keep things in the bedroom, Duggan argues, the "new homonormativity" has developed from and enthusiastically embraced the political ramifications of neoliberalism and the attendant cultural and economic privatization.[58] Building on both of these works, in the aftermath of the September 11 attacks Jasbir Puar began pointing to a convergence of homonormativity and nationalism, a phenomenon that she terms homonationalism, in which the privatization of sex is an option only for certain queer populations, meaning both that for some it is not optional and that for some it is not attainable. While race, nationality, and class constitute important factors in Puar's analysis, so does religion since, she argues, Sikhs and Muslims in the United States, especially those who are queer, were placed after September 11, 2001, in the position of either being forced to adopt nationalism and homonationalism or being prevented from adopting either.[59]

If homonormativity and homonationalism entail a promise to "keep it in the bedroom," a privatization of queer sex in the broad sense of non- or anti-normative sex, homonationalism adds in the privatization of religion. As with the privatization of sex, though, in Puar's formulation the privatization of religion entails keeping only nondominant religions behind closed doors. Christianity, particularly its Protestant form, whose cultural footprints are evident throughout mainstream U.S. culture, has not suffered the same sentence. In fact, scholars of queer studies in religion wrote about this connection even earlier than did Puar. In their landmark study of the rhetoric of religious tolerance in the United States, Janet Jakobsen and Ann Pellegrini point out that "the predominant understanding of religious freedom in the United States depends on the privatization of religion." Importantly, they add, "religious *difference* is acceptable—is tolerated—if it is contained in the private sphere."[60] Puar's and Jakobsen and Pellegrini's observations, drawn through queer theoretical analysis of neoliberalism, differ significantly from many of the arguments about religious privatization and secularization that pervade the study of religion, and they indicate that there may be an important link between neoliberal politics, the privatization of queer sex, and the privatization of nondominant religions—including the privatization of resistance to and critique of dominant religions. I have argued elsewhere that this double privatization affecting (among others) queer bodies and practices—sexual, religious, and both—can be understood as an enforcement of a neoliberal "separation of church and sex" that explains a great deal of the discomfort and outright opposition generated by the Sisters among social conservatives in LGBTQ as well as straight and cisgender communities.[61]

The understandings and expressions of spirituality and religion that the various Sisters and Guards whom I interviewed described to me both participate in and resist the neoliberalization of religion and sex. The significant number of interviewees who draw on subjective-life spirituality, and especially those members of the order who explained to me that they refuse to talk directly about religion when they are in face, are taking part in the privatization of religion. At the same time, it is critical not to lose sight of the fact that the subjective approaches to religion identified by Heelas and Woodhead, whether practiced individually or communally, have played a central role in creating religious and spiritual spaces for queer people, not just in the West but increasingly around the world. As Martikainen, Gauthier, and Woodhead indicate, there is no one-size-fits-all analysis of neoliberal religion, and I would add that one must be particularly wary of one-dimensional critiques of queer participation in what Carrette and King call "consumerist spirituality" because of the tendency for queer people of all genders to be painted with the same misogynistic brush. If Carrette and King's anxiety over corporate spirituality is tinged with "nostalgia . . . for more traditional gender relations," as Martikainen, Gauthier, and Woodhead so delicately put it, one must question to what extent it is also tinged with nostalgia for more traditional genders and sexualities.

Whether the Sisters take part in the privatization of sex is an intriguing question. At first it is tempting to offer an easy negative. After all, one of the key functions of the order has long been to educate people around safer sex—thus possibly contributing as well to the biopolitical management of queer bodies that Gregory Tomso has argued barebacking cultures may be resisting—and many Sisters and Guards play up the sexual connotations of their names and of the order itself in order to promote the Sisters' mission of promulgating joy and expiating guilt.[62] On closer examination, however, one must also consider the resistance in many houses to sexual activity in habit, and therefore the implied acceptance of the neoliberal separation of religion and sex.

One might even argue that those houses that focus primarily on fundraising and safer-sex promotion are deeply engaged in neoliberal logic, particularly in the United States, where there is almost no social safety net precisely because of the privatization—including outsourcing to socially conservative, homophobic, transphobic, and sexist religious organizations—of government social programs. In helping government workers to provide HIV testing and safer-sex education, in raising money for private support services that receive inadequate funding from the government and that are necessary because those services are not provided by the state, do the Sisters participate in the state surveillance and control of queer bodies? Do they participate in and thereby help to prop up the privatization of social services? That argument certainly could be made. But such an argument would ignore several countervailing points. First, regarding the biopolitical control of queer bodies, it may be worth considering that the Sisters follow a harm reduction model in which they offer to their communities information and tools but do not dictate behavior or condone and condemn certain actions. Having matured as an order during the worst of the AIDS years in white, gay communities, they are understandably passionate about preventing HIV infection, because for at least the first ten years of the order's existence an HIV-positive diagnosis was akin to a death sentence and state disregard of HIV and AIDS in the United States rapidly led to the decimation of gay and other oppressed communities. Likewise, while in the United States the Sisters' grants often support organizations and services that a government with a social safety net would provide by itself, many of the causes for which they provide support also would not be— and are not—supported by more socialist states. Even if they were, such support might be accompanied by such extensive state surveillance that it would be useless to the communities it intended to serve. As activists for many different nondominant communities have discovered over the years, there is a fine and very unclear line between resistance from within a system and complicity with it. Walking that line sometimes entails unwittingly stepping over it; quite a few communities of Sisters have struggled with that balance in the past, and many continue to do so today.

What to make, then, of Sister Cuminja's claim that the Sisters are "secular nuns"? Debates over the privatization of religion have gone hand in hand with the by-now tired argument over modernity and secularization, and attempts to resolve this argument by discussing religion as a whole within a particular society generally miss their mark because such approaches often fail to take into account the fact that the privatization of religion does not apply to the dominant religion. Some sociologists, for example, have argued for decades that Europe is becoming "secular," thereby ignoring the glaring public and often state presence of Christianity. Moreover, in marking Europe, perhaps more prescriptively than descriptively, as secular, the same scholars have marked religious people, many of them from nondominant and minority religions, as non-European. Such misreadings have dire consequences; for instance, they partly undergird much of the Islamophobia that plagues Europe today.

In the United States, which shares with Europe a violent and widespread Islamophobia as well as a resurgent anti-Semitism, misreadings of secularization have had a somewhat different result. For many years, sociologists singled out the United States as the curious exception to the rule that economic modernization leads to secularization, even as they continued to argue over what secularization meant and whether it was even happening at all. Yet conservative Christians in the United States are in general quite certain that secularization has taken place, removing Christianity and God from their proper places as the guiding ethos and sovereign of the country and restricting Christians' religious liberties by forcing them not to discriminate against those they consider heretics and sinners. In a context of rampant global neoliberalism, it is hardly surprising that the most successful claims to the "religious liberty" of discrimination have involved corporations and small businesses, with the most high-profile U.S. case being the 2014 Supreme Court decision in *Burwell v. Hobby Lobby*.[63]

It is often claimed that the late twentieth century saw a "resurgence" of religion that has continued to grow into the twenty-first century. Leaving aside the disturbing images of irresistible and destructive tsunami waves or military invasions that are evoked by the language of resurgence, it may be worth considering that such phenomena exist primarily in the eye of the beholder. In the 1960s, as new religious movements blossomed in unprecedented numbers and a generation of youth "tuned in, turned on, and dropped out" of mainstream society, mainstream observers—among them no small number of sociologists of religion—kept their vision focused firmly on mainstream Protestantism. Wearing those sizeable blinkers, they saw only the death of religion, when in fact it had in many ways simply relocated. When some of the groups to which it had moved, such as the Jesus People, grew into a larger movement and formed both churches and denominations, religion seemed to have "resurged." Perhaps religion is more mobile and agile than we generally think; perhaps, as others have argued, there is no "post-secular" because there was never, in fact, a "secular" in the sense of an "exterior" to religion.[64]

So where does that leave the question of "secular nuns"? If one defines the term "secular" as "not formally affiliated with a religion," then the Sisters are in fact secular. But as the "none nuns" have demonstrated, a lack of affiliation with religion hardly equates to a strictly secular outlook. So maybe they are secular as an order, even if individual members may not be? Such a claim encounters the problem of defining the secular, and by connection the sacred. Although some Sisters would say that the order has nothing to do with religion, spirituality, or the sacred, many others see aspects of the sacred in their work. Maybe the problem lies, then, in the dichotomy itself. Does a sharp line between the sacred and the secular, a line so clearly drawn from Roman Catholic doctrine, make sense in the Sisters? Or is this another opportunity, perhaps one that some have already taken up, for serious parody to queer religion?

The term "secular" is widely used in the order, but "sacred" is not its opposite in such usage except perhaps by implication. In the Sisters, the opposite of "secular" is "Sister" or "Guard." Members of the order in most countries speak of their "Sister name" or "Guard name" and their "secular name"; they contrast or compare their "Sister self" or "Guard self" with their "secular self."[65] Perhaps this implies simply that Sisters and Guards are sacred, but that argument does not explain the situation fully; for most of those with whom I spoke, their secular selves are not actually secular, at least in the sense of being irreligious. Thus, the distinction between "secular" and "Sister" or "Guard," drawn as it is from Roman Catholic language, is itself serious parody. The Sisters, then, are neither secular nor post-secular nuns. As they make clear nearly every time they explain the order, they are *queer* nuns—not just in terms of sexuality and gender, particularly because some are cisgender and heterosexual, but in the deeper, activist sense of queering as troubling, resisting the normative, acting/ACTing UP, religionfuck. As queer nuns, the Sisters both partake in and trouble contemporary, neoliberal patterns of religion, spirituality, and sexuality. They queer the sacred, the secular, and the sometimes-artificial divide that analysts have placed between the two, living out a reality that is far more complex.

Conclusion

New World Order?

"If I can wax sort of traditionally as a missionary," Reverend Sister Merry Peter said enthusiastically, "I think there are new missionary fields. But unlike the missionaries of the Christian church . . . *we're* not going out preaching a gospel. *We're* going out opening up a path." What is the difference, for this Sister, between these two forms of evangelism? "Whatever's inherent is coming out" where the Sisters open a path, she explained. She offered the example of an organization in Colombo, Sri Lanka, that had received funding from the San Francisco house to organize a Pride celebration.

> I'm like, "How do you have Pride in Sri Lanka?" You fly kites on the beach. I would never have thought of that in a million years. We're having this wonderful dialogue. A lot of what's going on in Colombo is about gender variance. . . . There may never be a Sri Lankan Sister, but the Sisters here and the people in Sri Lanka are thinking about things very differently.

In Saint Petersburg, Russia, Sister Merry Peter went on, local activists have connections to the Sisters despite the lack of Russian houses. Consequently, she sometimes learns about developments regarding LGBTQ communities in Russia from the various networks within the order before she learns about them from the media. She also noted that the Sisters had recently been receiving inquiries about the order from countries as widespread as Japan, India, Costa Rica, and Peru.[1] While the Sisters of Perpetual Indulgence have been known internationally since the early 1980s, the worldwide spread of social media and rapidly growing access to such media through smart phones even in fairly remote areas have enabled the Sisters to bypass sensationalist reports on "drag nuns" and to counter the homophobic screeds of scandalized social and religious conservatives with their own interpretations and representations of their ministry.

As extensive scholarship on globalization has made clear, such developments never take place outside the dynamics of political, economic, cultural, and neocolonial power. Founded in one of the wealthiest and most powerful countries on the planet, and with the vast majority of its members in Western European and settler colonial countries, the order is in a position to be caught up or even to actively participate in those dynamics of power. Its history is rooted, in part, in the very forms of feminism and gay politics that today drive global North attempts to control and shape global South political realities and activist goals. Yet the order has also been significantly influenced by the more radical wing of the gay liberation movement, and that movement, at its best moments, has been actively involved in anti-imperialist and antiracist struggles. Joanildo Burity's argument in the context of religion can be applied to serious religious parody as well: "It is only through the actual entanglements and intimations of global/local dynamics that one can properly capture the complex configuration of the relationship of religion and neoliberalism in globalizing times."[2] My concluding reflections on the wider applicability of serious parody as an activist strategy begin, therefore, with an examination of these "entanglements and intimations."

The Sisters and Global Politics

"For the moment," reflected Sister Rowena Keeper of the Holy Doiley,

> one of the pities is, we're probably not as politically sharp as we used to be. There [were] probably more causes . . . in the past . . . to get involved with. But that doesn't mean that they've gone away. I can think of some things that still need to be addressed around the world. And in particular, in some places, gay and lesbian rights are still terribly trammeled upon.

He gave the example of Russia, which was very much in the international public eye at the time of our interview during the lead-up to the Winter Olympic Games in Sochi, and he also mentioned Uganda and Jamaica. At home in Australia, by contrast, he found himself rather disinterested in the main LGBT political issue of the day: same-sex marriage rights. Although he imagined that the order might have a place in that struggle, Sister Rowena explained, "at a personal level . . . I don't have a strong opinion of it. I don't have a strong support for it or against it."[3] For those without a personal stake in the potential rewards offered by the marriage rights movement, the ongoing incarceration, battery, and execution of same-sex–attracted and gender-variant people may make the importance of same-sex marriage pale in comparison.

Shortly after we concluded our conversation, Sister Rowena forwarded to me an email he had sent to a reporter in 2008, on the occasion of Pope Benedict's visit to Sydney for World Youth Day. The Sydney house had joined a coalition called No to Pope, which opposed the visit, and Hugh Armitage of the *Gay Times* had written to request further details about the Sisters' objections. Sister Rowena responded by sending the reporter a copy of the basic information about the house from its website, including the mission statement and the Four Tenets of the Order of Perpetual Indulgence. Below these statements, he elaborated on their application to the policies of the Roman Catholic Church. His nine points addressed the status of same-sex eroticism and same-sex desire in Church doctrine, teachings regarding the safer sex practices that are so central to the work of the order, access to contraception and abortion, and guilt, all with an emphasis on the global influence of the Church. His argument was summed up in the final point: "9. Pope Benedict called abortion, birth control and same-sex marriage an *obstacle to world peace*. There you have it, all the people that don't fit into the Church's narrow view of the world are single handedly responsible for all its woes and troubles. Anyone for a large dollop of Catholic guilt?"[4]

Other long-standing members of the order also noted significant changes in the focus and stakes of activism in their communities. These changes are so highly evident in part because the order has historically served white, cisgender male communities in wealthy, internationally powerful countries, communities that have achieved a relatively high degree of protections and rights and whose attention in recent years has turned largely to issues of assimilation. These shifts in focus have inspired the more radical members of the order to look beyond bar ministry, safer-sex education, and fundraising to other communities in need, be they local—such as queer women's communities, transgender communities, and queer communities of color—or global.

When Is a Habit Like a Burqa?

As with questions of race and gender within the order, engagement in global politics can catch the Sisters up in precisely the sorts of power dynamics suggested above. Three cases from three different continents, all involving the Sisters and conservative Muslim women's attire, illustrate this point.

Case 1: Sister Rowena related that he had of late been approached "a couple of times" by people offended by what they perceived to be the Sisters' mockery of the Roman Catholic Church. " 'I bet you wouldn't be game to do that to the Muslims,' [they say,] as in, dress up in a burqa and pretend that you're a woman, offending the Islamic faith." While Sister Rowena did not say exactly what "the Islamic faith" might have meant to his non-Muslim challengers, who clearly were assuming that both Islam and Christianity are fairly monolithic religions, he did acknowledge that this was "an interesting point" and that his reply "took a little bit of thinking." However, he explained that "the response that I've formulated to this now is that it's not culturally relevant. I come from an Anglo-Saxon, Christian, Judaic background, and this is where my cultural reference lies. If a Muslim person wants to take on their faith, we would welcome that and go on a coalition exercise with them if they wanted." Moreover, he added evidence that such challengers might already exist: the participation of the group Muslims Against Homophobia in the past two Mardi Gras parades in Sydney. "There's actually been . . . clearly what are Middle Eastern men who've dressed up in burqas or similar attire, but very festive and party-like, sequins and brightworks and things like that."[5]

Case 2: According to Brother Bimbo del Doppio Senso, the Convent of Dunn Eideann had faced strikingly similar challenges, but had responded very differently. "We've had death threats from a group claiming to be Roman Catholic," she explained. "But the local cardinal has disowned them completely." As part of the threatening messages, the group told the Sisters, "You wouldn't dare put one of your members in a burqa." "So," Brother Bimbo concluded, "we did." The Edinburgh Sisters have henchpeople rather than Guards, people who lack the time to fully commit to the order but want to help out when they can. One of these henchpeople became what Brother Bimbo called a "crypto-Sister," wearing a burqa and using the name Sister Alice Qaeda.[6]

Case 3: "Toward the end of his life," reads one of the obituaries for Jack Fertig, known at one time as Sister Boom Boom, "he embraced Islam."[7] A few years before his death, after more than two decades of keeping the Sisters mostly at arm's length, Fertig again began attending events with the San Francisco house. This time, Sister Vish told me, she came in a chador, presumably also wearing a niqab, since Sister Vish explained that she had "just a slit" in the garment "so she can see out of it."[8]

In the weeks leading up to the U.S. invasion of Afghanistan in 2001, news media audiences in the United States were regaled with repeated images and stories of Afghan women who had been forced by the Taliban to wear burqas. Many of these media consumers learned the word *burqa* during those weeks, and many quickly came to associate it with all forms of Muslim veiling. As the war dragged on, a regime desperate for images of decisive victory headlined women's participation in Afghan elections, showing image after image of bareheaded women at the ballot box. "Voting = democracy," the images symbolically proclaimed; "bare heads = freedom"; "the United States has liberated the oppressed women of Afghanistan." Framed as they were in the language of women's liberation, these claims appealed to many non-Muslim feminists in the United States and also in the countries that joined in the wars in Afghanistan and eventually in Iraq; such stories have abounded in BBC coverage of the wars, for example. Jasbir Puar remarks that "serious liberal feminists . . . , having already foregrounded Islamic fundamentalism as the single greatest violent threat to women, were perfectly poised to capitalize on the missionary discourses that reverberated after the events of September 11."[9]

The cases involving Sisters and full-body Islamic veiling practices took place in the context of a war in which Australia and the United Kingdom were both involved at the behest of the United States, a war justified as a feminist and democratic (despite being externally imposed) revolution. Perhaps the critics who challenged the Sydney and Edinburgh houses perceived Islam as a far greater threat to queer people than Christianity could ever be; in their offense at what they perceived to be the Sisters' mockery of Roman Catholicism, they might have been accusing the order of missing its mark. Perhaps, too, there is more than implicit Islamophobia in the comments about burqas; perhaps these challengers are among those Christians who believe their own religion to be the last socially condoned target of bias in Western cultures. From such a perspective, they might have been outraged that the Sisters felt free to "mock" Roman Catholicism but not to take equal aim at Islam. In response, and working in quite different local contexts, the Convent of Dunn Eideann elected to demonstrate its willingness to challenge all religious conservatism, while in Sydney Sister Rowena decided that it was most relevant for people from Christian backgrounds to take on Christianity and that the Sisters should make themselves available as allies to queer Muslims who wished to take on Islam in similar ways.

This analysis leaves open the more complex issue of a white, gay convert to Islam and a famous Sister of Perpetual Indulgence donning a chador and a niqab for Sister events. Particularly given the political setting of the United States in the final years of Fertig's life, the racialization that permeates popular images of Islam in many non-Muslim majority countries, and the widespread Islamophobia that permeates non-Muslim LGBTQ communities just as much as it has saturated non-Muslim communities in the United States more broadly, for a white convert to engage in serious parody of Islam runs some of the same risks that Reverend Mother's use of blackface did in the early 1980s. Context is always critical to the effectiveness of performative protest, and in this case the context may not have been conducive to anything more than the promulgation of Islamophobia. A similar conclusion may be warranted in the case of Sister Alice Qaeda, although the appearance of a reveler in a sequined red burqa and rhinestone-studded sunglasses in the Muslims Against Homophobia contingent of Sydney's 2016 Mardi Gras parade raises provocative questions about when, where, and by whom such serious parody of Islam may be appropriate rather than appropriative.[10]

Serious Parody Meets Blasphemy Laws

In the spring of 2016, word went out in Sister networks that a member of the order had manifested in Poland and subsequently had been brought up on blasphemy charges. Sister Unity seems to have broken the story with posts on Facebook and Twitter on April 14; she followed up later that day with the added information that the trial would be in June but that the Sister in question expected the charges to be dropped.

The Sisters have been edging toward Eastern Europe for quite some time; after all, one of the earliest European houses came to maturity in the very recently reunited city of Berlin. The German-speaking order has supported the formation of houses in Switzerland and Austria; more recent German-sponsored missions include one that opened in Odessa, Ukraine, in 2014 and one in Prague, Czech Republic, that started in 2016. There is no house in Poland as of this writing, but there are a small number of individual Sisters living there.

Despite Poland's membership in the European Union since 2004, which should have protected freedom of expression, Polish scholar Iwona Lepka writes that "Article 196 of the Criminal Code provides that anyone found guilty of insulting religious sentiment through public calumny of an object or place of worship is liable to a fine or maximum two-year prison sentence."[11] Importantly, she adds that "despite the principle which proposes that the national institutions should be kept apart from those religious ones, the separation of Church and State has been frequently infringed" by widespread support of Roman Catholicism in government institutions.[12] Thus, there is a strong likelihood that charges arising from Article 196 will focus specifically on the perceived "public calumny" of the Roman Catholic Church, or of Christianity more broadly. Indeed, Poland's first case involving this article was brought in 2004 against an artist who made use of an Orthodox cross in her work; it took five years for her to be acquitted. This case, Lepka argues, along with two others she considers having to do with gay pride parades and open criticism of the pope, "set dangerous precedents."[13] In their aftermath, and also in the context of the country's currently widespread cultural conservatism and organized far right movement, a queer nun was charged with blasphemy.

The Polish blasphemy case raises questions about the role of the Sisters' serious parody in religiously conservative societies, particularly in cases where one religion, especially Christianity, is established either de jure or de facto. This awareness of the impact of Christian religious establishment on the order is shared by Hermana Dolores Raimunda of the Orden de San Felipe y Santiago de Montevideo. He has pondered, he told me, why more houses of the Sisters have not formed in Latin America, eventually reaching the conclusion that "Uruguay tiene características *muy* particulares. Es un estado laico, en el cual la iglesia y el estado están separados. ¿Bien? Cosa que no sucede en Argentina, . . . en México, . . . en Brasil. . . . Y pienso que tanto en Argentina, en Brasil, y en México les cuesta poco más largarse a formar conventos." (Uruguay has *very* particular characteristics. It's a secular state, in which the church and the state are separated. Right? Something that doesn't happen in Argentina, . . . in Mexico, . . . in Brazil. And I think that as much in Argentina [as] in Brazil and in Mexico it takes a little more to get out and form convents.) Hermana Dolores credits the successful founding and the long life of the Montevideo house to the secular state, but also to cultural factors. "Por las características de Uruguay," he explained, "de estado e iglesia estar separado, me da la impresión como que el católico uruguayo no es *tan* fervoroso como un católico mexicano, como un católico brasilero, o de otras partes de América Latina." (Because of Uruguay's characteristics of state and church being separated, I have the impression that the Uruguayan Catholic is not as fervent as a Mexican Catholic, as a Brazilian Catholic, or [a Catholic] from other parts of Latin America.)[14]

It may be more difficult and more dangerous to start a house in a fervently Catholic culture or in a country with an explicitly Christian state, but it is worth asking whether difficulty and danger translate to lack of effectiveness. It should be clear that this question in no way dismisses the severity of such dangers; Lepka notes, for example, that the first artist to be charged under Poland's Article 196 faced widespread threats and harassment after her case was made public, and that homophobic violence remains a significant problem in the country as it does in much of Eastern Europe.[15] However, since the main intended audiences of the Sisters' serious parody are the communities who are subject to that violence, it may be that their ministry can be effective in deeply important ways among queer communities in conservative—likely specifically conservative *Christian*—settings.

Orthodox Serious Parody

It may not be coincidental that Eastern European queer communities have recently developed a fascinating example of queer serious parody of religion, not through performance as with the Sisters, but through art. The Orthodox Calendar, which is produced in Romania, has been titillating queer audiences and advocating for queer-positive and feminist stances in the Orthodox Churches since 2013.[16] Using mostly Eastern European, Orthodox Christian models, the calendar offers erotic photographs that draw on Orthodox imagery, often including altars, religious symbols, icons, and men dressed as priests, along with critiques of the church that can be both subtle and searing. The 2015 calendar, titled "S.A.L.I.G.I.A." after the Latin acronym for the seven deadly sins, includes an image featuring a naked man viewed from the back. He kneels in front of a fresco of the Virgin Mary holding the infant Jesus, surrounded by images of saints. Painted in black down his back is an Orthodox cross. In the same black paint these words are scrawled, in capital letters and in English, across the fresco: "Oh Mary if you only knew all the evil things that they did to me oh Mary you would hold me naked in your arms."[17] The artistic team writes on its website, "While recognizing that change might not come quickly to the official Orthodox Church position, OC [the Orthodox Calendar] nonetheless believes that at least it can encourage people (believers or not) to reflect and realize that there is an urgent need for an update in values as part of the modern society."[18] While several of the images in the 2015 calendar emphasize the impact of homophobia—one model has bloody wounds on his back and another becomes an altar table, lit candles dripping wax across his body, in a possible reference to the binding of Isaac—others retain the joy and fun that are critical to serious parody. In one image, for instance, a stately altar draped in gold and red cloths fills the center of the picture while quite a few naked, entangled legs protrude from underneath.[19]

In a striking reminder of the political context in which the Orthodox Calendar models and production team work, the promotional short films for the 2014, 2015, and 2016 calendars open with the following notice, labeled "DISCLAIMER" in red at the top of the screen:

This video contains images of men who appear therein as priests. Viewers are free to accept or reject this. By posting this video, we are not confirming or denying the identity of these men. However, we consider irrelevant the true identities of these men. What is important—as with the Pussy Riot debate—are discussions generated by this video in respect of the role of gay men in religious orders, corruption in organized religions, treatment of minorities by society, etc.[20]

Although neither notice appears anywhere on the Orthodox Calendar website, at least as of this writing, *Huffington Post* articles about the calendar carry this disclaimer, reportedly emailed to the publication by a "calendar official" sometime after the press release for the 2014 calendar: "This product is not intended to be used for religious purposes. It is a work of artistic expression and political and social commentary promoting the modernity and dynamism of persons involved in the Orthodox Church."[21]

Given the prominent role of the Sisters in developing serious religious parody, it is particularly fascinating that the 2016 calendar, "Sancta Paraphilia," features on its cover two men wearing white pancake makeup. An article in the *Huffington Post*, which faithfully reports on each year's new calendar, explains that the image is of "Russian President Vladimir Putin and Moscow's Patriarch Kirill I, two long-standing opponents of lesbian, gay, bisexual and transgender (LGBT) rights, depicted as each other's brides in briefs and skimpy lingerie." Related artwork from the same series, titled *Golden Calf*, shows both figures astride a gilded statue of a bull, in reference not only to Putin's infamous bare-chested horseback riding pictures but also, and most importantly, to idolatry (see figure 7 of the color insert). The article does not explain the white makeup, and neither does the Orthodox Calendar website, so whether it is a reference to the Sisters is unclear. Regardless of any direct association with or inspiration by the Sisters, both the Orthodox Calendar and the sequined burqa worn by a member of Muslims Against Homophobia in the 2016 Sydney Mardi Gras parade demonstrate that queer serious parody of religion is not only alive and well, it is applicable well beyond the Sisters' serious parody of Roman Catholicism.

Serious Parody as Performative Protest

In the final paragraph of *Acts of Gaiety*, Sara Warner writes that "in an era of homoliberalism, a call to acts of gaiety serves as a heuristic device to explore what a more euphoric and ecstatic world might feel like."[22] Writing two years earlier, Benjamin Shepard offers a similar observation: "In the face of police, illness, carnage, and war, play helps activists engage with power as they take on the unsurmountable. . . . Play is . . . a resource that sustains, supports, and advances the aims of social movements."[23] Shepard adds later that "queers have always known plea-sure is a resource."[24] The Sisters of Perpetual Indulgence discovered this ludic resource on Easter Saturday of 1979, and since that day they have pursued "the promulgation of universal joy" with delight, camp, and fun.

Every ludic movement also has its serious side. Warner writes that as a "gesture of radical openness, gaiety shows us that what hurts, what causes us shame, and what we feel is wrong with the world is not neces-sary or inevitable, and it gives us license to unmake and remake it in other guises."[25] Her remarks echo those of Reverend Sister Merry Peter: "Joy is what's left in the crucible after you throw in all the tears and all the anger and all the shame and you burn it at a high temperature for five hours. And what comes out is the luster of joy."[26] But beyond the seriousness of the injustices and the harms that queer activists seek to undo, in the Sisters there lies another layer of seriousness: they are deeply serious about being queer nuns. Through play, camp, humor, and parody, when they are at their best they stand as prophetic figures call-ing out social wrongs and demanding social justice. Claiming the moral high ground from the Roman Catholic Church and decrying that insti-tution's injustices, they nonetheless understand themselves as emulating the nuns they admire, and they draw parallels between their own min-istry and those of Roman Catholic nuns and priests who have become outspoken leaders on social justice issues.

Through their serious religious parody, the Sisters of Perpetual Indulgence engage seriously with a tradition of religious figures leading the struggle for justice while using parody, play, and pleasure to queer those traditions and to push back against their own often vituperative ex-clusion from the very traditions they emulate. As a form of religious rev-olution, the act of claiming aspects of a tradition one finds valuable and criticizing those one perceives as harmful is hardly new. But the approach of emulating while decrying, of playfully and parodically excoriating one's oppressors while simultaneously laying claim to the truly faithful enactment of the still-valuable aspects of the oppressors' tradition—that approach appears to be novel. It may well be the case that the ludic queer activism of the 1970s was a necessary precursor to the development of the

Sisters' serious parody, but it is also likely that serious parody can be an effective strategy beyond specifically religious or queer contexts because of the opportunity it affords activists to challenge culturally dominant institutions on the basis of those institutions' own proclaimed values and with the disarming and empowering tools of humor.

Furthermore, it is possible that serious parody is already taking place more widely than we are aware, and that it simply has escaped notice or has been assigned, as the Sisters have been until now, to the category of ludic activism without regard to its serious aspect. Indeed, the persistent characterization of the Sisters of Perpetual Indulgence in studies of queer history and queer activism as being engaged solely in religious parody, and their characterization in some sources on queer spirituality as being engaged solely in religious practice, betray the deeply impoverished nature of existing models for understanding the intersections of religion, queerness, activism, and performance. It is high time for queer studies to relinquish its conviction that religion is only, always and everywhere, the opiate of the queers, and to recall that even Antonio Gramsci held open the possibility for religion to serve as a foundation for counter-hegemony.[27] Queer activists across the world are engaging in serious religious parody with hilarious, titillating, and profound results. Be they queer Muslims engaged in critical fabulousness (or fabulous criticism), photographers and models drawing on a tradition that does not mandate celibacy for its priests in order to create queer space in Orthodox Christian communities, or queer nuns for the twenty-first century, these provocative yet deeply serious queer engagements with religion demonstrate a much more complex and nuanced relationship between religion, queerness, performance, play, and justice than either queer studies or religious studies has been willing to comprehend to date. Perhaps, in taking serious parody *seriously*, these fields will come to a sharper understanding of their powerful intersections in the ongoing struggle for justice.

Last Rites

In a book about an order of nuns who are larger than life, sometimes literally with their platform boots and soaring coronets, it seems only appropriate to give the Sisters the final word—the last rites of this book, if you will. At the end of my interviews, I often asked whether the Sister or Guard persona had anything to add. Below, in no particular order, are the blessings and the words of wisdom they offered.

***

Work it, bitch! 'Cause if you ain't happy with yourself, ain't nobody else gonna be happy with you.
—Sister Daya Reckoning, The Abbey of St. Joan

Enjoy your naughtiness! And just embrace it.
—Sister Nadia Ahnwilda, The Abbey of St. Joan

In this moment, right now, you're perfect.
—Sister VixXxen, The Abbey of St. Joan

Love everybody. No matter what.
—Sister Ohna Fuckin' Tirade, Order of Benevolent Bliss

Just be yourself, do it for yourself, don't do it for other reasons. Don't let anyone hold you back.
—Sister Polly Amorous, Order of Benevolent Bliss

You are more beautiful than you think you are.
—Anonymous blessing at the 2011 Portland Conclave

If you don't love yourself, you're not going to be able to fully understand how to love others. But if you're willing to accept the love of others, in that process you will love yourself.
—Sister Reva Lation, Order of Benevolent Bliss

Party! If you can't lose yourself in the music, then what's the point of listening? Music will open your heart and work a lot of wonders and do a lot of healing. Just open your heart and dance, and don't care that anyone's looking, and don't care that anyone's listening. Be yourself.
—Novice Sister Spinna DeVinyl, Order of Benevolent Bliss

Single. Eight inches. Just saying. Put that in the book, 'cause I need someone to help me through retirement.
—Sister Unity Divine, Los Angeles House

Fear is the mind killer, and fear is the little death. You should allow that to pass over you, and you shall find the truth.
—Sister Jonbennet Gesserit

Life is pretty!
—Sister Trystina T. Rhume

Life is.
—Guard Inya, Asylum of the Tortured Heart

It's about the moment, all we have is the moment. And be as pretty and as fabulous as we can possibly be in the moment. And if we are living in joy by choice in that moment, before we know it we've spent a lifetime living in joy.
—Sister Kali Vagilistic X.P. Aladocious, Asylum of the Tortured
    Heart

Live life now, and act with love.
—Sister Angelpopstitute

Arrr!
—Sister Sorenda 'da Booty, Russian River Sisters

Spread the joy. It's worth living. Have fun, and in spite of all the things that happen in the world, there's always joy you can count on.
—Novice Sister Petunia Encarnata, Abbey of the Long Cedar
    Canoe

It's been a long journey, and the girl is here. She is here, she is here with a force, she's given it her all, and to borrow from her sister RuPaul, she's gonna work!
—Sista' Anita Lynchin', Order of Benevolent Bliss

Always be yourself. No matter what. Life is too short to hide who you are.
—Sister Betti Crotcher, Order of Benevolent Bliss

May these sinners on their knees
Be kept free from all disease.
When they take their shags to bed,
May they always keep their heads.
And remember the important issues:
Box of condoms, lube, and tissues.
Like Cuminja may they be
Non-stick and forever STI free.
Remember those who've gone before;
Go forth, be safe, and sin some more!
—Sister Cuminja Wrasse, London House of Common Sluts

As the Faeries would say: So mote it be.

APPENDIX A

Blooper Reel

Transcribing interviews is a grueling and thankless task, made all the more difficult when the audio files contain unfamiliar cultural or historical references. With deep gratitude and respect for all those who assisted me with the transcription of these interviews—Liam Mina, Jack MacNichol, Carly Johnson, Caroline Carr, Luís Alba-Sánchez, Inés Arenas-Embarcadero, Letta Page, Jeanne Crawford, and Michelle Thorla—I offer here the best of the best in the occasional hilarity that ensues when people try to figure out what exactly someone else has said. Errors are not attributed in order to preserve the dignity of the transcriptionist. Corrections are included in square brackets.

"January of '87, Ratzinger, who's the current Pope, was the head of the Congregation for the Doctrine of the Gays." [Congregation for the Doctrine of the *Faith*]—Grand Mother Vicious Power Hungry Bitch

With reference to working in the seminary store: "We would bring a record player in on days we were stalking the merchandise, and listen to Broadway show tunes." [*stocking* the merchandise]—Sister Soami

In reference to Roman Catholic nuns: "I am a person like this venereal tradition we're honoring." [*venerable* tradition]—Sister Soami

"Radical Ferries" [Radical Faeries, but perhaps there are radical ferries sailing the San Francisco Bay?]—Sister Soami

"One of the best books I've seen that really celebrates the paddle play of human male sexuality and deems it with spirit . . ." [the *panoply* of human male sexuality]—Sister Soami

"And, you know, the misery of gay life hasn't really hit them in the full, you know, they haven't known betrayal and the wonton nature of gay men." [the *wanton* nature of gay men]—Sister Benedikta

"The Catholic clone look, the whole reason that the Sisters, those four guys put on nuns' habits in 1979, was they were tired of the clones, they were tired of the demand to be the same, and wanted something different." [the *Castro* clone look]—Sister MaryMae Himm

"I think once he went as Barbara Butch and I went as Marilyn Quayle to a straight couples' party out in San Bernardino." [Barbara *Bush*]—Sister Unity Divine

APPENDIX B

Studying the Sisters

Although I had been considering a book project on the Sisters since I met a member of the Los Angeles house as part of an earlier research project,[1] I barely missed the Sisters' thirtieth anniversary celebration, some of which is featured in the Austrian documentary *The Sisters*.[2] On sabbatical for the fall semester of 2009, having obtained approval from my institutional review board, and ready to explore the possibility of writing a book on the Sisters of Perpetual Indulgence, I contacted the house that was closest to me at the time: the Order of Benevolent Bliss in Portland, Oregon. Sister Dixie Rupt invited me to attend a business meeting and explain my project. On September 16, 2009, I did so, and was approved to begin research with the Portland house. Exactly eight months later, on May 16, 2010, I met with members of Seattle's Abbey of St. Joan over breakfast the morning after a fundraising event they had organized at the small-town gay bar about an hour's drive from the rural college where I was teaching at the time. Again I explained the project and received approval to expand my work to the Seattle house. That summer, after some conversation regarding fair use and the applicability of the Sisters of Perpetual Indulgence trademark agreement to scholars, the San Francisco house also approved the project and thereby eased my way to contact other houses around the world.

I conducted research with the Sisters for four years and seven months, officially concluding the research phase of the project at the end of the Sisters' thirty-fifth anniversary party in April 2014. My approach was multi-methodological, incorporating archival work, oral history, participant observation, one-on-one interviews, and focus group interviews. All of the houses with which I worked were happy to have me interview fully professed members, but only the Order of Benevolent Bliss allowed me to interview novices by themselves. Some focus groups included novices, allowed to participate because at least one FP was also present, and when I interviewed members of missions I was of necessity interviewing novices, since all members of a house in formation are themselves considered to be in formation as well. No order permitted members in earlier stages of formation to interview with me, although all members were free to talk with me informally at any time.

Occasionally two members who were a couple in their "secular" lives wished to interview together, and I learned important perspectives from their conversation with each other as well as with me. The larger focus group interviews, on the other hand, were all conducted out of necessity. The 2011 international Conclave of the Sisters of Perpetual Indulgence was held in Portland, Oregon, with Sisters from across North America and even from Europe in attendance. Wanting to take maximum advantage of the opportunity to interview members of the order across this wide geographic range in a very short period of already tightly scheduled time, I requested individual interviews but was also willing to interview members of a house together if they preferred that approach. The Russian River, Eureka, Dallas–Fort Worth, San Diego, and Las Vegas houses all chose the latter option. All of the interviews in this study were conducted in person except for the interviews with Sisters in Montevideo, Uruguay and Sydney, Australia, to which cities I was unable to travel at the time of the interviews. These were conducted via videoconference, or over the phone if the former was unavailable. Due to a miscommunication when I was in Los Angeles for research, I also interviewed Sister Unity Divine via videoconferencing. An eleventh-hour interview with Mother Ethyl Dreads-a-Flashback was also conducted via videoconference.

In all, I conducted interviews with ninety-one members of the order, from houses in North America (both the United States and Canada), Europe (Switzerland, Germany, France, England, and Scotland), Australia, and Uruguay. Most of the interviews were semistructured and followed the list of questions included at the end of this appendix; five were conducted as oral history interviews, and several more with Sisters outside North America were conducted as a hybrid of the two approaches. Interviews ranged widely in length, between twenty-seven minutes and four hours and forty-two minutes;

the longest interview and one other interview were both conducted over the space of two days. The average length of the interviews was eighty-six minutes.

I conducted my most extensive fieldwork with the Order of Benevolent Bliss, and secondly with The Abbey of St. Joan. I also conducted fieldwork with the San Francisco house; the Music City Sisters in Nashville, Tennessee; the London House of Common Sluts; the Couvent de Paris; and the Erzmutterhaus Sankta Melitta Iuvenis zu Berlin. In total, my fieldwork resulted in over 100 single-spaced pages of fieldnotes and the interviews in nearly 1,700 single-spaced pages of transcripts. These, along with archival materials, artifacts gathered during my fieldwork, and the Sisters' own writings, blogs, and other publications, constitute the primary materials on which my analysis of the Sisters is based.

Interview Schedule

Demographics

1. How old are you?
2. What is the highest academic degree you hold?
3. What do you do for work, if you work?
4. How do you identify in terms of race or ethnicity?
5. Would you consider yourself to be working-class, middle-class, upper-class, or something else?
   a. If something else, what?
6. Would you say you were brought up in the same class as you are now, or a different one?
   a. If different, what?
7. How do you identify in terms of gender and gender history?
8. How do you identify in terms of sexual orientation?
9. Do you have a partner or significant other?

The Sisters

1. Check correct pronoun for Sister/Guard persona
2. What house do you belong to?

3. Have you been a member of other houses aside from this one? Which ones, and when?

4. Who is/are your Mother(s)/Big Sister(s)/sponsor(s) in the house?

5. When did you become a postulant? A novice? When did you take your vows?

6. (Fully professed only) Tell me about your vows. Do you remember what they were? What was it like becoming a fully professed Sister/guard?

7. Why did you choose to be a Sister and not a Guard (or a Guard and not a Sister)?

8. What was your novice project?

9. Had you ever dressed in drag (leather) before you became a Sister (Guard)?

10. How did you become interested in the Sisters?

11. Tell me about choosing your name. How and why did you choose it?

12. (Except for Guards) Do you consider yourself a nun? Why or why not?

13. What's it like to wear whiteface?

14. What's the most important part, for you, of being a Sister/Guard?

15. What would you say the central values of the Sisters are?

16. Do you have a favorite memory or memories from your time as a Sister/Guard? Tell me about it/them.

17. Are there any disadvantages of being a Sister/Guard? If so, what are they?

18. What kinds of things cause tension within or among houses? Can you give me examples?

19. Tell me about the relationship, broadly construed, between the Sisters and the Catholic Church.

Religion

1. Do you consider yourself religious? Spiritual? Both? Neither?

2. If religious or spiritual, how do you describe your religion or spirituality to others?

3. Tell me about the roles, if any, that religion or spirituality has played in your life.

4. Do you see any connection between your religion/spirituality/atheism and your being a Sister/Guard? If so, tell me about that connection.
5. What is your personal relationship, if any, to the Catholic Church?

In Closing

1. Is there anything we haven't covered that you'd like to add?
2. Would Sister/Guard____have anything to add?

NOTES

INTRODUCTION

1 Sister Cuminja Wrasse, London House of Common Sluts, interview with the author, 28 May 2011.

2 "House" is a term of art, likely drawn from drag usage of the term as well as from traditional Roman Catholic monastic communities and no doubt indebted at least in part to the drag ball traditions of queer communities of color. No houses in the order are actually residential, although Sisters certainly share living space at times as roommates or as partners, and some have designated as their "convent" or "priory" the space in which they regularly meet or don their habits.

3 Sister Glo Euro N'Wei, The Abbey of St. Joan (Seattle), interview with the author, 10 April 2011.

4 Although many members of the order refer to their white makeup as "whiteface," the term is not intended as a reference either to blackface minstrel traditions in the United States or to the history of subversive "whiteface" performance by actors of color. Nonetheless, the use of such makeup does have racial meanings and ramifications that are just as complex as they are often unintended.

5 Sometimes those differences are not just between countries or regions but within them as well, and disagreements over institutional authority can be a key source of conflicts or tensions both within and between houses.

6 Dates in this chapter are drawn when possible from interviews and archival materials, and cross-checked with information the Sisters have made available online. At times they are drawn solely from those online sources, although I always cross-check between online sources as well when possible. The online sources are the "SisTree," a genealogical tree of the entire worldwide order maintained by Sister Titania Humperpickle and available at www.perpetualindulgence.org, and the "Sistory" maintained by the San Francisco house, originally compiled by two former Mistresses of Archives, Sister Phyllis Stein the Fragrant and Sister Kitty Catalyst, O.C.P., with input from Sister Vish, available at thesisters.org.

7 According to the Archabbess, founder of the German-speaking order, the Heidelberg house merged with the new mission in Berlin in 1997, making Berlin the Archabbey (now called Erzmutterhaus or Archmother-house) of that order. The Archabbess, interview with the author, 23 March 2012.

8 All population data are from the U.S. Census Bureau, www.census.gov, last accessed 14 July 2015.

9 Welzer-Lang, Le Talec, and Tomolillo, *Un mouvement gai*, 269–70.

10 Sister Odora Flatulotta D'Pew, Grand Canyon Sisters of Perpetual Indulgence, interview with the author, 19 August 2011.

11 To briefly summarize the Seattle case: the city's original house split in 1996; the new house survived and the older one faded away but reemerged at the end of the 2000s. Now known as the Sisters of the Mother House of Washington, or SOM-HOW, the original Seattle house is not recognized by San Francisco, while the newer house, The Abbey of St. Joan, is. I did not have the opportunity to formally interview Sisters from SOMHOW, as they were just beginning to reemerge during my time conducting fieldwork in Seattle, but I have had conversations with a few members of the house, particularly Sister Angela Mercy.

12 Welzer-Lang, Le Talec, and Tomolillo, *Un mouvement gai*, 269.

13 Sœur Rose, Paname Couvent des Sœurs (Paris), interview with the author, 27 May 2011.

14 "De longues négociations." Welzer-Lang, Le Talec, and Tomolillo, *Un mouvement gai*, 270. I reference Le Talec here as primary author because this book began as his doctoral dissertation; his advisor is listed as first author as a professional courtesy and Tomolillo contributed to one chapter of the book. Thus, sociological authorship conventions aside, the argument made here is Le Talec's.

15 Hermana Dolores Raimunda, Hermanas de la Perpetua Indulgencia del Uruguay, Orden de San Felipe y Santiago de Montevideo, interview with the author, 17 December 2013; Hermana Prudencia Ernestina Simona Cruciphija Cienfuegos, Hermanas de la Perpetua Indulgencia del Uruguay, Orden de San Felipe y Santiago de Montevideo, interview with the author, 10 December 2013. See also Marcelo Otero's 2011 film on the Uruguay house, *Que me digan loca . . .* The film is available on YouTube, but sadly, as of 2015 the audio track had been removed due to copyright issues.

16 According to the *Oxford English Dictionary*, the term "exequatur" can mean "an official recognition of a consul or commercial agent by the government of the country to which he [sic] is accredited, authorizing him to exercise his power." However, the term also has a usage specific to the navigation of royal and papal powers in Europe. Again quoting from the *OED*: "An authorization granted by a temporal sovereign for the exercise of episcopal functions under Papal authority, or for the publication of Papal bulls. Hence, the right of insisting on the necessity of such authorization."

17 Sister Katie Kizum, The Abbey of St. Joan (Seattle), interview with the author, 24 July 2011.

18 Hermana Dolores Raimunda, Hermanas de la Perpetua Indulgencia del Uruguay, Orden de San Felipe y Santiago de Montevideo, interview with the author, 17 December 2013; Hermana Prudencia Ernestina Simona Cruciphija Cienfuegos, Hermanas de la Perpetua Indulgencia del Uruguay, Orden de San Felipe y Santiago de Montevideo, interview with the author, 10 December 2013.

19 Sœur Rose, Paname Couvent des Sœurs (Paris), interview with the author, 27 May 2011; Sœur Néfertata, Couvent de Paris, interview with the author, 27 May 2011.

20 Brother Bimbo del Doppio Senso, Convent of Dunn Eideann (Edinburgh), interview with the author, 20 August 2011.

21 Sœur Néfertata, Couvent de Paris, interview with the author, 27 May 2011. The newly invested convent in Montréal appears to be following the same tradition; see the convent's Facebook page, Les Sœurs de la Perpétuelle Indulgence—Couvent de Paris, www.facebook.com (last accessed 19 December 2016).

22 Hermana Prudencia Ernestina Simona Cruciphija Cienfuegos, Hermanas de la Perpetua Indulgencia del Uruguay, Orden de San Felipe y Santiago de Montevideo, interview with the author, 10 December 2013.

23 The latter example was Sister Baba Ganesh's novice project, and the resulting procession now takes place regularly at the Sisters' anniversary celebration on Easter weekend in San Francisco. Sister Baba Ganesh, Sisters of Perpetual Indulgence—San Francisco House, interview with the author, 11 July 2012.

24 Mother Inferior, Order of Perpetual Indulgence—Sydney House, interview with the author, 10 October 2013. See also Sister Cum Dancing, "Sisters of P.I. Chronology (draft only)," n.d., Bruce Belcher Papers, box 1, folder 3 of 13, Australian Lesbian and Gay Archives, Melbourne.

25 Mother Inferior, Order of Perpetual Indulgence—Sydney House, interview with the author, 10 October 2013; Sister Mary Arse Licked and Old Lace, Order of Perpetual Indulgence—Sydney House, interview with the author, 9 December 2013; Mother Premonstratensia, Order of Perpetual Indulgence—Sydney House (formerly of the Adelaide House), interview with the author, 12 December 2013; Sister Rowena Keeper of the Holy Doiley, Order of Perpetual Indulgence—Sydney House, interview with the author, 15 November 2013; Sister Salome of the 9th Mystic Rhinestone, Order of Perpetual Indulgence—Sydney House, interview with the author, 29 November 2013 and 5 December 2013.

26 Father Oh, Mary!, Sister Nova Aggra, and Novice Sister Gaia T., Abbey of the Big Red Wood (Eureka, California), interview with the author, 20 August 2011. The Cockettes, a San Francisco–based group active from 1969 to 1972, were widely known for, among other aspects of their performances, their use of skag drag, or drag in which no effort is made to conceal the socially prescribed incongruence between the sex of the body doing drag and the gender being presented. The Sisters, particularly male-bodied Sisters and female-bodied members embodying male personas, often thrive on exactly this kind of skag or "genderfuck" drag, not to mention the exuberant use of glitter and rhinestones, which were also part of the Cockettes' signature look. See, for instance, Shepard, "Play as World-Making."

27 Order of Perpetual Indulgence—Sydney House, "Our Background," www.universaljoy.com.au (last accessed 21 September 2016). Thanks to Sister Rowena Keeper of the Holy Doiley for bringing this statement to my attention.

28 Mother Inferior, Order of Perpetual Indulgence—Sydney House, interview with the author, 10 October 2013.

29 Brother Bimbo del Doppio Senso, Convent of Dunn Eideann (Edinburgh), interview with the author, 20 August 2011.

30 Welzer-Lang, Le Talec, and Tomolillo, *Un mouvement gai*, 83 (translation mine).

31 Jean-Yves Le Talec, personal communication with the author, 26 July 2015.

32 Brother Bimbo del Doppio Senso, Convent of Dunn Eideann (Edinburgh), interview with the author, 20 August 2011. According to Brother Bimbo, this "crypto-Sister" was called Sister Alice Qaeda. She wore a burqa rather than a habit, in response to a challenge from a conservative Catholic group that "you wouldn't dare put one of your members in a burqa." The racial and religious politics involved in this entire story are of course quite fraught.

33 Sister Mary-Kohn, Sisters of Perpetual Indulgence—Los Angeles House, interview with the author, 20 August 2011.

34 This is true, for instance, of a few of the Sisters in San Diego's Asylum of the Tortured Heart. Guard Inya, Sister Kali Vagilistic X.P. Aladocious, Asylum of the Tortured Heart (San Diego), and Sister Trystina T. Rhume, interview with the author, 17 August 2011.

35 Sister Unity Divine, Sisters of Perpetual Indulgence—Los Angeles House, interview with the author, 29 October 2013.

36 Mother Premonstratensia, Order of Perpetual Indulgence—Sydney House, interview with the author, 12 December 2013.

37 To that end, in this book I use the secular name of a living Sister only if I have been given explicit, written permission to do so. I do use secular names for Nuns of the Above (Sisters who have passed away), but only in cases where those names appear in publicly accessible archives. In some cases, participants have asked that I use their secular first names but not their last names; others have allowed both first and last names to be used, and some have requested that I use only their Sister or Guard names. Since all Sisters and Guards are public figures, I do reference members of the order by their actual Sister or Guard names even when I do not have written permission to do so. Jason Crawford made a similar choice to use the actual Sister and Guard names of his participants in his 2011 dissertation. He writes,

> To respect their "creative human artistry," I use the Sisters' chosen names when I refer to specific individuals. . . . I have also chosen to do this because the Sister names perform the humour and characteristics of each Member [*sic*] of the Order—I could not, with all my creative capabilities, do justice to their own names by weaving pseudo-sisterly names as the actual names. (Crawford, "'Go Forth and Sin Some More!,'" 52)

The separation of Sister and secular names and identities also placed the Sisters among those vocally protesting Facebook's decision in 2014 to require all users to list their "real [legal] name" on their profiles. While objections to this policy came from various quarters, including domestic violence victims and their advocates, trans communities and activists, and professionals such as psychologists who need to keep their personal lives private from their clients, among the Sisters the policy effectively prevented any Sister or Guard from having a Facebook page in their own right. Given that social media is one route for the Sisters' ministry, and that anonymity of their secular selves is an important tool for that ministry, the legal name policy has presented serious difficulties for many of the order's members.

38 Sister Katie Kizum, The Abbey of St. Joan (Seattle), interview with the author, 24 July 2011.

39 Sister Krissy Fiction, Order of Benevolent Bliss (Portland, Oregon), interview with the author, 1 November 2009.

40 Sister Dire-Reahh, London House of Common Sluts, interview with the author, 28 May 2011.

41 Sister Mary-Kohn, Sisters of Perpetual Indulgence—Los Angeles House, interview with the author, 20 August 2011. Sister Mary-Kohn has changed her name since I interviewed her in 2011; she now goes by Sister Mama-Kohn-Gusto. I am not aware of the reason for the change, but I find it interesting, given that she shared with me that some of the Sisters in her house were uncomfortable with what they perceived to be the harshness of the term *maricón*. If this Sister did indeed change her name due to the discomfort of other members of the house, her situation would make an interesting contrast with the apparent lack of concern in the Portland house over Sista' Anita Lynchin's name; see chapter 4.

42 Sister Mary Ralph, PN (Proper Nun), Sisters of Perpetual Indulgence—San Francisco House, interview with the author, 9 July 2011.

43 Mother Loosy Lust Bea Lady, Sister Gloria-Areola all over Gluttony, and Sister Sioux St. Semen Sloth, Sin Sity Sisters (Las Vegas), interview with the author, 20 August 2011.

44 Sister Angelpopstitute, traveling (unaffiliated) Sister, interview with the author, 28 May 2011.

45 Sister Connie Pinko, Sisters of Perpetual Indulgence—San Francisco House, interview with the author, 16 August 2011.

46 Most non-Native people know the term *heyoka* from Neihardt, *Black Elk Speaks*. One chapter of the book addresses the "heyoka ceremony" and the people who "act as heyokas." It explains the ceremony as follows:

> In the heyoka ceremony, everything is backwards, and it is planned that the people shall be made to feel jolly and happy first, so that it may be easier for the power to come to them. You have noticed that the truth comes into this world with two faces. One is sad with suffering; and the other laughs, but it is the same face, laughing or weeping. When people are already in despair, maybe the laughing face is better for them; and when they feel too good and are too sure of being safe, maybe the weeping face is better for them to see. And so I think that is what the heyoka ceremony is for. (145)

Scholars of comparative mythology have since included the figure of the heyoka in their cross-cultural category of "tricksters," a category with which some Sisters identify the work of their order. As Scott Lauria Morgensen points out, appropriating Native American roles and images has constituted a prominent strategy of non-Native LGBTQ activists for a number of decades; the role of such appropriations in the Sisters is one of the potential pitfalls of their serious parody. See Morgensen, *Spaces between Us*. I discuss the question of sacred clowns further in chapter 4.

47 Guard Inya, Sister Kali Vagilistic X.P. Aladocious, Asylum of the Tortured Heart (San Diego), and Sister Trystina T. Rhume, interview with the author, 17 August 2011.

48 Novice Sister Edna Daze, Order of Benevolent Bliss (Portland, Oregon), interview with the author, 23 January 2010.

49 Sister Anna Wrecks-Ya, Order of Benevolent Bliss (Portland, Oregon), interview with the author, 2 November 2009.

50 Sister Nadia Ahnwilda, The Abbey of St. Joan (Seattle), interview with the author, 9 April 2011.

51 The classic work on this topic remains Weston's *Families We Choose*. See, for instance, her discussion of community on pp. 122–29 of that volume.

52 Also relevant here is the explicitly familial structure of drag houses, which have a mother and sometimes a father, children, and siblings.

53 This claim is true as well for transgender and other gender-nonconforming communities at least through the end of the twentieth century, because of the ways definitions of homosexuality incorporated gender nonconformity and thereby blurred distinctions between the two as separate sources of identity. See, for instance, Valentine, *Imagining Transgender*.

54 Tim Dean offers a nuanced exploration of barebacking culture and the attendant debates in *Unlimited Intimacy*. The debates I describe here among the Sisters have been further complicated by the development of and ongoing discussions over pre-exposure prophylaxis, or PrEP; however, the questions of what constitutes safer sex and when a Sister is vowed to adhere to such practices remain at the heart of such concerns, whether the conversation is about PrEP, condom use, or both.

55 Gregory Tomso makes a related argument regarding public efforts to encourage gay men to use oral prophylactics in "Viral Sex and the Politics of Life."

56 Sister Loganberry Frost, Sister Mary Media, and Sister Σplace., Sisters of Perpetual Indulgence—San Francisco House, interview with the author, 19 April 2014.

CHAPTER 1. "IT WAS LIKE THIS ASTEROID BELT"

1 Sister Soami, Missionary Order of Perpetual Indulgence, interview with the author, 9 June 2012.

2 Susan Short Gilbert, aka Saint Suzie of The Bust-a-Doozy, untitled and undated narrative, courtesy of Sister Vish-Knew. According to Gilbert, the habits were donated by a teacher from her Catholic school days who heard that they were needed for a theatrical production and assumed that the show in question was *The Sound of Music*. "I never corrected her," recalls Gilbert. "If I ever go to hell, it will be for this, I suspect."

3 Sister Vish-Knew, Sisters of Perpetual Indulgence—San Francisco House, personal communication with the author, 31 January 2016.

4 Weissman and Weber, *The Cockettes*. Though space limitations preclude any in-depth discussion of this aspect of the Sisters' story, both the Cockettes and Divine—star of *Pink Flamingos* and a onetime Cockette—have had an important impact on the Sisters of Perpetual Indulgence. One former Cockette, Goldie Glitters, even joined the Sisters for a time in the early 1980s, as Sister Quaelewd (or Quaalude—sources disagree on the spelling) Conduct.

5 On San Francisco's gay history, see Stryker and Van Buskirk, *Gay by the Bay*; and Boyd, *Wide-Open Town*; on Transcendental Meditation, see Williamson, *Transcendent in America*; on Harry Hay and the Radical Faeries, see Roscoe, *Radically Gay*. Thoughtful analyses of the Radical Faeries can be found in Herring, "Out of the Closets" (this article notably focuses on the emergence of the periodical *RFD* from the same Iowa farmhouse in which Ken Bunch lived for a time, and its evolution into the publication in which Sister Soami is closely involved); Stover, "When Pan Met Wendy"; Hennen, *Faeries, Bears, and Leathermen*; and Morgensen, *Spaces between Us*.

6 Grand Mother Vicious Power Hungry Bitch, Sisters of Perpetual Indulgence—San Francisco House, interview with the author, 21 November 2011.

7 Ibid.

8 Ibid.

9 Ibid.

10 Sister Hysterectoria, The NYC (dis)Order, interview with the author, 22 December 2012.

11 Grand Mother Vicious Power Hungry Bitch, Sisters of Perpetual Indulgence—San Francisco House, interview with the author, 21 November 2011. Sister Soami recalls that the two ran their pom-poms up the flagpole instead of their veils (personal communication with the author, 16 December 2016).

12 Grand Mother Vicious Power Hungry Bitch, Sisters of Perpetual Indulgence—San Francisco House, interview with the author, 21 November 2011. The same Sister, who now uses the name Sister Vish-Knew, recalls that Reverend Mother had been given this moniker years before "because of his spiritual and motherly personality. In fact, the first 2 years I knew him, I did not know his birth name. That is how often he was referred to as 'RM.'" Sister Vish-Knew, Sisters of Perpetual Indulgence—San Francisco House, personal communication with the author, 29 November 2015.

13 Sister Hysterectoria, The NYC (dis)Order, interview with the author, 22 December 2012.

14 Sister Soami, Missionary Order of Perpetual Indulgence, interview with the author, 9 June 2012.

15 Sister Hysterectoria, The NYC (dis)Order, interview with the author, 22 December 2012.

16 Ibid.

17 Sister Hysterectoria, The NYC (dis)Order, personal communication with the author, 4 August 2015.

18 Sister Hysterectoria, The NYC (dis)Order, interview with the author, 22 December 2012.

19 Ibid.

20 Kenkelen, "'Sisters of Perpetual Indulgence.'" Kenkelen's description of the cloistered sisters as "Mexican immigrant nuns" is also interesting, although a full examination of the function of this description in an article lambasting the Sisters of Perpetual Indulgence is beyond the scope of this chapter.

21 Sister Soami, Missionary Order of Perpetual Indulgence, interview with the author, 9 June 2012.

22 Sister Soami, Missionary Order of Perpetual Indulgence, personal communication with the author, 16 December 2016.

23 Sister Hysterectoria, The NYC (dis)Order, interview with the author, 22 December 2012; Grand Mother Vicious Power Hungry Bitch, Sisters of Perpetual Indulgence—San Francisco House, interview with the author, 21 November 2011; Sister Soami, Missionary Order of Perpetual Indulgence, interview with the author, 9 June 2012.

24 Grand Mother Vicious Power Hungry Bitch, Sisters of Perpetual Indulgence—San Francisco House, interview with the author, 21 November 2011.

25 Sister Soami, Missionary Order of Perpetual Indulgence, personal communication with the author, 16 December 2016.

26 Sister Soami, Missionary Order of Perpetual Indulgence, interview with the author, 9 June 2012.

27 Ibid.

28 See Erzen, *Straight to Jesus*, esp. chap. 1.

29 Sister Soami, Missionary Order of Perpetual Indulgence, interview with the author, 9 June 2012.

30 Kyper, "The Week the Evangelists Tried to 'Save Sin City.'"

31 Sister Soami, Missionary Order of Perpetual Indulgence, interview with the author, 9 June 2012.

32 Sister Loganberry Frost, Sister Mary Media, and Sister Σplace., Sisters of Perpetual Indulgence—San Francisco House, interview with the author, 19 April 2014.

33 E.g., Sister Soami, Missionary Order of Perpetual Indulgence, interview with the author, 10 June 2012.

34 On MCC, see my earlier work, *Coming Out in Christianity*.

35 Caen, "Friday's Fractured Flicker."

36 Soiffer, "Big Gay Protest at USF"; Neary, "Gays Demonstrate at USF's Open House."

37 Sisters of Perpetual Indulgence, "Mainstream Exiles."

38 Sister Missionary Position, "A Litany for Justice for All (Delivered Thanksgiving Evening, November 27, 1980 at the March against Violence in Memory of Harvey Milk & George Moscone, SF Civic Center)," courtesy of Sister Soami.

39 Hansen, "Male Nuns Spread Joy"; Day, "The Sisters of Perpetual Indulgence"; Thompson, "Not Wholly Nunsense."

40 "A Gay Day for a Parade."

41 Newman, *Altered Habits*.

42 "Headlines First Annual Dog Show Parade."

43 "Escándalo gay en U.S.A."; Starr, "Indulging the Sisters"; Starr, "Getting It from Both Sides." The initial Starr column was in response to an earlier *Examiner* article: Snider, "The Sisters of Perpetual Indulgence."

44 "The Sisters of Perpetual Indulgence Present a Crusade."

45 White, "Illegal Indulgences."

46 An internal document from the early Toronto house states that the house's first manifestation took place "at Toronto's first Lesbian and Gay Pride Day in June, 1981," and that event was on June 28. Sisters of Perpetual Indulgence (Toronto Chapter), n.d., untitled document courtesy of Sister Soami. This document is also available online, under the title "Sisters' Handbook."

47 Ibid.

48 Sister Hysterectoria, The NYC (dis)Order, interview with the author, 22 December 2012.

49 Romanovsky, "Welcome to the Archives" (italics and all spelling in original).

50 Sister Soami, Missionary Order of Perpetual Indulgence, interview with the author, 10 June 2012.

51 Gary Schliemann/Sister Mae Call of the Wilde, personal communication with the author, 25–26 November 2016.

52 Mother Inferior, Order of Perpetual Indulgence—Sydney House, interview with the author, 10 October 2013.

53 Ibid.

54 See Sister Cum Dancing, "Sisters of P.I. Chronology."

55 Mother Inferior, Order of Perpetual Indulgence—Sydney House, interview with the author, 10 October 2013.

56 Sister Cum Dancing, "Sisters of P.I. Chronology."

57 I learned a great deal about the importance of the Gay Liberation Quire at the "Beyond the Culture Wars: LGBTIQ History Now" conference at La Trobe University, 25–26 November 2016. Special thanks to Tim Jones, who organized the conference and invited me to attend, and to Paul Van Reyk, a former Quire member whose conference presentation, "The Queen of Heaven Don't Pump Gas!," was particularly enlightening.

58 Mother Inferior, Order of Perpetual Indulgence—Sydney House, interview with the author, 10 October 2013.

59 Ibid.

60 Allec, "No More Guilt!"; Welch, "Body Politic Article"; "'Nuns' Offend Homosexuals Council Told."

61 Sister Cum Dancing, "Sisters of P.I. Chronology."

62 "The Sisters of Perpetual Indulgence Wish to Announce."

63 Reverend Sister Merry Peter, Sisters of Perpetual Indulgence—San Francisco
House, interview with the author, 11 July 2012. Sister Flirtatious Romanovsky of
Middlesex, who was one of the five remaining members when the decision was
taken to close the house, shared a similar perspective when I asked what people
should know about the Toronto house. "Although many groups do not move past
Mission House status (or even achieve it)," he wrote,

> I firmly believe that in addition to the usual group dynamics/personal-
> ity issues that all groups face, the oh-so British attitude of civility even as
> one discriminates ("he's one of *those* people" "poor soul—such a burden")
> contributes its own challenges. The attitude, also often seen as "Canadian
> politeness," avoids the messy confrontation which can be a catalyst for more
> open discussion. (Sister Flirtatious Romanovsky of Middlesex, personal
> communication with the author, 29 August 2015.)

64 On the early history of HIV and AIDS, see Altman, *AIDS in the Mind of America*,
also published as *AIDS and the New Puritanism*; and Patton, *Sex and Germs*.
While Randy Shilts's *And the Band Played On* is often cited as the classic work in
this area, the slanted argument that provides the underlying narrative to Shilts's
generally accurate recitation of facts was immediately critiqued by activists and
other commentators. See Crimp, "How to Have Promiscuity in an Epidemic." Altman, working partly in San Francisco while being based in Melbourne, offers one
of the few mentions of the Sisters in AIDS histories—an impressively accurate if
fleeting reference to the order as "a group of male nuns, albeit one not recognized
by the official Catholic Church" that "had made STD education a priority even
before AIDS was named" (*AIDS and the New Puritanism*, 161). Altman clearly
had, or had access to, a copy of the San Francisco Sisters' 1982 *Play Fair!* pamphlet
(on which see below).

65 Sister Soami, Missionary Order of Perpetual Indulgence, interview with the
author, 9 June 2012.

66 Richard Berkowitz and Michael Callen's "How to Have Sex in an Epidemic" is
often mistakenly described as the first safer-sex guide for gay men authored by
gay men, but it was published in New York City in 1983.

67 Romanovsky, "Welcome to the Archives."

68 The 1982 version cautions that "the information in this brochure is relevant to
current health needs of the gay male community. It is not intended to relate to the
situation for women."

69 London House of Common Sluts, *Play Fair!*

70 Grand Mother Vicious Power Hungry Bitch, Sisters of Perpetual Indulgence—San
Francisco House, interview with the author, 21 November 2011.

71 Ibid.; Sister Soami, Missionary Order of Perpetual Indulgence, personal communication with the author, 16 December 2016.

72 Sisters of Perpetual Indulgence, "The Sisters of Perpetual Indulgence Present:
!SCORE!"

73 Grand Mother Vicious Power Hungry Bitch, Sisters of Perpetual Indulgence—San Francisco House, interview with the author, 21 November 2011.

74 Ibid.; Sister Soami, Missionary Order of Perpetual Indulgence, interview with the author, 10 June 2012 and personal communication with the author, 23 December 2015.

75 Sisters of Perpetual Indulgence, "Mayor's Quip to Sisters."

76 Ibid.

77 Grand Mother Vicious Power Hungry Bitch, Sisters of Perpetual Indulgence—San Francisco House, interview with the author, 21 November 2011.

78 E.g., ibid.; Sister Soami, Missionary Order of Perpetual Indulgence, interview with the author, 10 June 2012.

79 Reiterman, "Russian Center's Ladies."

80 Grand Mother Vicious Power Hungry Bitch, Sisters of Perpetual Indulgence—San Francisco House, interview with the author, 21 November 2011.

81 Fertig, oral history interview, 87–88. Thanks to Drew Bourn for bringing this transcript to my attention.

82 Sister Hysterectoria, The NYC (dis)Order, interview with the author, 22 December 2012.

83 E.g., Sandbach, "Sister Boom Boom."

84 A copy of this poster can be seen in the archives of the San Francisco house.

85 Ludlow, "S.F.'s Zany Cheerleader."

86 Grand Mother Vicious Power Hungry Bitch, Sisters of Perpetual Indulgence—San Francisco House, interview with the author, 21 November 2011.

87 Sisters of Perpetual Indulgence, "Constitution and Rules of Order."

88 Sister Soami, Missionary Order of Perpetual Indulgence, interview with the author, 9 June 2012.

89 Sister Hysterectoria, The NYC (dis)Order, interview with the author, 22 December 2012.

90 Sister Hysterectoria, The NYC (dis)Order, personal communication with the author, 19 January 2017.

91 Grand Mother Vicious Power Hungry Bitch, Sisters of Perpetual Indulgence—San Francisco House, interview with the author, 21 November 2011.

92 Margaret Taylor (Sister Very Maculate), interview for History Inverted, 66 mins., 1996, DVD 502, Australian Lesbian and Gay Archives (ALGA), Melbourne. Digitized and transcribed by ALGA.

93 Fertig, oral history interview, 94.

94 Grand Mother Vicious Power Hungry Bitch, Sisters of Perpetual Indulgence—San Francisco House, interview with the author, 21 November 2011; Sister Soami, Missionary Order of Perpetual Indulgence, personal communication with the author, 23 December 2015; Nolte, "Jack Fertig."

95 Sister Soami, Missionary Order of Perpetual Indulgence, interview with the author, 9 June 2012.

96 Kelley, "Walking on the Waters of Babylon."

97 Fertig, "Doing What the Sisters Do Best." Much more generous coverage of the tenth anniversary, published admittedly before the party, came from Huston, "Holy Habits, Batman!"

98 Huston, "Holy Habits, Batman!" The other new members listed are Sister Luscious Lashes, Sister There's No Place Like Rome, Sister Dana Van Iquity, Sister Marquesa de Sade, and Sister Juanita La Bufadora de Insane Diego. Several of these Sisters are still active in the San Francisco house, some under slightly altered names, as of this writing.

99 See, e.g., Welzer-Lang, Le Talec, and Tomolillo, *Un mouvement gai*, 245.

100 The following history of the London house is taken from Sister Mary-Anna Lingus, Sisters of Perpetual Indulgence—London House, interview with the author, 16 December 2016. Documented traces of this house appear in Varnden, "Sister Love"; and Lucas, "The Color of His Eyes." According to Sister Mary-Anna Lingus, Lucas was himself a member of the London house.

101 Welzer-Lang, Le Talec, and Tomolillo, *Un mouvement gai*, 71.

102 Ibid., 89.

103 Sister Mary-Anna Lingus, Sisters of Perpetual Indulgence—London House, interview with the author, 16 December 2016.

104 Thompson, "Children of Paradise." The Sisters appear only on pp. 60–61.

105 The Archabbess, interview with the author, 23 March 2012.

106 Another early member of the Heidelberg house and the second Guard in the international order, Guard Ambrosio de Membro Sancto, recalls that the Heidelberg house arose out of "a circle of spiritual gay men who held Pink Masses and performed Energy Circles at sacred Celtic locations in our neighbourhood" and "named ourselves GAYA, an amalgam of Gay and Gaia, the Greek goddess personifying Earth." See McCartney, "Sistory of the Guard Tradition."

107 Hermana Dolores Raimunda, Hermanas de la Perpetua Indulgencia del Uruguay, Orden de San Felipe y Santiago de Montevideo, interview with the author, 17 December 2013.

108 Couvent de Paname, International Conclave papers.

109 Welzer-Lang, Le Talec, and Tomolillo, *Un mouvement gai*, 92.

110 Order of Perpetual Indulgence, First National Convocation flyer; Mother Premonstratensia, Order of Perpetual Indulgence—Sydney House, interview with the author, 12 December 2013.

111 Humperpickle, "SisTree"; Wafer, "Uncle Doreen's Family Drag Album"; Terzon, "The Sisters of Perpetual Indulgence." Thanks to Nick Henderson for bringing the latter article to my attention.

112 "No More Guilt but Plenty of Indulgence"; "Queen City Report."

113 Sister Unity Divine, Sisters of Perpetual Indulgence—Los Angeles House, interview with the author, 29 October 2013.

114 Cherry, "Elevation of the Convent in Montreal."

CHAPTER 2. "WE ARE NUNS, SILLY!"

1 Welzer-Lang, Le Talec, and Tomolillo, *Un mouvement gai*, 57; Sister Soami, Missionary Order of Perpetual Indulgence, interview with the author, 9 June 2012.

2 Sisters of Perpetual Indulgence, "Mass in a Time of War against V.D." The model for this prayer is the Roman Catholic Our Father, used in a slightly truncated version as the Lord's Prayer in Protestant churches as well.

3 Church Ladies for Choice, "Starter Kit" (New York, 1993), 7, qtd. in Cohen-Cruz, "At Cross-Purposes," 91.

4 *Church Ladies Song Book*, n.d., qtd. in Shepard, *Queer Political Performance and Protest*, 121.

5 See Kalb, "The Gospel According to Billy"; Shepard, *Queer Political Performance and Protest*, 235–36.

6 The Abbey of St. Joan, "About Us," theabbey.org (last accessed 4 August 2015).

7 Warner, *Acts of Gaiety*; Shepard, *Queer Political Performance and Protest*.

8 In *Queer Political Performance and Protest*, the Sisters appear almost as a backdrop; they are always part of the scene, yet the eye seems to slide over them before stopping on another group for analysis. The same is true, surprisingly, of one of the definitive histories of queer communities in San Francisco, Stryker and Van Buskirk's *Gay by the Bay*, in which the Sisters appear four times as passing references, part of the psychedelically queer wallpaper of the city but apparently not meriting concerted attention.

9 Muñoz, *Disidentifications*, 11.

10 Ibid., 28, 31.

11 Ibid., 103–11.

12 Ibid., 181–200.

13 Hutcheon, *A Theory of Parody*, 6.

14 Denisoff, *Aestheticism and Sexual Parody*, 3–4.

15 Sister Krissy Fiction, Order of Benevolent Bliss (Portland, Oregon), interview with the author, 1 November 2009.

16 Previous commentators on the Sisters have noted their parody but have tended to downplay its serious aspect or have not explored this combination of seriousness and parody at length. See Lucas, "The Color of His Eyes"; Welzer-Lang, Le Talec, and Tomolillo, *Un mouvement gai*; Glenn, "Queering the (Sacred) Body Politic"; and Crawford, "'Go Forth and Sin Some More!'"

17 Welzer-Lang, Le Talec, and Tomolillo, *Un mouvement gai*, 135 (translation mine, italics in original).

18 Ibid., 290 (translation mine). I have chosen the word "mimesis" rather than "mimicry" to translate *mimétisme* because I think it better captures both Le Talec's meaning and the *serious* parody of the Sisters through the time-honored use of the term *mimesis* in theoretical work on art, literature, and performance.

19 Petro, *After the Wrath of God*, 93.

20 Grand Mother Vicious Power Hungry Bitch, Sisters of Perpetual Indulgence—San Francisco House, interview with the author, 21 November 2011.

21 Photos by John Entwistle, courtesy of Sister Soami.

22 Several Sydney Sisters told me of this event; a photograph with a brief caption appears in Humphries and McDonald, *Barry Humphries' Flashbacks*, 175. Thanks to Will Visconti for sending this source my way. Other images of the Fred Nile effigy are among the holdings of the Australian Lesbian and Gay Archives (ALGA).

23 Several Sisters recounted this event; the most complete versions come from Sister Krissy Fiction, Order of Benevolent Bliss (Portland, Oregon), interview with the author, 1 November 2009; Sister Reva Lation, Order of Benevolent Bliss (Portland, Oregon), interview with the author, 1 November 2009; and Sister Stella Standing, The Abbey of St. Joan (Seattle), interview with the author, 18 July 2010.

24 Richardson, *Words Kill*.

25 Welzer, Le Talec, and Tomolillo, *Un mouvement gai*, 87 (translation mine).

26 Ibid. The Mass was said in English, and Le Talec reproduces the text in that language.

27 Ibid.

28 Ibid., 87–88; Sister X, "I Took the Vow" (1991); "I Took the Vow" (1993).

29 See, for instance, Goss, *Queering Christ*. For a broader historical overview of eroticism in Christian devotion, see Rambuss, *Closet Devotions*.

30 Gould, *Moving Politics*, 137–38.

31 Sisters of Perpetual Indulgence, *Play Fair!*

32 E.g., Cvetkovich, *An Archive of Feelings*; Ahmed, *The Cultural Politics of Emotion*; Gould, *Moving Politics*; Shepard, *Queer Political Performance and Protest*; and Warner, *Acts of Gaiety*. For a discussion of affect in religious politics, see Moon, *God, Sex, and Politics*.

33 Sister Mona Little-Moore, Order of Benevolent Bliss (Portland, Oregon), interview with the author, 7 February 2010.

34 Jordan, *The Silence of Sodom*, 182.

35 I intentionally do not include drag kings in this list, because Sister personas are feminine. While masculine personas are also a form of drag, they are rarer and are often ignored by the gay male community. Masculine drag performed by female-bodied people occurs most commonly among Guards, but is in general a rarity in the order as a whole.

36 See "The Sisters of Perpetual Indulgence Wish to Announce." A similar argument has returned of late, but with a new twist: some members of transgender communities consider drag queen acts to be offensive; see, for instance, Gander, "Drag Queens Banned." It will be interesting to watch this dynamic as it unfolds, specifically with reference to possible future critiques of the Sisters. The order does have transgender members, but has at times struggled to be as welcoming of them as some members would like to be, and there have been tensions between the San Francisco house and some trans women activists in recent years.

37 Sisters of Perpetual Indulgence—San Francisco House, greeting card, n.d. Sisters of Perpetual Indulgence archives, San Francisco, California.

38 Grand Mother Vicious Power Hungry Bitch, Sisters of Perpetual Indulgence—San Francisco House, interview with the author, 21 November 2011.

39 Sister Soami, Missionary Order of Perpetual Indulgence, interview with the author, 10 June 2012.

40 Sister Rowena Keeper of the Holy Doiley, Order of Perpetual Indulgence—Sydney House, interview with the author, 15 November 2013.

41 To reiterate, I am concerned here with stereotypes and am not making claims about the actual characteristics of drag queens.

42 Sister Anna Wrecks-Ya, Order of Benevolent Bliss (Portland, Oregon), interview with the author, 2 November 2009.

43 Hermana Prudencia Ernestina Simona Cruciphija Cienfuegos, Hermanas de la Perpetua Indulgencia del Uruguay, Orden de San Felipe y Santiago de Montevideo, interview with the author, 10 December 2013 (translation mine).

44 Sister Soami, Missionary Order of Perpetual Indulgence, interview with the author, 10 June 2012.

45 My thoughts on sacrilege in the Sisters have been influenced in part by Le Talec, who distinguishes between blasphemy and sacrilege and rightly places the order firmly in the latter camp. See, in particular, Welzer-Lang, Le Talec, and Tomolillo, *Un mouvement gai*, 144–45. My thinking on the erotics of sacrilege owes a great deal to Mark Jordan's book *The Silence of Sodom*, particularly his chapter "Reiteration, or The Pleasures of Obedience."

46 Sister Dominé Trix, The Abbey of St. Joan (Seattle), interview with the author, 9 April 2011.

47 Sister Pure Heart, The Abbey of St. Joan (Seattle), interview with the author, 24 July 2011.

48 Sister Maria Caffeina Mochalatte, The Abbey of St. Joan (Seattle), interview with the author, 19 August 2011.

49 Order of Perpetual Indulgence—Sydney House, "Why Do We Exist?"

50 Novice Sister Petunia Encarnata, Abbey of the Long Cedar Canoe (Vancouver), interview with the author, 16 August 2011.

51 Sister Baba Ganesh, Sisters of Perpetual Indulgence—San Francisco House, interview with the author, 11 July 2012.

52 Guard Noah Shame and Guard Lance Boyles, Order of Benevolent Bliss (Portland, Oregon), interview with the author, 25 March 2010.

53 Sister Maya Poonani, Order of Benevolent Bliss (Portland, Oregon), interview with the author, 1 November 2009. As Rohit Dasgupta reminded me in conversation (24 July 2015), Sister Maya's last name is Hindi slang for female genitalia. This is but one small hint of the larger global dynamics of power in which the Sisters often unwittingly take part.

54 Sister Nadia Ahnwilda, The Abbey of St. Joan (Seattle), interview with the author, 9 April 2011.

55 Sister Dominé Trix, The Abbey of St. Joan (Seattle), interview with the author, 9 April 2011.

56 Sister Alma Children, Order of Benevolent Bliss (Portland, Oregon), interview with the author, 1 November 2009.

57 Sister Glo Euro N'Wei, The Abbey of St. Joan (Seattle), interview with the author, 10 April 2011.

58 Sister Odora Flatulotta D'Pew, Grand Canyon Sisters of Perpetual Indulgence, interview with the author, 19 August 2011.

59 Sister Loganberry Frost, Sister Mary Media, and Sister Σplace., Sisters of Perpetual Indulgence—San Francisco House, interview with the author, 19 April 2014.

60 Cleto, "Introduction: Queering the Camp," 3 (italics in original).

61 Such as the story, prominently featured in both the documentary *The Sisters* and the film's widely available trailer but repudiated by every early Sister with whom I spoke, that some early members of the order were sex workers who needed to hide their identities as Sisters from their clients. The story was told by a Sister who joined the order after the period in question, but because of the popularity of the documentary among members of the order and the seniority of the Sister who made the claim, it has become widely taken as truth and was related to me multiple times with varying levels of amusement, seriousness, and discomfort. Hoschek and Smejkal, *The Sisters/Die Schwestern*. The segment in question is at 39:33–39:43.

62 Sister Mona Little-Moore, Order of Benevolent Bliss (Portland, Oregon), interview with the author, 7 February 2010.

63 This definition parallels that offered by the *Oxford English Dictionary*: "The policy of active participation or engagement in a particular sphere of activity; spec. the use of vigorous campaigning to bring about political or social change."

64 Sœur Rose, Paname Couvent des Sœurs (Paris), interview with the author, 27 May 2011.

65 Emma Goldman, *Living My Life*, abridged by M. Brody (London: Penguin, 2006), 42, qtd. in Thompson, *Performance Affects*, 1.

66 Thompson, *Performance Affects*, 136, 140.

67 Reverend Sister Merry Peter, Sisters of Perpetual Indulgence—San Francisco House, interview with the author, 11 July 2012.

68 Sister Unity Divine, Sisters of Perpetual Indulgence—Los Angeles House, interview with the author, 29 October 2013.

69 Warner, *Acts of Gaiety*, 192.

CHAPTER 3. "A SACRED, POWERFUL WOMAN"

1 Sister VixXxen, The Abbey of St. Joan (Seattle), interview with the author, 17 July 2010. Sister VixXxen is of Mexican and Scandinavian descent; by "among my tribe" she likely means within the queer community.

2 E.g., Philia, "Dragphobia!"

3 Sister Soami, Missionary Order of Perpetual Indulgence, interview with the author, 9 June 2012.

4 See, for instance, Jones, "Open Letter."

5 Sister Honey, BE!, Sisters of Perpetual Indulgence—San Francisco House, interview with the author, 11 July 2012.

6 Mother Katharina Lætitiam Donans, OSPI, Erzmutterhaus Sankta Melitta Iuvenis zu Berlin, interview with the author, 23 March 2012. *Tunte* is, in that regard, similar to the French *folle*, a category in which Le Talec includes the Sisters and in which Sœur Rose includes herself. See Le Talec, *Folles de France*; Sœur Rose, Paname Couvent des Sœurs (Paris), interview with the author, 27 May 2011.

7 Sister Urania, interview with the author.

8 See Hennen, *Faeries, Bears, and Leathermen.*

9 See Rupp, *Sapphistries*, 146–51.

10 See ibid., 198; and Stein, *Rethinking the Gay and Lesbian Movement*, 56–57.

11 See Stein, *Rethinking the Gay and Lesbian Movement.*

12 Meyerowitz, *How Sex Changed*, 225–26.

13 Valentine, *Imagining Transgender*, 202 (italics in original).

14 Timmons, *The Trouble with Harry Hay.*

15 Heilbroner and Davis, *American Experience: Stonewall Uprising*, 44:55–45:15. The speaker is Richard Inman, president of the Mattachine Society of Florida. According to the film, the clip is taken from a 1966 program called "The Homosexual," aired by WTVJ in Miami, Florida.

16 See Valentine, *Imagining Transgender*, esp. chap. 4, for both an overview and a critique of this movement; for a conversation between Native Two-Spirit people, both activists and anthropologists, and non-Native anthropologists about the harm done by these overarching theories and their appropriation by non-Native activists and anthropologists, see Jacobs, Thomas, and Lang, *Two-Spirit People.*

17 Hay, "Toward the New Frontiers of Fairy," 254.

18 Sister Urania, interview with the author.

19 Mother Belleza Tulips@analia and Sister Benedikta, Swiss Order of Perpetual Indulgence, interview with the author, 6 September 2010.

20 Novice Sister Petunia Encarnata, Abbey of the Long Cedar Canoe (Vancouver), interview with the author, 16 August 2011.

21 Sister Honey, BE!, Sisters of Perpetual Indulgence—San Francisco House, interview with the author, 11 July 2012.

22 Sister Maria Caffeina Mochalatte, The Abbey of St. Joan (Seattle), interview with the author, 19 August 2011.

23 See, for instance, Stein, *Rethinking the Gay and Lesbian Movement*, 83.

24 Sister MaryMae Himm, Sisters of Perpetual Indulgence—San Francisco House, interview with the author, 9 July 2012.

25 Sister Connie Pinko, Sisters of Perpetual Indulgence—San Francisco House, interview with the author, 16 August 2011.

26 Novice Sister Jen Derfukt, Order of Benevolent Bliss (Portland, Oregon), interview with the author, 7 February 2010.

27 Fieldnotes, Berlin, Germany, 24 March 2012.

28 Novice Sister Betti Crotcher, Order of Benevolent Bliss (Portland, Oregon), interview with the author, 26 March 2010.

29 Guard Noah Shame and Guard Lance Boyles, Order of Benevolent Bliss (Portland, Oregon), interview with the author, 25 March 2010.

30 Hermana Prudencia Ernestina Simona Cruciphija Cienfuegos, Hermanas de la Perpetua Indulgencia del Uruguay, Orden de San Felipe y Santiago de Montevideo, interview with the author, 10 December 2013. Notice that Hermana Prudencia uses the masculine form of the adjective "feminine" (*femenino*) to emphasize her masculine identity. Thanks to Nicole Pitsavas for this insight.

31 Mother Inferior, Order of Perpetual Indulgence—Sydney House, interview with the author, 10 October 2013.

32 Sister Rowena Keeper of the Holy Doiley, Order of Perpetual Indulgence—Sydney House, interview with the author, 15 November 2013.

33 Mother Inferior, Order of Perpetual Indulgence—Sydney House, interview with the author, 10 October 2013.

34 Brother Bimbo del Doppio Senso, Convent of Dunn Eideann (Edinburgh), interview with the author, 20 August 2011.

35 Sister Rhoda N'Lytenment, The Abbey of St. Joan (Seattle), interview with the author, 10 April 2011.

36 Sœur Néfertata, Couvent de Paris, interview with the author, 27 May 2011.

37 Sister Katie Kizum, The Abbey of St. Joan (Seattle), interview with the author, 24 July 2011.

38 Sister Ohna Fuckin' Tirade, Order of Benevolent Bliss (Portland, Oregon), interview with the author, 25 March 2010.

39 Thanks to Sister Krissy for the exact wording; Sister Krissy Fiction, Order of Benevolent Bliss (Portland, Oregon), personal communication with the author, 13 June 2016.

40 Sister Benedikta, in Mother Belleza Tulips@analia and Sister Benedikta, Swiss Order of Perpetual Indulgence, interview with the author, 6 September 2010.

41 Sister Maya Poonani, Order of Benevolent Bliss (Portland, Oregon), interview with the author, 1 November 2009.

42 Sister Krissy Fiction, Order of Benevolent Bliss (Portland, Oregon), interview with the author, 1 November 2009.

43 For the classic articulation of this theory, see Butler, *Gender Trouble*, esp. 163–90. For a more accessible articulation, see Butler, "Performative Acts and Gender Constitution."

44 Sister MaryMae Himm, Sisters of Perpetual Indulgence—San Francisco House, interview with the author, 9 July 2012.

45 Sister Babylon Anon, The Abbey of St. Joan (Seattle), interview with the author, 16 July 2010.

46 Sister Rhoda N'Lytenment, The Abbey of St. Joan (Seattle), interview with the author, 10 April 2011.

47 Possibly NYer, "What Will He Tell Them?"

48 Sister Loganberry Frost, Sister Mary Media, and Sister Σplace., Sisters of Perpetual Indulgence—San Francisco House, interview with the author, 19 April 2014.

49 E.g., LaBarbera, "San Francisco Catholic Archbishop"; KnowTrth, *Catholic Church Condones Homosexuality*. The original video was removed from online circulation; this version is spliced together with written commentary.

50 Sister Loganberry Frost, Sister Mary Media, and Sister Σplace., Sisters of Perpetual Indulgence—San Francisco House, interview with the author, 19 April 2014.

51 See, e.g., "Talk: Sisters of Perpetual Indulgence"; LaBarbera, "San Francisco Catholic Archbishop"; and Hewing, "The Desecration of the Blessed Sacrament."

52 Similar accusations of sacrilege, and similar refusals to take activists' quite nuanced and thoughtful analyses into account, attended the Stop the Church protest and especially the actions of ACT UP affiliates inside St. Patrick's Cathedral in 1989; probably quite a few of those reacting to the news of the Sisters' attendance at Most Holy Redeemer had that protest in mind. Anthony Petro offers a nuanced rereading of the Stop the Church protest, and in particular the profoundly theological act of crumbling a consecrated communion wafer, in *After the Wrath of God*.

53 Sister Daya Reckoning, The Abbey of St. Joan (Seattle), interview with the author, 18 July 2010.

54 One male persona who received particularly strong public condemnation was Mother Inferior's alter ego, Monsignor Porka Madonna, Apostolic Delegate to the Gay Community. "But it was accidental radicalism," Mother Inferior laughed. Although of Italian descent, he explained, "I wasn't as aware, because we didn't grow up speaking Italian, that Porka Madonna is . . . when you type it out, 'the Madonna is a pig,' it's pretty shocking!" Mother Inferior, Order of Perpetual Indulgence—Sydney House, interview with the author, 10 October 2013.

55 This was Sister Vibrata Electric of the Flaming Labia, who also manifested as Cardinal Packin' Pecker. I interviewed her for a previous project; Wilcox, *Queer Women*. Sister Vibrata was later excommunicated from the Los Angeles house for reasons of which I am unaware; I have been unable to contact her for many years.

56 Puar, *Terrorist Assemblages*. On embodiment, sexualization, and desexualization, see also McRuer, *Crip Theory*; and Kafer, *Feminist, Queer, Crip*.

57 My wording here is intentionally quite careful. Some forms of predatory and pedophilic heterosexuality are accepted in mainstream Western cultures, as is evidenced by the infantilization of women fashion models, the sexualization of girls, and the persistent sexualization and valorization of rape in popular culture. But images of gender-nonconforming heterosexual predation, which all tellingly exist solely in the world of heterosexual, cisgender fantasy, are represented as specifically pathological both through and because of the aspect of gender nonconformity.

58 Sister Mary Tyler Moore, interview with the author, 28 November 2016; Johnston, "Black and White TVs."
59 Grand Mother Vicious Power Hungry Bitch, Sisters of Perpetual Indulgence—San Francisco House, interview with the author, 21 November 2011.
60 See Oxx, *The Nativist Movement in America*, 52.
61 Winning Democrats, Facebook post, 22 May 2016, facebook.com (last accessed 13 June 2016).

CHAPTER 4. "SISTER OUTSIDERS"

1 Lorde, *Sister Outsider*.
2 Ganesh, "SISTERS OUTSIDER: A Love Letter."
3 U.S. Census Bureau, "U.S. Census Bureau Projections."
4 The percentage of San Francisco's population claiming solely Native American or Alaska Native ancestry is closer to 0.7 percent than to 0.07 percent; Sister Baba's figure may be a typo. See U.S. Census Bureau, "Quick Facts: San Francisco."
5 Ganesh, "SISTERS OUTSIDER: A Love Letter."
6 Ganesh, "SISTER OUTSIDERS: The Song of Sister Chiquieata Banenea."
7 Ganesh, "SISTER OUTSIDERS: 'A GIRL?'"
8 Ganesh, "Sisters Outsider: Fuck Diversity Training 101" (emphasis in original). Sister Baba's strategies involve reconceptualizing the process by which dominant groups learn about power and privilege, being open about the order's interest in involving transgender people and people of color, and—specifically for Sisters of color and trans Sisters—not giving up on the order.
9 Ganesh, "Sisters Outsider: Coming Home."
10 Fieldnotes, 18 July 2010. My own position in this situation was also difficult, as I found the comment troubling but was reluctant to put the novice in an even more awkward situation with a superior by calling out the latter.
11 Kleinhaus, "Taking Out the Trash," 195.
12 Morgensen, *Spaces between Us*, 45.
13 Ganesh, "Sisters Outsider: Coming Home."
14 Ganesh, "SISTER OUTSIDERS: The Song of Sister Chiquieata Banenea."
15 Sister Jonbennet Gesserit, interview with the author, 16 August 2011. Sister Jonbennet had no house at the time of our interview; she had been veiled independently by a member of the San Francisco house while both were caretakers at the Wolf Creek Radical Faerie Sanctuary in southern Oregon.
16 Sister Baba Ganesh, Sisters of Perpetual Indulgence—San Francisco House, interview with the author, 11 July 2012.
17 Mother Inferior, Order of Perpetual Indulgence—Sydney House, interview with the author, 10 October 2013.
18 While many people in the United States who trace their ancestry to Latin America consider their racial identity (most commonly white, black, or indigenous, but quite often also Asian) to be separate from their national heritage, that heritage is often treated in the United States as being itself racially distinct from

whiteness. Some Latinx people (a gender-neutral version of the terms "Latina," "Latino," and "Latina/o" or "Latin@") thus find it both productive and reflective of their own experiences to identify as people of color in the United States even when they might very well be considered white in their country of ancestral origin.

19 Novice Sister Spinna DeVinyl, Order of Benevolent Bliss (Portland, Oregon), interview with the author, 19 June 2010. Sister Spinna was elevated to FP shortly after this interview.

20 Guard Inya, Sister Kali Vagilistic X.P. Aladocious, Asylum of the Tortured Heart (San Diego), and Sister Trystina T. Rhume, interview with the author, 17 August 2011.

21 Use of the term "gayborhood" has expanded rapidly since the publication of Amin Ghaziani's book *There Goes the Gayborhood?* On class segregation, see, e.g., Barrett and Pollack, "Whose Gay Community?; on racial segregation, see, e.g., Green, "On the Horns of a Dilemma."

22 Fieldnotes, 17 April 2010.

23 U.S. Census Bureau, "Quick Facts: Portland."

24 Novice Sister Jen Derfukt, Order of Benevolent Bliss (Portland, Oregon), interview with the author, 7 February 2010.

25 Bonilla-Silva, *Racism without Racists.*

26 Sister Odora Flatulotta D'Pew, Grand Canyon Sisters of Perpetual Indulgence, interview with the author, 19 August 2011.

27 Ganesh, "SISTER OUTSIDERS: The Song of Sister Chiquieata Banenea."

28 Sister MaryMae Himm, Sisters of Perpetual Indulgence—San Francisco House, interview with the author, 9 July 2012.

29 Reverend Sister Merry Peter, Sisters of Perpetual Indulgence—San Francisco House, interview with the author, 11 July 2012.

30 "Neo-Nuns Rout Neo-Christians." The photo appeared on the front page of the *San Francisco Sentinel* in late August or early September 1980 as a teaser for an article penned by Reverend Mother entitled "Sisters to the Rescue."

31 Sister Soami, Missionary Order of Perpetual Indulgence, interview with the author, 9 June 2012.

32 Sister Hysterectoria, The NYC (dis)Order, interview with the author, 22 December 2012.

33 Sister Soami, Missionary Order of Perpetual Indulgence, interview with the author, 10 June 2012.

34 Sister Vish-Knew, Sisters of Perpetual Indulgence—San Francisco House, personal communication with the author, 17 June 2016.

35 See, for instance, Nolte, "Jack Fertig."

36 Sister Vish-Knew, Sisters of Perpetual Indulgence—San Francisco House, personal communication with the author, 17 June 2016.

37 Sister Soami, Missionary Order of Perpetual Indulgence, interview with the author, 10 June 2012.

38 Sista' Anita Lynchin', Order of Benevolent Bliss (Portland, Oregon), interview with the author, 24 March 2010; Sister Pure Heart, The Abbey of St. Joan (Seattle), interview with the author, 24 July 2011.

39 Hoschek and Smejkal, *The Sisters/Die Schwestern*. The film traveled the LGBT film festival circuit to no small acclaim, but to my knowledge was never commercially released other than on Vimeo.

40 Grand Mother Vicious Power Hungry Bitch, Sisters of Perpetual Indulgence—San Francisco House, interview with the author, 21 November 2011.

41 Sister Hysterectoria, The NYC (dis)Order, interview with the author, 22 December 2012.

42 Sister Angelpopstitute, traveling Sister, interview with the author, 28 May 2011; Mother Belleza Tulips@analia and Sister Benedikta, Swiss Order of Perpetual Indulgence, interview with the author, 6 September 2010.

43 Hermana Prudencia Ernestina Simona Cruciphija Cienfuegos, Hermanas de la Perpetua Indulgencia del Uruguay, Orden de San Felipe y Santiago de Montevideo, interview with the author, 10 December 2013 (translation mine).

44 Hermana Dolores Raimunda, Hermanas de la Perpetua Indulgencia del Uruguay, Orden de San Felipe y Santiago de Montevideo, interview with the author, 17 December 2013 (translation mine).

45 Sister Saviour Applause, Russian River Sisters of Perpetual Indulgence (Guerneville, California), interview with the author, 16 August 2011; Sister Dominé Trix, The Abbey of St. Joan (Seattle), interview with the author, 9 April 2011.

46 Sister GreezElda GreedLay, Order of Benevolent Bliss (Portland, Oregon), interview with the author, 20 August 2011.

47 Novice Sister D'Wanna DeWitt, Order of Benevolent Bliss (Portland, Oregon), interview with the author, 11 August 2011.

48 Novice Sister Gaia T., Sister Nova Aggra, and Father Oh, Mary!, Abbey of the Big Red Wood (Eureka, California), interview with the author, 20 August 2011.

49 Sister MaryMae Himm, Sisters of Perpetual Indulgence—San Francisco House, interview with the author, 9 July 2012.

50 Sister Pure Heart, The Abbey of St. Joan (Seattle), interview with the author, 24 July 2011.

51 Novice Sister Jen Derfukt, Order of Benevolent Bliss (Portland, Oregon), interview with the author, 7 February 2010.

52 Sister Jonbennet Gesserit, interview with the author, 16 August 2011.

53 Sister Baba Ganesh, Sisters of Perpetual Indulgence—San Francisco House, interview with the author, 11 July 2012.

54 Sister Mary-Kohn, Sisters of Perpetual Indulgence—Los Angeles House, interview with the author, 20 August 2011.

55 McAllister, *Whiting Up*, 11, 18. See also Muñoz, "The White to Be Angry: Vaginal Creme Davis's Terrorist Drag," in *Disidentifications*, 93–115.

56 Sista' Anita Lynchin', Order of Benevolent Bliss (Portland, Oregon), interview with the author, 24 March 2010.

57 Sister Unity Divine, "Sister Unity's Bear Attack," YouTube, 8 July 2007 (last accessed 23 June 2016).

58 Sister Unity Divine, "Berdache, The Holy Gay," YouTube, 1 November 2007 (last accessed 23 June 2016).

59 De Becker, *The Other Face of Love.* Sister Unity notes the publication date as 1964, which is when the book first appeared in French.

60 Sister Unity Divine, "Berdache, the Holy Gay."

61 E.g., Williams, *The Spirit and the Flesh*; Roscoe, *The Zuni Man-Woman*; and Roscoe, *Queer Spirits*, among quite a few others. Scott Morgensen's *Spaces between Us* offers an extended analysis of the role played by the berdache story in *RFD*, a periodical closely associated with the Sisters not only through the Radical Faeries but also because it was founded, prior to the existence of either Sisters or Faeries, in the Iowa farmhouse commune in which Ken Bunch lived at the time.

62 Grahn's *Another Mother Tongue* was instrumental in bringing these ideas into lesbian communities, still often quite separate from their gay male counterparts when the book was originally published in 1984. Arthur Evans's book *Witchcraft and the Gay Counter-Culture* may have initiated the trend of reading the berdache story into neopaganism, and Eisler's book *The Chalice and the Blade* produced both of the above-mentioned effects. For an example of the integration of "homosexuals" and "Faeries" into the Burning Times narrative, see Starhawk, *The Spiral Dance*, 21. For transgender activists' adoption of the berdache story, one need look no further than Leslie Feinberg's iconic book, *Transgender Warriors*.

63 Morgensen, *Spaces between Us*, 127–59.

64 Thompson, *Gay Spirit.*

65 Grahn, *Another Mother Tongue.* Morgensen argues that Grahn's book "narrated U.S. lesbian and gay history as a colonial desire of non-Natives for a sense of place on Native land" (Morgensen, *Spaces between Us*, 4–12).

66 Sister Urania, interview with the author.

67 Morgensen, *Spaces between Us.*

68 Sister Unity Divine, Sisters of Perpetual Indulgence—Los Angeles House, interview with the author, 29 October 2013.

69 Sister Hysterectoria, The NYC (dis)Order, interview with the author, 22 December 2012.

70 Sister MaryMae Himm, Sisters of Perpetual Indulgence—San Francisco House, interview with the author, 9 July 2012.

71 Mother Belleza Tulips@analia and Sister Benedikta, Swiss Order of Perpetual Indulgence, interview with the author, 6 September 2010.

72 Sister Angelpopstitute, traveling Sister, interview with the author, 28 May 2011; Guard Inya, Sister Kali Vagilistic X.P. Aladocious, Asylum of the Tortured Heart (San Diego), and Sister Trystina T. Rhume, interview with the author, 17 August 2011.

73 Sister Vish-Knew, Sisters of Perpetual Indulgence—San Francisco House, personal communication, 31 January 2016.

74 Morris, "'Cabaret,'" 152–53.
75 Belletto, "'Cabaret' and Antifascist Aesthetics," 615–16.
76 Ibid., 616.
77 Ibid., 618. Belletto relies here on Adorno's essay "Commitment," in *Notes to Literature*, vol. 2, ed. Rolf Tiedemann, trans. Shierry Weber Nicholsen (New York: Columbia University Press), 76–94.
78 Lott, *Love and Theft*, 29.
79 McAllister, *Whiting Up*, 18.
80 Siegel, "Clown Politics"; Fletcher, "Of Minutemen and Rebel Clown Armies."
81 Muñoz, *Disidentifications*, esp. chap. 4.
82 Brightman, "Traditions of Subversion," 272.
83 Ibid., 284.
84 Ibid., 278.
85 Ibid.
86 Ibid., 284.

CHAPTER 5. "A SECULAR NUN"

1 Sister Cuminja Wrasse, London House of Common Sluts, interview with the author, 28 May 2011.
2 Heelas and Woodhead, *The Spiritual Revolution*. On secularization and post-secularism, see, e.g., Berger, "The Desecularization of the World"; Bruce, "The Curious Case of the Unnecessary Recantation"; Habermas, "Notes on Post-Secular Society"; Gorski and Altinordu, "After Secularization?"; and Furani, "Is There a Postsecular?"
3 Glenn Vernon may have been the first to call attention to the relevance of the religiously unaffiliated and to dub them the "religious 'nones'"; see Vernon, "The Religious 'Nones.'" Since at least the mid-2000s, scholarship in this area has been burgeoning. For just a few selected examples, see Lim, MacGregor, and Putnam, "Secular and Liminal"; Singleton, "Are Religious 'Nones' Secular?"; and Wilkins-Laflamme, "How Unreligious Are the Religious 'Nones'?"
4 A good survey of this literature is Yip, "Coming Home from the Wilderness."
5 On the Protestant and colonial roots of religious studies as a field, see, e.g., Asad, *Genealogies of Religion*; and Masuzawa, *The Invention of World Religions*. On the debates over the meaning of religious freedom, see Michaelson, *Redefining Religious Liberty*; and Clarkson, *When Exemption Is the Rule*. This movement was foreshadowed by the political developments analyzed by Jakobsen and Pellegrini in *Love the Sin*.
6 Heelas and Woodhead, *The Spiritual Revolution*. For an analysis of the role of gender in what Heelas and Woodhead call the "subjective turn," see Sointu and Woodhead, "Spirituality, Gender, and Expressive Selfhood." On my work with other study participants, see Wilcox, *Queer Women*.
7 For a review of this literature, see Pollack, Müller, and Pickel, *The Social Significance of Religion*, 1–14.

8 Much of the data on patterns of youth religiosity in the United States have come from the landmark National Study of Youth and Religion; for a recent examination of these data, see Hardie, Pearce, and Denton, "The Dynamics and Correlates of Religious Service Attendance." On LGBTQ identity and religious attendance patterns, see Wilcox, *Queer Women*.

9 E.g., Tolliver, "Comments on Snorton's 'Negotiating the Glass Closet'"; and Snorton, "A Response to Tolliver."

10 Sista' Anita Lynchin', Order of Benevolent Bliss (Portland, Oregon), interview with the author, 24 March 2010.

11 Sister Nadia Ahnwilda, The Abbey of St. Joan (Seattle), interview with the author, 9 April 2011.

12 Guard Inya, Sister Kali Vagilistic X.P. Aladocious, Asylum of the Tortured Heart (San Diego), and Sister Trystina T. Rhume, interview with the author, 17 August 2011. To reiterate, the Sisters consider their work to be a form of ministry; thus, Sister Trystina is a fourth-generation minister, even though she is not a fourth-generation *Methodist* minister.

13 Sister Sorenda 'da Booty, Russian River Sisters of Perpetual Indulgence (Guerneville, California), interview with the author, 16 August 2011.

14 Sister Kerianna Cross, Sister Amanda de Flower, and Sister Ophelia Nutz, DFW Sisters, Abbey of the Lone Star, interview with the author, 19 August 2011.

15 Mother Loosy Lust Bea Lady, Sister Gloria-Areola all over Gluttony, and Sister Sioux St. Semen Sloth, Sin Sity Sisters (Las Vegas), interview with the author, 20 August 2011.

16 Sister Unity Divine, Sisters of Perpetual Indulgence—Los Angeles House, interview with the author, 29 October 2013.

17 The Center for Spiritual Living is a metaphysical religious movement that is related to the non-Christian descendants of Christian Science, such as Religious Science and Science of Mind.

18 Sister Polly Amorous, Order of Benevolent Bliss (Portland, Oregon), interview with the author, 7 February 2010.

19 Sister Prudence Improper, Russian River Sisters of Perpetual Indulgence (Guerneville, California), interview with the author, 16 August 2011.

20 Mother Inferior, Order of Perpetual Indulgence—Sydney House, interview with the author, 10 October 2013.

21 The term "bricolage" comes originally from Claude Lévi-Strauss; see *The Savage Mind*, 16–22. On its use in the study of religion see, for example, Hervieu-Léger, "Bricolage vaut-il dissémination?" I discuss the utility of this term in *Queer Women*, 83.

22 E.g., Bibby and Archambault, "La religion à la carte au Québec."

23 Sister Stella Standing, The Abbey of St. Joan (Seattle), interview with the author, 18 July 2010; Sister Golden Hair Surprise, Order of Benevolent Bliss (Portland, Oregon), interview with the author, 2 November 2009; Sister Nadia Ahnwilda, The Abbey of St. Joan (Seattle), interview with the author, 9 April 2011.

24 Sister Golden Hair Surprise, Order of Benevolent Bliss (Portland, Oregon), interview with the author, 2 November 2009.

25 Hermana Prudencia Ernestina Simona Crucifija Cienfuegos, Hermanas de la Perpetua Indulgencia del Uruguay, Orden de San Felipe y Santiago de Montevideo, interview with the author, 10 December 2013.

26 Sister Urania, interview with the author.

27 Mother Belleza Tulips@analia and Sister Benedikta, Swiss Order of Perpetual Indulgence, interview with the author, 6 September 2010.

28 See Killen and Silk, *Religion and Public Life in the Pacific Northwest*.

29 Sister Krissy Fiction, Order of Benevolent Bliss (Portland, Oregon), interview with the author, 1 November 2009.

30 Sister Krissy Fiction, Order of Benevolent Bliss (Portland, Oregon), personal communication with the author, 17 December 2015. On the broader Antinouan movement, see White, "The New Cultus of Antinous."

31 As one reviewer rightly noted, this claim to be nondogmatic appears dubious when one considers a broader definition of the term "dogma" and a functional definition of religion. The Sisters certainly do not tell their members what to believe, but they have sometimes dogmatic approaches to the rules and regulations, written and unspoken, that shape the order, and they certainly engage in a great deal of ritual practice—serious, parodic, and both.

32 Sister Soami, Missionary Order of Perpetual Indulgence, interview with the author, 10 June 2012.

33 Guard Inya, Sister Kali Vagilistic X.P. Aladocious, Asylum of the Tortured Heart (San Diego), and Sister Trystina T. Rhume, interview with the author, 17 August 2011.

34 Sister Maria Caffeina Mochalatte, The Abbey of St. Joan (Seattle), interview with the author, 19 August 2011.

35 Novice Sister Spinna DeVinyl, Order of Benevolent Bliss (Portland, Oregon), interview with the author, 19 June 2010.

36 Sœur Néfertata, Couvent de Paris, interview with the author, 27 May 2011.

37 Sœur Rose, Paname Couvent des Sœurs (Paris), interview with the author, 27 May 2011.

38 Sister Loganberry Frost, Sister Mary Media, and Sister Σplace., Sisters of Perpetual Indulgence—San Francisco House, interview with the author, 19 April 2014.

39 Sister Mary Arse Licked and Old Lace, Order of Perpetual Indulgence—Sydney House, interview with the author, 9 December 2013.

40 Sister Babylon Anon, The Abbey of St. Joan (Seattle), interview with the author, 16 July 2010.

41 Sister Stella Standing, The Abbey of St. Joan (Seattle), interview with the author, 18 July 2010.

42 Sister Loganberry Frost, Sister Mary Media, and Sister Σplace., Sisters of Perpetual Indulgence—San Francisco House, interview with the author, 19 April 2014.

43 Reverend Sister Merry Peter, Sisters of Perpetual Indulgence—San Francisco House, interview with the author, 11 July 2012.

44 Sister Maya Poonani, Order of Benevolent Bliss (Portland, Oregon), interview with the author, 1 November 2009.

45 Sister Constance Lee Craving, Sisters of Perpetual Indulgence—San Francisco House, interview with the author, 11 July 2012. A short film of the first such darshan is available on Vimeo: Derrick, *2007 First Friday Darshan*.

46 Sister Constance Lee Craving, Sisters of Perpetual Indulgence—San Francisco House, interview with the author, 11 July 2012.

47 See Gould, *Moving Politics*.

48 Sœur Rose, Paname Couvent des Sœurs (Paris), interview with the author, 27 May 2011.

49 McGuire, *Lived Religion*.

50 Heelas and Woodhead, *The Spiritual Revolution*.

51 Roof, *Spiritual Marketplace*; Bruce, *Religion in Modern Britain*.

52 Gauthier, Martikainen, and Woodhead point out the neoliberal overtones of such sociological metaphors in "Introduction: Religion in Market Society," 6–7.

53 Carrette and King, *Selling Spirituality*, 53.

54 Bellah et al., *Habits of the Heart*.

55 Gauthier, Martikainen, and Woodhead, "Introduction: Religion in Market Society," 6.

56 Ibid., 9.

57 Berlant and Warner, "Sex in Public."

58 Duggan, "The New Homonormativity."

59 Puar, *Terrorist Assemblages*; see esp. chap. 3.

60 Jakobsen and Pellegrini, *Love the Sin*, 117 (italics mine).

61 Wilcox, "The Separation of Church and Sex."

62 Tomso, "Viral Sex and the Politics of Life."

63 Burwell v. Hobby Lobby Stores, Inc., 573 U.S. ___ (2014).

64 Furani, "Is There a Postsecular?"; see also Jakobsen and Pellegrini, "Introduction: Times Like These."

65 The only telling exception to this rule is the French order, which distinguishes instead between "in face" or "in habit" and *en civil* (in civilian clothes).

CONCLUSION

1 Reverend Sister Merry Peter, Sisters of Perpetual Indulgence—San Francisco House, interview with the author, 11 July 2012.

2 Burity, "Entrepreneurial Spirituality," 21.

3 Sister Rowena Keeper of the Holy Doiley, Order of Perpetual Indulgence—Sydney House, interview with the author, 15 November 2013.

4 Sister Rowena Keeper of the Holy Doiley, Order of Perpetual Indulgence—Sydney House, personal communication with the author, 15 November 2013 (emphasis in original).

5 Sister Rowena Keeper of the Holy Doiley, Order of Perpetual Indulgence—Sydney House, interview with the author, 15 November 2013. Muslims Against Homophobia, founded by Alice Aslan, is still active in Sydney. See Brook, "Gay Muslims."

6 Brother Bimbo del Doppio Senso, Convent of Dunn Eideann (Edinburgh), interview with the author, 20 August 2011.

7 Nolte, "Jack Fertig."

8 Grand Mother Vicious Power Hungry Bitch, Sisters of Perpetual Indulgence—San Francisco House, interview with the author, 21 November 2011.

9 Puar, *Terrorist Assemblages*, 6.

10 Brook, "Gay Muslims."

11 Lepka, "Freedom of Expression," 628. See also Hall, "Questioning Secularization?," esp. 123–24; and Szymanowski and Lowe, "Court Rules against Polish Rock Musician."

12 Lepka, "Freedom of Expression," 629.

13 Ibid., 634.

14 Hermana Dolores Raimunda, Hermanas de la Perpetua Indulgencia del Uruguay, Orden de San Felipe y Santiago de Montevideo, interview with the author, 17 December 2013 (translation mine).

15 Lepka, "Freedom of Expression."

16 See Orthodox Calendar, "About Us."

17 Image available in Wong, "Romanian 'Orthodox Priests' Calendar."

18 Orthodox Calendar, "About Us."

19 See Wong, "Romanian 'Orthodox Priests' Calendar."

20 E.g., Orthodox Calendar, *O.C. 2015 Promo.*

21 E.g., "Orthodox Calendar 2014."

22 Warner, *Acts of Gaiety*, 193.

23 Shepard, *Queer Political Performance and Protest*, 12.

24 Ibid., 21.

25 Warner, *Acts of Gaiety*, 192.

26 Reverend Sister Merry Peter, Sisters of Perpetual Indulgence—San Francisco House, interview with the author, 11 July 2012.

27 Gramsci, *Selections from the Prison Notebooks.*

APPENDIX B

1 See Wilcox, *Queer Women.*

2 Hoschek and Smejkal, *The Sisters/Die Schwestern.*

BIBLIOGRAPHY

Ahmed, Sara. *The Cultural Politics of Emotion*. New York: Routledge, 2004.

Allec, John. "No More Guilt! A Tour of the Territory of Perpetual Indulgence." *Body Politic*, no. 81 (March 1982): 29–31. Photocopy in the author's possession, courtesy of Sister Soami.

Altman, Dennis. *AIDS in the Mind of America*. New York: Anchor/Doubleday, 1986.

Asad, Talal. *Genealogies of Religion: Discipline and Reasons of Power in Christianity and Islam*. Baltimore: Johns Hopkins University Press, 1993.

Balass, Joe, dir. *Joy! Portrait of a Nun*. 72 mins. Montréal, QC: Films du 3 Mars, 2013.

Barrett, Donald C., and Lance M. Pollack. "Whose Gay Community? Social Class, Sexual Self-Expression, and Gay Community Involvement." *Sociological Quarterly* 46, no. 3 (Summer 2005): 437–56.

Bellah, Robert N., Richard Madsen, William M. Sullivan, Ann Swidler, and Steven M. Tipton. *Habits of the Heart: Individualism and Commitment in American Life*. Berkeley: University of California Press, 1985.

Belletto, Steven. "'Cabaret' and Antifascist Aesthetics." *Criticism* 50, no. 4 (2008): 609–30.

Berger, Peter L. "The Desecularization of the World: A Global Overview." In *The Desecularization of the World: Resurgent Religion and World Politics*, edited by Peter L. Berger, 1–18. Grand Rapids, MI: Eerdmans, 1999.

Berlant, Lauren, and Michael Warner. "Sex in Public." *Critical Inquiry* 24, no. 2 (1998): 547–66.

Bibby, Reginald W., and Isabelle Archambault. "La religion à la carte au Québec: Un problème d'offre, de demande, ou des deux?" *Globe: Revue Internationale d'Études Québecoises* 11, no. 1 (2008): 151–79.

Bonilla-Silva, Eduardo. *Racism without Racists: Color-Blind Racism and the Persistence of Racial Inequality in the United States*. Lanham, MD: Rowman and Littlefield, 2003.

Boyd, Nan Alamilla. *Wide-Open Town: A History of Queer San Francisco to 1965*. Berkeley: University of California Press, 2003.

Brightman, Robert. "Traditions of Subversion and the Subversion of Tradition: Cultural Criticism in Maidu Clown Performances." *American Anthropologist*, n.s., 101, no. 2 (June 1999): 272–87.

Brook, Benedict. "Gay Muslims, Out Olympians, Pirate Drag Queens, and Lots of Ruby Rose Lookalikes—Welcome to Mardi Gras." *News.com.au*, 3 March 2016. www.news.com.au. Last accessed 28 July 2016.

Brown, Mark. Letter to Ken Bunch. 9 April 1982. Sisters of Perpetual Indulgence, ONE Subject Files Collection, 2012.001, ONE Archives, Los Angeles.

Bruce, Steve. "The Curious Case of the Unnecessary Recantation: Berger and Secularization." In *Peter Berger and the Study of Religion*, edited by Linda Woodhead, 87–100. New York: Routledge, 2001.

———. *Religion in Modern Britain*. New York: Oxford University Press, 1995.

Burity, Joanildo A. "Entrepreneurial Spirituality and Ecumenical Alterglobalism: Two Religious Responses to Global Neoliberalism." In *Religion in the Neoliberal Age: Political Economy and Modes of Governance*, edited by Tuomas Martikainen and François Gauthier, 21–36. Burlington, VT: Ashgate, 2013.

Butler, Judith. *Gender Trouble: Feminism and the Subversion of Identity*. New York: Routledge, [1990] 1999.

———. "Performative Acts and Gender Constitution: An Essay in Phenomenology and Feminist Theory." *Theatre Journal* 40, no. 4 (1988): 519–31.

Caen, Herb. "Friday's Fractured Flicker." *San Francisco Chronicle*, 17 October 1980. Sisters of Perpetual Indulgence, ONE Subject Files Collection, 2012.001, ONE Archives, Los Angeles.

Carrette, Jeremy, and Richard King. *Selling Spirituality: The Silent Takeover of Religion*. New York: Routledge, 2005.

Cherry, Sœur. "Elevation of the Convent in Montreal." 12 November 2016. Les Sœurs de Montréal. soeursdemontreal.ca. Last accessed 20 December 2016.

Clarkson, Frederick. *When Exemption Is the Rule: The Religious Freedom Strategy of the Christian Right*. Somerville, MA: Political Research Associates, 2016.

Cleto, Fabio. "Introduction: Queering the Camp." In *Camp: Queer Aesthetics and the Performing Subject: A Reader*, 1–42. Ann Arbor: University of Michigan Press, 1999.

Cohen-Cruz, Jan. "At Cross-Purposes: The Church Ladies for Choice." In *Radical Street Performance: An International Anthology*, edited by Jan Cohen-Cruz, 90–99. New York: Routledge, 1998.

Couvent de Paname. International Conclave papers, 1996–1997. Photocopy in the author's possession, courtesy of Sister Soami.

Crawford, Jason B. "'Go Forth and Sin Some More!' A Performance Geography of the San Francisco Sisters of Perpetual Indulgence." Ph.D. diss., Concordia University, 2011.

Crimp, Douglas. "How to Have Promiscuity in an Epidemic." *October* 43 (1987): 237–71.

Cvetkovich, Ann. *An Archive of Feelings: Trauma, Sexuality, and Lesbian Public Cultures*. Durham: Duke University Press, 2003.

Day, Greg. "The Sisters of Perpetual Indulgence." *Alternate*, January 1981, 12–16. Sisters of Perpetual Indulgence, ONE Subject Files Collection, 2012.001, ONE Archives, Los Angeles.

Dean, Tim. *Unlimited Intimacy: Reflections on the Subculture of Barebacking*. Chicago: University of Chicago Press, 2009.

de Becker, Raymond. *The Other Face of Love*. Trans. Margaret Crosland and Alan Daventry. New York: Grove, 1969.

DeLight, Sister Missionary (formerly Sister Missionary Position). Letter to German Sisters of Perpetual Indulgence. Holy Saturday, 1992. Photocopy in the author's possession, courtesy of Sister Soami.

Denisoff, Dennis. *Aestheticism and Sexual Parody, 1840–1940.* New York: Cambridge, 2001.

Derrick, Rena, dir. *2007 First Friday Darshan.* 4 mins. 2016. vimeo.com. Last accessed 10 October 2016.

Duggan, Lisa. "The New Homonormativity: The Sexual Politics of Neoliberalism." In *Materializing Democracy: Toward a Revitalized Cultural Politics,* edited by Russ Castronovo and Dana D. Nelson, 175–94. Durham: Duke University Press, 2002.

Eisler, Riane. *The Chalice and the Blade: Our History, Our Future.* San Francisco: Harper SanFrancisco, 1987.

Erzen, Tanya. *Straight to Jesus: Sexual and Christian Conversions in the Ex-Gay Movement.* Berkeley: University of California Press, 2006.

"Escándalo gay en U.S.A.: ¡Monjas travestis!" *Marcha: La Revista Explosiva,* no. 2 (7 July 1981). Sisters of Perpetual Indulgence, ONE Subject Files Collection, 2012.001, ONE Archives, Los Angeles.

Evans, Arthur. *Witchcraft and the Gay Counter-Culture.* Boston: Fag Rag Books, 1978.

Feinberg, Leslie. *Transgender Warriors: Making History from Joan of Arc to RuPaul.* Boston: Beacon, 1996.

Fertig, Jack. "Doing What the Sisters Do Best." *Bay Times,* May 1989, 9. Photocopy in the author's possession, courtesy of Sister Soami.

———. Oral history interview with Roland Schambari. 29 May 1998. GLBT Historical Society, San Francisco.

Fletcher, John. "Of Minutemen and Rebel Clown Armies: Reconsidering Transformative Citizenship." *Text and Performance Quarterly* 29, no. 3 (2009): 222–38.

Furani, Khaled. "Is There a Postsecular?" *Journal of the American Academy of Religion* 83, no. 1 (2015): 1–26.

Gander, Kashmira. "Drag Queens Banned from Performing at Free Pride Glasgow Event over Fears Acts Will Offend Trans People." *Independent,* 21 July 2015. www.independent.co.uk. Last accessed 6 August 2015.

Ganesh, Sister Baba/Joël Barraquiel Tan. "SISTER OUTSIDERS: 'A GIRL? A REAL GIRL?' a.k.a. Nv. Sister Leigh Viticus + the 2-Headed Calf." *Baba's Blog,* 31 May 2014. joelbtan.tumblr.com. Last accessed 17 June 2016.

———. "SISTER OUTSIDERS: The Song of Sister Chiquieata Banenea from the A.T.L." *Baba's Blog,* 19 May 2014. joelbtan.tumblr.com. Last accessed 17 June 2016.

———. "Sisters Outsider: Coming Home for Sister Freida Peoples." *Baba's Blog,* 9 February 2015. joelbtan.tumblr.com. Last accessed 20 June 2016.

———. "Sisters Outsider: Fuck Diversity Training 101 + 3 Tips for 2043." *Baba's Blog,* 4 December 2014. joelbtan.tumblr.com. Last accessed 20 June 2016.

———. "SISTERS OUTSIDER: A Love Letter to Sisters of Color on Race + 2043." *Baba's Blog,* 13 May 2014. joelbtan.tumblr.com. Last accessed 17 June 2016.

Gauthier, François, Tuomas Martikainen, and Linda Woodhead. "Introduction: Religion in Market Society." In *Religion in the Neoliberal Age: Political Economy and Modes of Governance*, edited by Tuomas Martikainen and François Gauthier, 1–17. Burlington, VT: Ashgate, 2013.

"A Gay Day for a Parade." *San Francisco Examiner*, 29 June 1981, D11. Sisters of Perpetual Indulgence, ONE Subject Files Collection, 2012.001, ONE Archives, Los Angeles.

Ghaziani, Amin. *There Goes the Gayborhood?* Princeton: Princeton University Press, 2014.

Glenn, Cathy B. "Queering the (Sacred) Body Politic: Considering the Performative Cultural Politics of the Sisters of Perpetual Indulgence." *Theory and Event* 7, no. 1 (2003), n.p.

Gorski, Philip S., and Ateş Altinordu. "After Secularization?" *Annual Review of Sociology* 34 (2008): 55–85.

Goss, Robert. *Queering Christ: Beyond "Jesus Acted Up."* Cleveland: Pilgrim, 2002.

Gould, Deborah B. *Moving Politics: Emotion and ACT UP's Fight against AIDS.* Chicago: University of Chicago Press, 2009.

Grahn, Judy. *Another Mother Tongue: Gay Words, Gay Worlds.* Boston: Beacon, 1984.

Gramsci, Antonio. *Selections from the Prison Notebooks of Antonio Gramsci.* Ed. and trans. Quintin Hoare and Geoffrey Nowell Smith. New York: International Publishers, 1971.

Green, Adam Isaiah. "On the Horns of a Dilemma: Institutional Dimensions of the Sexual Career in a Sample of Middle-Class, Urban, Black, Gay Men." *Journal of Black Studies* 37, no. 5 (May 2007): 753–74.

Habermas, Jürgen. "Notes on Post-Secular Society." *New Perspectives Quarterly* 25, no. 4 (2008): 17–29.

Hall, Dorota. "Questioning Secularization? Church and Religion in Poland." In *The Social Significance of Religion in the Enlarged Europe: Secularization, Individualization, and Pluralization*, edited by Detlef Pollack, Olaf Müller, and Gert Pickel, 121–41. Burlington, VT: Ashgate, 2012.

Hansen, Vinnie. "Male Nuns Spread Joy and Absurdity." *San Francisco Neighborhood Perspective* 1, no. 7 (December 1980): 1. Sisters of Perpetual Indulgence, ONE Subject Files Collection, 2012.001, ONE Archives, Los Angeles.

Hardie, Jessica Halliday, Lisa D. Pearce, and Melinda Lundquist Denton. "The Dynamics and Correlates of Religious Service Attendance in Adolescence." *Youth and Society* 48, no. 2 (2016): 151–75.

Hay, Harry. "Toward the New Frontiers of Fairy Vision . . . subject-SUBJECT Consciousness." In *Radically Gay: Gay Liberation in the Words of Its Founder*, edited by Will Roscoe, 254–64. Boston: Beacon, 1996.

"Headlines First Annual Dog Show Parade." 7 June 1981. Flyer in the author's possession, courtesy of Sister Soami.

Heelas, Paul, and Linda Woodhead. *The Spiritual Revolution: Why Religion Is Giving Way to Spirituality.* Malden, MA: Blackwell, 2005.

Heilbroner, David, and Kate Davis, dirs. *American Experience: Stonewall Uprising*. 84 mins. Public Broadcasting Service, 2005.

Hennen, Peter. *Faeries, Bears, and Leathermen: Men in Community Queering the Masculine*. Chicago: University of Chicago Press, 2008.

Herring, Scott. "Out of the Closets, into the Woods: RFD, Country Women, and the Post-Stonewall Emergence of Queer Anti-Urbanism." *American Quarterly* 59, no. 2 (2007): 341–72.

Hervieu-Léger, Danièle. "Bricolage vaut-il dissémination? Quelques réflexions sur l'opérationnalité sociologique d'une métaphore problématique." *Social Compass* 52, no. 3 (2005): 295–308.

Hewing, Bryan V. "The Desecration of the Blessed Sacrament in San Francisco and Archbishop George Niederauer." *Big B Files*, 27 March 2008. bigbfiles.wordpress .com. Last accessed 6 November 2015.

High, Sister Mary Juanita, and Sister Mary Timothy Simplicity. *The Sisters of Perpetual Indulgence, Part I: A Background*. 5 mins. In the Life Media, 2010. Available on YouTube. Last accessed 5 October 2016.

———. *The Sisters of Perpetual Indulgence, Part II: Personal Stories*. 6 mins. In the Life Media, 2010. Available on YouTube. Last accessed 5 October 2016.

———. *The Sisters of Perpetual Indulgence, Part III: Charity*. 6 mins. In the Life Media, 2010. Available on YouTube. Last accessed 6 October 2016.

Hoschek, Manfred, and Sigrid Smejkal, dirs. *The Sisters/Die Schwestern*. 73 mins. 2009. vimeo.com. Last accessed 11 September 2015.

Humperpickle, Sister Titania. "SisTree." N.d. www.perpetualindulgence.org. Last accessed 21 September 2016.

Humphries, Barry, and Roger McDonald. *Barry Humphries' Flashbacks*. London: HarperCollins, 1999.

Huston, Bo. "Holy Habits, Batman! It's Been Ten Years!" *Bay Times*, April 1989, 10. Photocopy in the author's possession, courtesy of Sister Soami.

Hutcheon, Linda. *A Theory of Parody: The Teachings of Twentieth-Century Art Forms*. 2nd ed. Champaign: University of Illinois Press, 2000.

"I Took the Vow." *Nun Issue* 1 (April 1993): 5. Sisters of Perpetual Indulgence, ONE Subject Files Collection, 2012.001, ONE Archives, Los Angeles.

Jacobs, Sue-Ellen, Wesley Thomas, and Sabine Lang, eds. *Two-Spirit People: Native American Gender Identity, Sexuality, and Spirituality*. Champaign: University of Illinois Press, 1997.

Jakobsen, Janet R., and Ann Pellegrini. "Introduction: Times Like These." In *Secularisms*, edited by Janet R. Jakobsen and Ann Pellegrini, 1–35. Durham: Duke University Press, 2008.

———. *Love the Sin: Sexual Regulation and the Limits of Religious Tolerance*. New York: New York University Press, 2003.

Johnston, Craig. "Black and White TVs: The Sisters of Perpetual Indulgence." *Star* 4, no. 8 (5 November 1982): 7. Australian Lesbian and Gay Archives, Melbourne.

Jones, Zinnia. "Open Letter: 350+ Trans Women and Transfeminine People Stand against Calpernia Addams and Andrea James." 14 April 2014. the-orbit.net. Last accessed 27 May 2016.

Jordan, Mark D. *The Silence of Sodom: Homosexuality in Modern Catholicism*. Chicago: University of Chicago Press, 2000.

Kafer, Alison. *Feminist, Queer, Crip*. Bloomington: Indiana University Press, 2013.

Kalb, Jonathan. "The Gospel According to Billy." *Theater* 31, no. 3 (2001): 161–67.

Kelley, Harry. "Walking on the Waters of Babylon: A Meditation on the Death of the Sisters of Perpetual Indulgence." *San Francisco Sentinel*, 3 April 1987, 17. Photocopy in the author's possession, courtesy of Sister Soami.

Kenkelen, Bill. "'Sisters of Perpetual Indulgence': Gays Poke Fun at 'Oppressive' Church." *National Catholic Reporter* 18, no. 6 (4 December 1981): 5.

Key, Sister Ann R., and Sister Phyllis Stein the Fragrant. "Sisters of Perpetual Indulgence." In *Gay Histories and Cultures: An Encyclopedia*, edited by George F. Haggerty, 822–23. New York: Garland, 2000.

Killen, Patricia O'Connell, and Mark Silk, eds. *Religion and Public Life in the Pacific Northwest: The None Zone*. Walnut Creek, CA: AltaMira, 2004.

Kleinhaus, Chuck. "Taking Out the Trash: Camp and the Politics of Parody." In *The Politics and Poetics of Camp*, edited by Moe Meyer, 182–201. New York: Routledge, 1994.

KnowTrth. *Catholic Church Condones Homosexuality*. 31 October 2007. Available on YouTube. Last accessed 1 June 2016.

Kyper, John. "The Week the Evangelists Tried to 'Save Sin City.'" *Gay Community News* 8, no. 8 (13 September 1980): 1. Sisters of Perpetual Indulgence, ONE Subject Files Collection, 2012.001, ONE Archives, Los Angeles.

LaBarbera, Peter. "San Francisco Catholic Archbishop George Niederauer Gives Communion to Blasphemous 'Sisters of Perpetual Indulgence.'" 9 October 2007. Americans for Truth About Homosexuality. americansfortruth.com. Last accessed 1 June 2016.

Lepka, Iwona. "Freedom of Expression in Post-Communist Poland." *Critique* 37, no. 4 (2009): 619–34.

Le Talec, Jean-Yves. *Folles de France: Repenser l'homosexualité masculine*. Paris: Éditions la Découverte, 2008.

———. "Soeurs de la Perpétuelle Indulgence, Les." In *Dictionnaire des cultures gays et lesbiennes*, edited by Didier Eribon, 442–43. Paris: Larousse, 2003.

Lévi-Strauss, Claude. *The Savage Mind*. Chicago: University of Chicago Press, 1966.

Lim, Chaeyoon, Carol Ann MacGregor, and Robert D. Putnam. "Secular and Liminal: Discovering Heterogeneity among Religious Nones." *Journal for the Scientific Study of Religion* 49, no. 4 (2010): 596–618.

London House of Common Sluts. *Play Fair! The Sisters' Guide to Safer Sex*. London, 2009. Original pamphlet in the author's possession.

Lorde, Audre. *Sister Outsider: Essays and Speeches*. Trumansburg, NY: Crossing, 1984.

Lott, Eric. *Love and Theft: Blackface Minstrelsy and the American Working Class*. New York: Oxford University Press, 1993.

Lucas, Ian. "The Color of His Eyes: Polari and the Sisters of Perpetual Indulgence." In *Queerly Phrased: Language, Gender, and Sexuality*, edited by Anna Livia and Kira Hall, 85–94. New York: Oxford University Press, 1997.

Ludlow, Lynn. "S.F.'s Zany Cheerleader: Sis Boom Boom, Rah." *San Francisco Examiner*, 13 July 1984, A1. Sisters of Perpetual Indulgence, ONE Subject Files Collection, 2012.001, ONE Archives, Los Angeles.

Masuzawa, Tomoko. *The Invention of World Religions, or, How European Universalism Was Preserved in the Language of Pluralism*. Chicago: University of Chicago Press, 2005.

McAllister, Marvin. *Whiting Up: Whiteface Minstrels and Stage Europeans in African American Performance*. Chapel Hill: University of North Carolina Press, 2011.

McCartney, Justice Aaron. "Sistory of the Guard Tradition as Written by Guard Ambrosio de Membro Sancto." 7 December 2016. www.facebook.com. Last accessed 20 December 2016.

McGuire, Meredith B. *Lived Religion: Faith and Practice in Everyday Life*. New York: Oxford University Press, 2008.

McRuer, Robert. *Crip Theory: Cultural Signs of Queerness and Disability*. New York: New York University Press, 2006.

Meyerowitz, Joanne. *How Sex Changed: A History of Transsexuality in the United States*. Cambridge: Harvard University Press, 2002.

Michaelson, Jay. *Redefining Religious Liberty: The Covert Campaign against Civil Rights*. Somerville, MA: Political Research Associates, 2013.

Moon, Dawne. *God, Sex, and Politics: Homosexuality and Everyday Theologies*. Chicago: University of Chicago Press, 2004.

Morgensen, Scott Lauria. *Spaces between Us: Queer Settler Colonialism and Indigenous Decolonization*. Minneapolis: University of Minnesota Press, 2011.

Morris, Mitchell. "'Cabaret,' America's Weimar, and Mythologies of the Gay Subject." *American Music* 22, no. 1 (2004): 145–57.

Muñoz, José Esteban. *Disidentifications: Queers of Color and the Performance of Politics*. Minneapolis: University of Minnesota Press, 1999.

Neary, Walter. "Gays Demonstrate at USF's Open House." *San Francisco Foghorn* 76, no. 7 (Halloween 1980): 2. Sisters of Perpetual Indulgence, ONE Subject Files Collection, 2012.001, ONE Archives, Los Angeles.

Neihardt, John G. *Black Elk Speaks*. Lincoln: University of Nebraska Press, [1932] 2000.

"Neo-Nuns Rout Neo-Christians." *San Francisco Sentinel*, August or September 1980, 1. Sisters of Perpetual Indulgence—San Francisco House archives, San Francisco, CA.

Newman, Marjorie, dir. *Altered Habits*. 3 mins. Stanford University, 1981. Available on YouTube. Last accessed 21 September 2016.

Nolte, Carl. "Jack Fertig—Sister Boom Boom—Dies," *SF Gate*, 7 August 2012. www.sfgate.com. Last accessed 30 December 2015.

"No More Guilt but Plenty of Indulgence: The Sisters of Perpetual Indulgence Flout Their Habits in Auckland." *OUT!*, August/September 1993, 25. Photocopy in the author's possession, courtesy of Sister Soami.

"'Nuns' Offend Homosexuals Council Told." *Toronto Star*, 26 February 1982, A6. Photocopy in the author's possession, courtesy of Sister Soami.

NYer, "What Will He Tell Them? (Archbishop Niederauer to Celebrate Mass at SF Drag Queen Parish)." *Free Republic*, 3 October 2007. www.freerepublic.com. Last accessed 13 June 2016.

Order of Perpetual Indulgence. First National Convocation. Flyer. 1994. Photocopy in the author's possession, courtesy of Sister Soami.

———. *Missionary Trail*. August 1989. Photocopy in the author's possession, courtesy of Sister Soami.

Order of Perpetual Indulgence—Sydney House. "Roll Call." N.d. www.universaljoy .com.au. Last accessed 20 August 2015.

———. "Why Do We Exist?" N.d. www.universaljoy.com.au. Last accessed 23 September 2016.

Orthodox Calendar. "About Us." N.d. www.orthodox-calendar.com. Last accessed 28 July 2016.

———. *O.C. 2015 Promo*. 4 mins. 11 September 2014. Available on YouTube. Last accessed 29 July 2016.

"Orthodox Calendar 2014: 'Romanian Priests' Get Sexy (and Gay) for Steamy Spread (NSFW)." *Huffington Post*, 5 November 2013. www.huffingtonpost.com. Last accessed 29 July 2016.

Otero, Marcelo, dir. *Que me digan loca . . .* 2011. 43 mins. Available on YouTube. Last accessed 21 September 2016.

Oxx, Katie. *The Nativist Movement in America: Religious Conflict in the Nineteenth Century*. New York: Routledge, 2013.

Patton, Cindy. *Sex and Germs: The Politics of AIDS*. Boston: South End, 1985.

Petro, Anthony M. *After the Wrath of God: AIDS, Sexuality, and American Religion*. New York: Oxford University Press, 2015.

Philia, Sister Xena. "Dragphobia!" *Nun Issue* 1, no. 1 (April 1983): 2.

Pollack, Detlef, Olaf Müller, and Gert Pickel, eds. *The Social Significance of Religion in the Enlarged Europe*. Burlington, VT: Ashgate, 2012.

Puar, Jasbir. *Terrorist Assemblages: Homonationalism in Queer Times*. Durham: Duke University Press, 2007.

"Queen City Report: Nuns on Bikes?" *OUT!*, February/March 1995, 50. Photocopy in the author's possession, courtesy of Sister Soami.

Rambuss, Richard. *Closet Devotions*. Durham: Duke University Press, 1998.

Reiterman, Tim. "Russian Center's Ladies See Too Much Red and Bad Habits." *San Francisco Examiner*, 18 May 1982, A14. Photocopy in the author's possession, courtesy of Sister Soami.

Richardson, Bob. *Words Kill*. 3 mins. 2009. Available on YouTube. Last accessed 22 September 2016.

Romanovsky, Sister Flirtatious of Middlesex. "Welcome to the Archives of the Order of Perpetual Indulgence Toronto, Ontario House (1980s)." N.d. sistersopitoronto.ca. Last accessed 11 September 2015.

Roof, Wade Clark. *Spiritual Marketplace: Baby Boomers and the Remaking of American Religion*. Princeton: Princeton University Press, 1999.

Roscoe, Will. *Queer Spirits: A Gay Men's Myth Book*. Boston: Beacon, 1995.

———, ed. *Radically Gay: Gay Liberation in the Words of Its Founder*. Boston: Beacon, 1996.

———. *The Zuni Man-Woman*. Albuquerque: University of New Mexico Press, 1991.

Rupp, Leila J. *Sapphistries: A Global History of Love between Women*. New York: New York University Press, 2009.

Sandbach, Lizanne. "Sister Boom Boom, Nun of the Above, Mounts Her Campaign for Supervisor." *Metro*, October/November 1982, 9. Sisters of Perpetual Indulgence, ONE Subject Files Collection, 2012.001, ONE Archives, Los Angeles.

Shepard, Benjamin. "Play as World-Making: From the Cockettes to the Germs, Gay Liberation to DIY Community Building." In *Hidden 1970s: Histories of Radicalism*, edited by Dan Berger and Brian Behnken, 177–94. New Brunswick: Rutgers University Press, 2010.

———. *Queer Political Performance and Protest: Play, Pleasure and Social Movement*. New York: Routledge, 2010.

Shilts, Randy. *And the Band Played On: Politics, People, and the AIDS Epidemic*. New York: St. Martin's, 1987.

Siegel, Fred. "Clown Politics: Report on the International Clown-Theatre Congress." *TDR* 36, no. 2 (1992): 182–86.

Singleton, Andrew. "Are Religious 'Nones' Secular? The Case of the Nones in Australia." *Journal of Beliefs and Values* 36, no. 2 (2015): 239–43.

Sisters of Perpetual Indulgence. "Constitution and Rules of Order." Ratified 27 July 1980. Sisters of Perpetual Indulgence, ONE Subject Files Collection, 2012.001, ONE Archives, Los Angeles.

———. "Mainstream Exiles: A Lesbian and Gay Men's Cultural Festival." Performance program. November 8, 1980. Photocopy in the author's possession, courtesy of Sister Soami.

———. "Mass in a Time of War against V.D." Original script. Photocopy in the author's possession, courtesy of Sister Soami.

———. "Mayor's Quip to Sisters Inspires Red Fertility Dance." Press release. 27 April 1982. Photocopy in the author's possession, courtesy of Sister Soami.

———. *Play Fair!* San Francisco, CA, 1982. Original pamphlet in the author's possession.

———. "The Sisters of Perpetual Indulgence Present: !SCORE! Basketball Game and Sock Hop, Friday, February 12." Flyer. Sisters of Perpetual Indulgence, ONE Subject Files Collection, 2012.001, ONE Archives, Los Angeles.

Sisters of Perpetual Indulgence—San Francisco House. "Sistory." N.d. thesisters.org. Last accessed 21 September 2016.

Sisters of Perpetual Indulgence, Toronto Chapter. "Sisters' Handbook." N.d. sistersopi-toronto.ca. Last accessed 11 September 2015.

"The Sisters of Perpetual Indulgence Present a Crusade: A Softball Benefit for the 1982 Gay Olympics, Sisters vs. Gay Men's Chorus, Sunday, October 25." Flyer. Sisters of Perpetual Indulgence, ONE Subject Files Collection, 2012.001, ONE Archives, Los Angeles.

"The Sisters of Perpetual Indulgence Wish to Announce That, as of October 1, 1986, the Order of Perpetual Indulgence (Toronto Chapter) Will Disband." *Body Politic*, November 1986, n.p. Photocopy in the author's possession, courtesy of Sister Soami.

Snider, Burr. "The Sisters of Perpetual Indulgence." *San Francisco Examiner*, 23 September 1981, E9. Sisters of Perpetual Indulgence, ONE Subject Files Collection, 2012.001, ONE Archives, Los Angeles.

Snorton, C. Riley. "A Response to Tolliver." In *Passing/Out: Sexual Identity Veiled and Revealed*, edited by Dennis R. Cooley and Kelby Harrison, 164–66. Burlington, VT: Ashgate, 2012.

Soami, Sister. "Angels-on-a-Pinhead: History of the Order of Perpetual Indulgence." *Ashé Journal* 7, no. 2 (2008): 127–30.

Soiffer, Bill. "Big Gay Protest at USF." *San Francisco Chronicle*, 20 October 1980. Photocopy in the author's possession, courtesy of Sister Soami.

Sointu, Eeva, and Linda Woodhead. "Spirituality, Gender, and Expressive Selfhood." *Journal for the Scientific Study of Religion* 47, no. 2 (2008): 259–76.

Starhawk. *The Spiral Dance: A Rebirth of the Ancient Religion of the Great Goddess*. 10th anniv. ed. San Francisco: HarperSanFrancisco, 1989.

Starr, Kevin. "Getting It from Both Sides." *San Francisco Examiner*, 21 October 1981, E13. Photocopy in the author's possession, courtesy of Sister Soami.

———. "Indulging the Sisters." *San Francisco Examiner*, 12 October 1981, E4. Sisters of Perpetual Indulgence, ONE Subject Files Collection, 2012.001, ONE Archives, Los Angeles.

Stein, Marc. *Rethinking the Gay and Lesbian Movement*. New York: Routledge, 2012.

Stover, John A. III. "When Pan Met Wendy: Gendered Membership Debates among the Radical Faeries." *Nova Religio: The Journal of Alternative and Emergent Religions* 11, no. 4 (2008): 31–55.

Stryker, Susan, and Jim Van Buskirk. *Gay by the Bay: A History of Queer Culture in the San Francisco Bay Area*. San Francisco: Chronicle, 1996.

Szymanowski, Grzegorz, and Christian Lowe. "Court Rules against Polish Rock Musician: Case Pits Catholic Values against Free Expression." *Edmonton Journal*, 31 October 2012, D8.

"Talk: Sisters of Perpetual Indulgence." Anonymous Wikipedia comment. 13 October 2007. en.wikipedia.org. Last accessed 6 November 2015.

Terzon, Emilia. "The Sisters of Perpetual Indulgence: Pink Nuns That Briefly Dominated the NT Gay Rights Movement." *ABC Darwin*, 26 May 2016. www.abc.net.au. Last accessed 21 September 2016.

Thompson, James. *Performance Affects: Applied Theatre and the End of Effect.* New York: Palgrave MacMillan, 2009.

Thompson, Mark. "Children of Paradise: A Brief History of Queens." In *Gay Spirit: Myth and Meaning*, edited by Mark Thompson, 49–68. New York: St. Martin's, 1987.

———, ed. *Gay Spirit: Myth and Meaning.* New York: St. Martin's, 1987.

———. "Not Wholly Nunsense from the Sisters of Perpetual Indulgence: Getting in the Habit to 'Give Up Guilt.'" *Advocate*, 19 February 1981, T11–13. Sisters of Perpetual Indulgence, ONE Subject Files Collection, 2012.001, ONE Archives, Los Angeles.

Timmons, Stuart. *The Trouble with Harry Hay: Founder of the Modern Gay Movement.* Boston: Alyson, 1990.

Tolliver, Willie. "Comments on Snorton's 'Negotiating the Glass Closet.'" In *Passing/ Out: Sexual Identity Veiled and Revealed*, edited by Dennis R. Cooley and Kelby Harrison, 154–58. Burlington, VT: Ashgate, 2012.

Tomso, Gregory. "Viral Sex and the Politics of Life." *South Atlantic Quarterly* 107, no. 2 (2008): 265–85.

U.S. Census Bureau. "2010 Census Interactive Population Search." N.d. www.census .gov. Last accessed 21 September 2016.

———. "Quick Facts: Portland City, Oregon, Race and Hispanic Origin." N.d. www .census.gov. Last accessed 20 June 2016.

———. "Quick Facts: San Francisco City, Race and Hispanic Origin." N.d. www.census .gov. Last accessed 20 June 2016.

———. "U.S. Census Bureau Projections Show a Slower Growing, Older, More Diverse Nation Half a Century from Now." Press release. 12 December 2012. www.census .gov. Last accessed 17 June 2016.

Valentine, David. *Imagining Transgender: An Ethnography of a Category.* Durham: Duke University Press, 2007.

Varnden, Richard. "Sister Love." *The Face*, n.d. Photocopy in the author's possession, courtesy of Sister Soami.

Vernon, Glenn M. "The Religious 'Nones': A Neglected Category." *Journal for the Scientific Study of Religion* 7, no. 2 (1968): 219–29.

Wafer, Jim. "Uncle Doreen's Family Drag Album: A Reading of Hunter Valley Social History from a Gay Man's Perspective." In *Out in the Valley: Hunter Gay and Lesbian Histories*, edited by Jim Wafer, Erica Southgate, and Lyndall Coan, 9–202. Newcastle History Monograph no. 15. Newcastle, NSW: Newcastle Region Library, 2000.

Warner, Sara. *Acts of Gaiety: LGBT Performance and the Politics of Pleasure.* Ann Arbor: University of Michigan Press, 2012.

Weissman, David, and Bill Weber, dirs. *The Cockettes.* Grandelusion, 2002. 106 mins.

Welch, Ted. "Body Politic Article: Furor over 'Nuns.'" *Toronto Sun*, 25 February 1982, 54. Photocopy in the author's possession, courtesy of Sister Soami.

Welzer-Lang, Daniel, Jean-Yves Le Talec, and Sylvie Tomolillo. *Un mouvement gai dans la lutte contre le SIDA.* Paris: L'Harmattan, 2000.

Weston, Kath. *Families We Choose: Lesbians, Gays, Kinship*. New York: Columbia University Press, 1991.

White, Allen. "Illegal Indulgences: Sisters Busted on Christmas Eve." *Bay Area Reporter*, 30 December 1981, 1. Sisters of Perpetual Indulgence, ONE Subject Files Collection, 2012.001, ONE Archives, Los Angeles.

White, Ethan Doyle. "The New Cultus of Antinous: Hadrian's Deified Lover and Contemporary Queer Paganism." *Nova Religio* 20, no. 1 (2016): 32–59.

Wilcox, Melissa M. *Coming Out in Christianity: Religion, Identity, and Community*. Bloomington: Indiana University Press, 2003.

———. *Queer Women and Religious Individualism*. Bloomington: Indiana University Press, 2009.

———. "The Separation of Church and Sex: Conservative Catholics and the Sisters of Perpetual Indulgence." *e-misférica* 12, no. 2 (2016), n.p.

Wilkins-Laflamme, Sarah. "How Unreligious Are the Religious 'Nones'? Religious Dynamics of the Unaffiliated in Canada." *Canadian Journal of Sociology* 40, no. 4 (2015): 477–500.

Williams, Walter. *The Spirit and the Flesh: Sexual Diversity in American Indian Culture*. Boston: Beacon, 1986.

Williamson, Lola. *Transcendent in America: Hindu-Inspired Meditation Movements as New Religion*. New York: New York University Press, 2010.

Wong, Curtis M. "'Orthodox Priests' Get Sexy (and Gay) for Steamy, NSFW Spread: Holy Smokes." *Huffington Post*, 9 October 2015. www.huffingtonpost.com. Last accessed 28 July 2016.

———. "Romanian 'Orthodox Priests' Calendar 2015 Pays Tribute to Social Tolerance." *Huffington Post*, 9 October 2014. www.huffingtonpost.com. Last accessed 29 July 2016.

X, Sister. "I Took the Vow." 1991. Original printed material in the author's collection, courtesy of Sister Soami.

Yip, Andrew K. T. "Coming Home from the Wilderness: An Overview of Recent Scholarly Research on LGBTQI Religiosity/Spirituality in the West." In *Queer Spiritual Spaces: Sexuality and Sacred Places*, edited by Sally Munt, Kath Browne, and Andrew K. T. Yip, 35–50. Burlington, VT: Ashgate, 2010.

INDEX

and Roman Catholicism, 38, 72, 84,
    92–93, 94, 111, 123, 129
and rumors of sex work, 154–155
as sacred clowns. *See* sacred clowns
as sacred women, 104
San Francisco die-in, 73
as "secular" nuns, 172–175, 209–210
sexualized, 135–137
sober, 27
spirituality, 176, 182–183, 192–199
spiritual role, 91
structure, 30
and subversiveness of ambiguity, 172
taking confession. *See* Sister moments
thirtieth anniversary celebration,
    198–199
trademarking of, 5
and transgender members, 147
twentieth anniversary, 64
United Nuns' Privy Council, 65, 66
US houses, 9
views on sin, 75
wearing of the habit, 32, 35, 46–47, 84
Sisters of the Mother House of Washing-
    ton (SOMHOW), 64, 236
Sisters Outsider (blog post), 140
Sistory, 9
SisTree, 9–10
skag drag, 32, 81
Slut Walk, 100
sobriety, impact on participation, 57
softball, gay league, 33–34
Soho, 1
SOS (Save Our Souls) campaign, 150, 152
South American houses, 1
spirituality, 25, 130, 174–175, 178, 179–180,
    181. *See also* Sisters of Perpetual Indul-
    gence: spirituality
as individual, 184–185
influenced by twelve-step movements,
    189
and neoliberalism, 204–205
shaped by The Golden Rule, 189, 196

Starr, Kevin, 44, 53
stigmatic guilt, 15
Stonewall Riots, 50, 63
Stores, Rick, *Figure 5*
subjective-life spirituality, 204, 206
Sugar Plum Fairies, 31, 33
sunglasses, 28, 37, 103
    Australian houses, 82, 97
Suzuki, D. T., 32
Swiss houses, 125, 217
Sydney house, 7, 17, 45, 47, 60, 89–90, 136,
    195
    Ancients, 47
    first manifestation, 47
    on Roman Catholic Church, 89–90
    sexual assault against, 136
syphilis, 1

third gender theory, 110, 111, 145
Thompson, Mark, 44, 62
"three asteroids," 31–32
Three Mile Island, 39, 42
Toronto house, 7, 45, 48, 51, 59
    failure of, 48–49
    original Sisters, 45
Transcendental Meditation, 19, 32
transgender rights movement, 108–109
transgender Sisters, 105
transmisogyny, 129, 139
transphobic laws, U.S., 138

U.K. houses
    Australian influence, 123
    mode of dress, 1
United Nuns' Privy Council (UNPC), 6, 9
    management of trademark, 9
universal joy, 15
University of Iowa, 31
    Gay Liberation Front, 31
U.S. houses
    as 501(c)(3) organizations, 8
    community service, 8
    growth of houses, 21st century, 65

ABOUT THE AUTHOR

Melissa M. Wilcox is Professor and Holstein Family and Community Chair of Religious Studies at the University of California, Riverside. Her research and teaching interests focus on the intersectional study of religion, power, and social justice, particularly within queer and trans communities.